AS A PEACE-LOVING GLOBAL CITIZEN

AS A
PEACE-LOVING
GLOBAL CITIZEN

REVEREND SUN MYUNG MOON

Original publication was in the Korean language by Gimm-Young Publishers, Inc. Seoul, Korea
March 9, 2009

Thanks to Mission Foundation for Family Federation for World Peace and Unification, and Gimm-Young Publishers Inc. for their permission and support for this English edition.

Manufactured in the United States of America. The paper used in this publication meets the minimum requirements of American National Standard for Information Sciences – Permanence of Paper for Printed Library Materials, ANSIZ39.481984.

Photographs courtesy of the HSA-UWC Photo Archives.

Produced in the United States of America
ISBN 978-0-9884879-0-1

Sixth printing, October 2012

TABLE OF CONTENTS

Foreword

Asteady spring rain fell all last night, ending a winter drought. It was so nice to have had the rain that I spent all this morning walking about in the garden. The ground had that fragrant aroma of moist earth I had missed all through the winter, and the weeping willow and cherry trees were showing signs of new spring buds. I felt I could hear the popping sounds of new life sprouting here and there around the garden. Before I knew it, my wife, who had followed me out, was picking young mugwort shoots that had managed to poke their heads up through the dry lawn. (Mugwort is a medicinal shrub with a wide range of healing properties.) The night's rain had turned the whole world into a fragrant spring garden.

No matter how much commotion there may be in the world, when the calendar turns to March, spring is on its way. The older I become, the more it means to me that in nature spring follows winter and brings with it flowers in full bloom. Who am I that God, in each season, allows the flowers to bloom and the snow to fall, so I might know the joy of being alive? Love wells up from within the deepest recesses of my heart, and I am overcome with emotion. I am moved to tears to think that everything of real value has been given to me freely.

In my life, I have circled the globe many times over in my efforts to bring about a world of peace, and yet it is here in this garden in spring that I am able to taste real peace. Peace too was given to us by God, but we lost it somewhere, and now we spend our lives looking for it in all the wrong places.

To bring a world of peace, I have spent my life going to the most lowly and secluded places. I met mothers in Africa who could only watch helplessly as their children died of hunger, and I met fathers in South America who lived by rivers full of fish but could not support their families by fishing. At first, all I did was simply share my food, but they granted me their love in return.

Intoxicated by the power of love, I went on to plant seeds and cultivate forests. Together we caught fish to feed hungry children, and the trees were used to build schools. I was happy fishing all through the night, even as mosquitoes bit me all over. I was happy even when I was sinking knee-deep into mud, because I could see the shadows of despair disappear from the faces of my neighbors.

Seeking the shortest path to a world of peace, I devoted myself to inspiring change in the political process and to changing people's ways of thinking. I met then-President Mikhail Gorbachev of the Soviet Union as part of my effort to bring reconciliation between communism and democracy, and I met then-President Kim Il Sung of North Korea for a serious discussion on how to bring peace to the Korean peninsula.

I went to a United States that was in moral decline and played the role of a fireman responding to a call in an effort to reawaken its Puritan spirit. I dedicated myself to resolving various conflicts in the world. In my work for peace among Muslims and Jews, I was not deterred by rampant terror. As a result of my efforts, thousands have gathered for rallies and peace marches, with Jews, Muslims, and Christians all joining together.

Sadly, however, the conflict continues. I see hope, though, that an age of peace is about to be inaugurated in my native land of Korea. The Korean peninsula has been trained through endless suffering and the tragedy of division, and I can feel in every cell of my body that a powerful energy has been stored here and is ready to burst out. In the same way that no one can stop a new season of spring from coming, no human power can stop heavenly fortune from coming to the Korean peninsula and spreading throughout the world. People need to prepare themselves so that they may rise with the tide of heavenly fortune when it arrives.

I am a controversial person. The mere mention of my name causes trouble in the world. I never sought money or fame but have spent my life speaking only of peace. The world, though, has associated many different phrases with my name, rejected me, and thrown stones at me. Many are not interested in knowing what I say or what I do. They only oppose me.

I have been unjustly imprisoned six times in my life — by imperial Japan, in Kim Il Sung's North Korea, by South Korea's Syngman Rhee government, and even in the United States — and at times I was beaten so hard that the flesh was torn from my body. Today, though, not even the slightest wound remains in my heart. Old wounds disappear easily in the presence of true love. Even enemies melt away without a trace in the presence of true love. True love is a heart that gives and gives and wants to continue giving. True love is a love that forgets it already gave love and gives love again.

I have lived my entire life intoxicated in such love. I wanted nothing aside from love, and I threw my entire being into the effort to share love with my impoverished neighbors. At times, the path of love was so difficult that my knees buckled under me, but even then I felt happy in my heart, dedicated to loving humanity.

Even now, I am filled with love that I have not yet been able to give. It is with a prayer that this love will become a river of peace saturating the drought-stricken land and flowing to the ends of the earth that I now place this book before the world.

Recently a growing number of people have been seeking to know more about me. For the sake of those who are curious, I have looked back on my life and recorded my candid recollections in this book. As for the stories that could not be included in this volume, I hope there will be other opportunities for me to convey them.

I send boundless love to all those who have put their faith in me, remained by my side, and lived their lives with me, especially to my wife, Hak Ja Han Moon, to whom I am deeply grateful for struggling with me to scale the most difficult peaks.

Finally, I would like to express my heartfelt gratitude to Eun Ju Park, president of Gimm-Young Publishers Inc., who poured out much sincerity and dedication in the process of bringing this book to publication, and to everyone in the publishing company who labored in editing the words I spoke so that the often complex content could be easily understood by readers.

Sun Myung Moon
Cheongpyeong, South Korea
March 1, 2009

THE KOREAN PENINSULA
.... Route of Sun Myung Moon
Journey to Pusan 1950-51

USSR

CHINA

NORTH KOREA

Jeongju Anju

⊙ HEUNGNAM

PYONGYANG

38th parallel

Kaesong

Chuncheon
Cheongpyeong

Yongmae Island

SEOUL

INCHEON

Moongyeong

East Sea
(Sea of Japan)

SOUTH KOREA

Yellow Sea

DAEGU

Kyongju

KWANGJU

Nampyeong

BUSAN

Yeosu

Jeju Island

South Sea

CHAPTER ONE

FOOD IS LOVE

What I Learned about Peace
while Being Carried on My Father's Back

I have lived my life with just one thought. I wanted to bring about a world of peace, a world where there are no wars and where all humankind lives in love. Perhaps some may say, "How is it possible that you were thinking about peace even when you were a child?" Is it so astonishing that a child would dream of a peaceful world?

In 1920, when I was born, Korea was under forced occupation by Japan. Even after liberation in 1945, there came the Korean War, the Asian financial crisis, and numerous other difficult crises. For many years, the land of Korea has not been closely associated with peace. But these times of suffering and confusion were not matters related only to Korea. The two world wars, the Vietnam War, and the wars in the Middle East show that people in the world continuously treat each other with enmity, point guns at each other, and bomb each other. Perhaps for people who experience these horrors of bloodied bodies and broken bones, peace has been something that could be imagined only in a dream. Peace, though, is not so difficult to accomplish. To begin with, we can find peace in the air we breathe, in the natural environment, and in the people around us.

As a child, I thought of the meadows as my home. As soon as I could wolf down my bowl of rice for breakfast, I would run out of the house and spend the entire day in the hills and streams. I could spend the day wandering about the forest with all the different birds and animals, eating herbs and wild berries, and I would never feel hungry. Even as a child, I knew that my mind and body were at ease anytime I went into the forest.

I would often fall asleep in the hills after playing there. My father would be forced to come find me. When I heard my father shouting in the distance, "Yong Myung! Yong Myung!" I couldn't help but smile, even as I slept. My name as a child was Yong Myung. The sound of his voice would awaken me, but I would pretend to still be asleep. He would hoist me onto his back and carry me home. That feeling I had as he carried me down the hill—feeling completely secure and able to let my heart be completely at ease—that was peace. That is how I first learned about peace, while being carried on my father's back.

The reason I loved the forest was also because all the peace in the world dwells there. Creatures in the forest do not fight each other. Of course, they eat one another and are eaten, but that is because they are hungry and need to sustain themselves. They do not fight out of enmity. Birds do not hate other birds. Animals do not hate other animals. Trees do not hate other trees. There needs to be an absence of enmity for peace to come. Human beings are the only ones who hate other members of the same species. People hate other people because their country is different, their religion is different, or their way of thinking is different.

I have been to almost two hundred countries. There were not many countries where I would land at the airport and think to myself, "This really is a peaceful and contented place." There were many places where, because of civil unrest, soldiers held their weapons high, guarding the airports and blocking the streets. The sound of gunfire could be heard day and night. Several times, I came close to losing my life in places where I went to talk about peace. In today's world, there is an endless series of conflicts and confrontations, large and small. Tens of millions suffer from hunger, without food. Yet, trillions of dollars are spent on weapons. The money spent on guns and bombs alone would be enough to end hunger for everyone.

I have dedicated my life to building bridges of peace between countries that hate each other and became enemies because of ideology or religion. I created forums where Muslims, Christians, and Jews could come together. I worked to reconcile the views of the United States and the Soviet Union when they were at odds with each other over Iraq. I have helped in the process of bringing reconciliation between North and South Korea. I did not do these things for money or fame. From the time I was old enough to know what was going on in the world, there has been only one objective for my life: that is for the world to live in peace, as one. I never wanted anything else. It has not been easy to live day and night for the purpose of peace, but that is the work that makes me most happy.

During the Cold War, we experienced the pain of having our world divided in two because of ideology. It seemed then that if only communism would disappear, peace would come. Yet, now that the Cold War is past, we find even more conflicts.

Not only do countries oppose each other across borders, but within those same countries, people are fractured by race, religion, and the place where they were born. People like this become enemies and never open their hearts to one another.

When we look at human history, we see that the most brutal and cruel wars were not those fought between nations but those between races. Among these, the worst were wars between ethnic groups where religion was used as a pretext. In the Bosnian civil war, one of the worst ethnic conflicts of the twentieth century, thousands, including many children, were brutally massacred. On September 11, 2001, thousands of innocent lives were lost as the World Trade Center buildings in New York were destroyed when passenger planes were crashed into them. Recently, too, in the Gaza Strip in Palestine as well as in southern Israel, hundreds have lost their lives as a result of the intense conflict there. Homes have been destroyed, and people are living on the brink of death. All this is the grim result of conflicts between ethnic groups and between religions.

What makes people hate and kill each other like this? Of course there are many reasons, but religious differences are almost always involved. This was true with the Gulf War. It is true with the Arab–Israeli conflict over control of Jerusalem. When racism uses religion as a pretext, the problem becomes extremely complex. The evil ghosts of the religious wars that we thought had ended in the Middle Ages continue to haunt us in the twenty-first century.

Religious wars continue to occur because many politicians use the enmity between religions to satisfy their selfish designs. In the face of political power, religions often waver and lose their way. They lose sight of their original purpose, which is to exist for the sake of peace. All religions have a responsibility to advance the cause of world peace. Yet, lamentably, we see that religions instead become a cause of conflict.

Behind this evil we find the machinations of politics, with its power and money. The responsibility of a leader, above all else, is to keep the peace. Yet leaders often seem to do the opposite and lead the world into confrontation and violence.

Leaders use the language of religion and nationalism to hide their selfish ambitions. Unless their hearts are set right, countries and nationalities will wander in confusion. Neither religion nor love of one's nation are evil in their essence. They are valuable if used to contribute to building a global human community. But when the claim is made that only a particular religion or ethnic group is right and other religions and ethnic groups are treated with disdain and attacked, religion and love of nation lose their value. When a religion goes so far as to trample on others and treat other religions as worthless, it no longer embodies goodness. The same is true when love of nation is used to emphasize the righteousness of a person's own country over others.

The truth of the universe is that we must acknowledge each other and help each other. Even the smallest animals know this. Cats and dogs do not get along, but if you raise them in the same household, they embrace each other's offspring and are friendly toward each other. We see the same thing in plants. The vine that winds its way up a tree depends on the trunk to support it. The tree, however, does not say, "Hey, what do you think you're doing, winding your way up my trunk?" The principle of the universe is for everyone to live together, for the sake of one another. Anyone who deviates from this principle faces certain ruin. If nationalities and religions continue to attack each other maliciously, humanity has no future. There will be an endless cycle of terror and warfare until one day we become extinct. But we are not without hope. Clearly there is hope.

I have lived my life without ever letting go of that hope and have always kept alive the dream of peace. What I want is to wipe away completely the walls and fences that divide the world in myriad ways and to create a world of unity. I want to tear down the walls between religions and races and fill in the gap between the rich and the poor. Once that is done, we can re-establish the world of peace that God created in the beginning. I am talking about a world where no one goes hungry and no one sheds tears. To heal a world where there is no hope, and which is lacking in love, we need to go back to the pure hearts that we had as children. To shed our desire to possess ever-increasing amounts of material wealth and restore our beautiful essence as human beings, we need to go back to the principles of peace and the breath of love that we learned as we were being carried on our fathers' backs.

The Joy of Giving Food to Others

I have very small eyes. I am told that when I was born, my mother wondered, "Does my baby have eyes, or not?" and spread my eyelids apart with her fingers. Then when I blinked, she said with joy, "Oh my, yes. He does have eyes, after all!" My eyes were so small that people often called me "Osan's Little Tiny Eyes," because my mother was from the village of Osan.

I cannot remember anyone saying, though, that my small eyes make me any less attractive. In fact, people who know something about physiognomy, the art of understanding a person's characteristics and fortune by studying facial features, say my small eyes give me the right disposition to be a religious leader. I think it is similar to the way a camera can focus farther as the aperture of its lens is reduced. A religious leader needs to be able to see farther into the future than do other people, and perhaps small eyes are an indication of such a quality. My nose is rather unusual as well. Just one look and it is obvious that this is the nose of a stubborn and determined man. There must be something to physiognomy, because when I look back on my life, these features of my face seem to parallel the way I have lived my life.

I was born at 2221 Sangsa Ri (village), Deokeon District, Jeongju City, Pyongan Province, as the second son of Kyung Yu Moon of the Nampyung Moon clan and Kyung Gye Kim of the Yeonan Kim clan. I was born on the sixth day of the first lunar month in 1920, the year after the 1919 independence movement of Korea from Japan.

I was told that our family settled in the village of Sangsa Ri during the life of my great-grandfather. My paternal great-grandfather worked the farm himself, producing thousands of bushels of rice and building the family fortune with his own hands. He never smoked or drank liquor, preferring instead to use the money to buy food for those in need. When he died, his last words were, "If you feed people from all the regions of Korea, then you will receive blessings from all those regions." So the guest room in our home was always full of people. Even people from other villages knew that if they came to our home, they could always count on being fed a good meal. My mother carried out her role of preparing food for all those people without ever complaining.

My great-grandfather was so active, he never wanted to rest. If he had some spare time he would use it to make pairs of straw footwear that he would then sell in the marketplace. When he grew old, in his merciful ways, he would buy several geese, let them go in the wild, and pray that all would be well with his descendants. He hired a teacher of Chinese characters to sit in the guest room of his home and provide free literacy lessons to the young people of the village.

The villagers gave him the honorific title "Sun Ok" (Jewel of Goodness) and referred to our home as "a home that will be blessed."

By the time I was born and was growing up, much of the wealth that my great-grandfather had accumulated was gone, and our family had just enough to get by. The family tradition of feeding others was still alive, however, and we would feed others even if it meant there wouldn't be enough to feed our family members. The first thing I learned after I learned to walk was how to serve food to others.

During the Japanese occupation, many Koreans had their homes and land confiscated. As they escaped the country to Manchuria, where they hoped to build new lives for themselves, they would pass by our home on the main road that led to Seoncheon in North Pyongan Province. My mother always prepared food for the passersby, who came from all parts of Korea. If a beggar came to our home asking for food and my mother didn't react quickly enough, my grandfather would pick up his meal and take it to the beggar. Perhaps because I was born into such a family, I too have spent much of my life feeding people. To me, giving people food is the most precious work. When I am eating and I see someone who has nothing to eat, it pains my heart and I cannot continue eating.

I will tell you something that happened when I was about eleven years old. It was toward the last day of the year, and everyone in the village was busy preparing rice cakes for the New Year's feast. There was one neighbor family, though, that was so poor they had nothing to eat. I kept seeing their faces in my mind, and it made me so restless that I was walking around the house, wondering what to do. Finally, I picked up an eight-kilogram bag of rice and ran out of the house. I was in such a hurry to get the bag of rice out of the house that I didn't even tie the bag closed. I hoisted the bag onto my shoulders and held it tightly as I ran along a steep, uphill path for about eight kilometers to get to the neighbor's home. I was excited to think how good it would feel to give those people enough food so they could eat as much as they wanted.

The village mill was next to our house. The four walls of the mill house were well built, so that the crushed rice could not fall through the cracks. This meant that in the winter it was a good place to escape the wind and stay warm. If someone took some kindling from our home's furnace and started a small fire in the mill house, it became warmer than an *ondol* room. (The *ondol* heating system from Korea warms the whole house by dispersing heat through channels beneath the floor.) Some of the beggars who traveled around the country would decide to spend the winter in that mill house. I was fascinated by the stories they had to tell about the world outside, and I found myself spending time with them every chance I got. My mother would bring my meals out to the mill house, and she would always bring enough for my beggar friends to eat as well. We would eat from the same dishes and share the same blankets at night. This is how I spent the winter. When spring came, they would leave for faraway places, and I could not wait for winter to come again so they would return to our home. Just because their bodies were poorly clothed did not mean that their hearts were ragged as well. They had a deep and warm love that showed. I gave them food, and they shared their love with me. The deep friendship and warmth they showed me back then continue to be a source of strength for me today.

As I go around the world and witness children suffering from hunger, I am always reminded of how my grandfather never missed a chance to share food with others.

Being a Friend to All

Once I set my mind to do something, I have to put it into action immediately. Otherwise, I cannot sleep. As a child, I would sometimes get an idea during the night but be forced to wait until morning before acting on it. I would stay awake and make scratches on the wall to pass the time. This happened so often that I would almost dig a hole in the wall, and chunks of dirt would pile up on the floor. I also couldn't sleep if I had been treated unfairly during the day. In such a case, I would get out of bed during the night, go to the culprit's home, and challenge him to come out and fight me. I am sure it must have been very difficult for my parents to raise me.

I could not stand to see someone treated unjustly. Whenever there was a fight among the children in the village, I would involve myself as though I were responsible to see that justice was served in every situation. I would decide which child in the fight was in the wrong, and I would scold that child in a loud voice. Once I went to see the grandfather of a boy who was a bully in the neighborhood. I said to him, "Your grandson has done this and that wrong. Please take care of it."

I could be wild in my actions, but nevertheless I was a child with a big heart. I would sometimes visit my married older sister in the home of her husband's family and demand they serve me rice cakes and chicken. The adults never disliked me for this because they could see that my heart was filled with a warm love.

I was particularly good at taking care of animals. When birds made a nest in a tree in front of our house, I dug a small water hole for them to drink water. I also scattered some hulled millet from the storeroom on the ground for them to eat. At first, the birds would fly away whenever someone came close. They soon realized, however, that the person giving them food was someone who loved them, and they stopped flying away when I approached.

Once I thought I would try raising fish. So I caught some fish and put them in the water hole. I also took a fistful of fish food and sprinkled it over the water. When I got up the next morning, though, I found that all the fish had died during the night. I was so looking forward to raising those fish. I stood there in astonishment, looking at them floating on top of the water. I remember that I cried all that day.

My father kept many bee colonies. He would take a large hive and fasten a basic foundation to the bottom of it. Then the bees would deposit their beeswax there to create a nest and store their honey. I was a curious child, and I wanted to see just how the bees built the hive. So I stuck my face into the middle of the hive and got myself stung severely by the bees, causing my entire face to swell tremendously.

I once took the foundations from the hive boxes and received a severe scolding from my father. Once the bees had finished building their hives, my father would take the foundations and stack them to one side. These foundations were covered with beeswax that could be used as fuel for lamps in place of oil. I took those expensive foundations, broke them up, and took them to homes that couldn't afford to buy oil for their lamps. It was an act of kindness, but I had done it without my father's permission, and so I was harshly reprimanded.

When I was twelve, we had very little in the way of games. The choices were a Parcheesi-like game called *yute*, a chess-like game called *janggi*, and card games. I always enjoyed it when many people would play together. I liked to play *yute* or fly my kite, and in the evenings I would make the rounds of the card games going on around the village. They were games in which the winner picked up 120 *won* (Korean currency) after each hand, and I could usually win at least once every three hands.

New Year's Eve and the first full moon of the new year were the days when the most gambling went on. On those days, the police would look the other way and never arrest anyone for gambling. I went to where grownups were gambling, took a nap during the night, and got them to deal me in for just three hands in the early morning, just as they were about to call it quits for the night. I took the money I had won and bought food, toys, candy, and gift packages for my friends and for poor children in all the surrounding villages. I didn't use the money for myself or to do anything bad. When my older sisters' husbands visited our home, I would ask permission and take money from their wallets. I would then use this money to buy sweets for children in need. I also bought them sweet syrup.

In any village it is natural that there are people who live well and those who don't. When I would see a child who had brought boiled millet to school for lunch, I couldn't eat my own better lunch of rice. So I would exchange my rice for his millet. I felt closer to the children from poor families than to those from rich families, and I wanted somehow to see to it that they didn't go hungry. This was a kind of game that I enjoyed most of all. I was still a child, but I felt that I wanted to be a friend to everyone. In fact, I wanted to be more than just friends; I wanted to have relationships where we could share our deepest hearts.

One of my uncles was a greedy man. His family owned a melon patch near the middle of the village, and every summer, when the melons were ripe and giving off a sweet fragrance, the village children would beg him to let them eat some. My uncle, though, set up a tent on the road next to the melon patch and sat there keeping guard, refusing to share even a single melon.

One day I went to him and asked, "Uncle, would it be all right if sometime I were to go to your patch and eat all the melon I want?" My uncle willingly answered, "Sure, that would be fine."

So I sent word to all the children that anyone wanting to eat melon should bring a burlap bag and gather in front of my house at midnight. At midnight I led them to my uncle's melon patch and told them, "I want all of you to pick a row of melons, and don't worry about anything." The children shouted with joy and ran into the melon patch. It took only a few minutes for several rows of melons to be picked clean. That night the hungry children of the village sat in a clover field and ate melons until their stomachs almost burst.

The next day there was big trouble. I went to my uncle's home, and it was in pandemonium, like a beehive that had been poked. "You rascal," my uncle shouted at me. "Was this your doing? Are you the one who ruined my entire year's work of raising melons?"

No matter what he said, I was not going to back down. "Uncle," I said, "don't you remember? You told me I could eat all the melons I wanted. The village children wanted to eat melons, and their desire was my desire. Was it right for me to give them the melons, or should I absolutely not have given them any?" When he heard this, my uncle said, "All right. You're right." That was the end of his anger.

A Definite Compass for My Life

The Moon clan originated in Nampyung, near Naju, Cholla Province, a town about three hundred twenty kilometers south of Seoul, in the southwest region of the country. My great-great-grandfather, Sung Hak Moon, had three sons. The youngest of these was my great-grandfather, Jung Heul Moon, who also had three sons: Chi Guk, Shin Guk, and Yoon Guk. My grandfather, Chi Guk Moon, was the oldest of the three.

Grandfather Chi Guk Moon was illiterate, as he did not attend either a modern elementary school or the traditional village school. His power of concentration was so great, however, that he was able to recite the full text of the Korean translation of *Sam Kuk Zhi* (a popular, widely known novel about the three kingdoms in classical Chinese history) just by having listened to others read it to him. And it wasn't just *Sam Kuk Zhi*. When he heard someone tell an interesting story, he could memorize it and retell it in exactly the same words. He could memorize anything after hearing it just once. My father took after him in this way; he could sing from memory the entire Christian hymnal, consisting of more than four hundred pages.

Grandfather followed the last words of his father to live his life with a spirit of giving, but he was not able to maintain the family fortune. This was because his youngest brother, my great-uncle Yoon Guk Moon, borrowed money against the family's property and lost it all. Following this incident, members of the family went through some very hard times, but my grandfather and father never spoke ill of Great-Uncle Yoon Guk. This was because they knew he had not lost the money by gambling or anything of that nature. Instead, he had sent the money to the Provisional Government of the Republic of Korea, based in Shanghai, China. In those days, seventy thousand won was a large sum, and this was the amount that my great-uncle donated to the independence movement.

Great-Uncle Yoon Guk, a graduate of Pyongyang Seminary and a minister, was an intellectual who was fluent in English and well versed in Chinese studies. He served as the responsible pastor for three churches, including Deok Heung Church in Deok Eon Myeon. He participated in the drafting of the 1919 Declaration of Independence, together with Nam Seon Choe.

When it was found, however, that three of the sixteen Christian leaders among the signatories were associated with Deok Heung Church, Great-Uncle voluntarily removed his name from the signers list. Seung Hoon Lee, one of the remaining signatories who worked with my great-uncle in establishing the Osan School, asked Great-Uncle Yoon Guk to take care of all his affairs in case the independence movement failed and he died at the hands of the Japanese colonial authorities.

On returning to our hometown, Great-Uncle Yoon Guk printed thousands of Korean flags and handed them out to the people who poured into the streets to shout their support for Korean independence. He was arrested on March 8 as he led a demonstration on the hill behind the Aipo Myeon administrative office. The demonstration in support of independence was attended by the principal, the faculty, and some two thousand students of the Osan School, some three thousand Christians, and some four thousand other residents of the area. He was given a two-year prison sentence and was sent to the Euiju prison. The following year he was released as part of a special pardon.

Even after his release, he could never stay long in one place, because of severe persecution by the Japanese police, and he was always on the run. He carried a large scar where the Japanese police had tortured him by stabbing him with a bamboo spear and carving out a piece of his flesh. He was speared in the legs and in the side of his ribs, but he said that he never gave in. When the Japanese found they couldn't break him, they offered him the position of county chief if he would pledge to stop participating in the independence movement. His response was to rebuke the Japanese in a loud voice: "Do you think I would take on a position and work for you thieves?"

When I was about seven or eight years old, Great-Uncle Yoon Guk was staying in our home for a short time and some members of the Korean independence army came to see him. They were low on funds and had traveled by night on foot through a heavy snowfall to reach our house. My father covered the heads of us children with a sleeping quilt so that we would not be awakened. However, I was already wide awake, and I lay there under the quilt, my eyes wide open, listening as best I could to the sounds of the adults talking. Though it was late, my mother killed a chicken and boiled some noodles to serve to the independence fighters.

To this day, I cannot forget the words that I heard Great-Uncle Yoon Guk speak as I lay there under the quilt, holding my breath in excitement. "Even if you die," he said, "if you die for the sake of our country, you will be blessed." He continued, "Right now, we can see only darkness before us, but the bright morning is sure to come." Because of the effects of torture, he did not have full use of his body, but his voice resonated with strength.

I also remember thinking to myself then: "Why did such a wonderful person as Great-Uncle have to go to prison? If only we were stronger than Japan, this wouldn't have happened."

Great-Uncle Yoon Guk continued to roam about the country, avoiding persecution by the Japanese police, and it was not until 1966, while I was in Seoul, that I received news of him again. Great-uncle appeared in a dream to one of my younger cousins and told him, "I am buried in Jeongseon, Kangwon Province." We went to the address he gave in the dream and found that he had passed away nine years before that. We found only a grave mound covered with weeds. I had his remains reburied in Paju, Kyeonggi Province, near Seoul.

In the years following Korea's liberation from Japan in 1945, communists in North Korea killed Christian ministers and independence fighters indiscriminately. Great-Uncle Yoon Guk, fearing his presence might cause harm to the family, escaped the communists by crossing south over the 38th parallel and settling in Jeongseon. No one in our family was aware of this. He supported himself in that remote mountain valley by selling calligraphy brushes. Later, we were told that he set up a traditional village school where he taught Chinese classics.

According to some of his former students, he often enjoyed spontaneously composing poems in Chinese characters. His students transcribed and preserved some one hundred thirty of these, including the following:

SOUTH NORTH PEACE

Ten years have passed since I left home to come South.
The flow of time speeds my hair to turn white.
I would return North, but how can I?
What was intended as a short sojourn
has been prolonged.

Wearing the long-sleeved ko-hemp clothing of summer
I fan myself with a silk fan
and consider what the autumn will bring.
Peace between South and North draws near.
Children waiting under the eaves,
You needn't worry so much.

Though separated from his family and living in Jeongseon, a land unfamiliar to him in every way, Great-Uncle Yoon Guk's heart was filled with concerns for his country. Great-Uncle also left this poetic verse:

When setting your goal in the beginning,
pledge yourself to a high standard.
Don't allow yourself
even the least bit of private desire.

My great-uncle's contributions to the independence movement were posthumously recognized by the Republic of Korea government in 1977 with a Presidential Award, and in 1990 with the Order of Merit for National Foundation. Even now, I sometimes recite his poetic verses.

They are infused with his steadfast love for his country even in the face of extreme adversity.

Recently, as I have grown older, I think about Great-Uncle Yoon Guk more often. Each phrase of his poetry expressing his heart of concern for his country penetrates into my heart. I have taught our members the song "Daehan Jiri Ga" (Song of Korean Geography), whose words were written by Great-Uncle Yoon Guk himself. I enjoy singing this song with our members. When I sing this song, from Mount Baekdu to Mount Halla, I feel relieved of my burdens.

SONG OF KOREAN GEOGRAPHY

The peninsula of Korea in the East,
positioned among three countries.
North, the wide plains of Manchuria,
East, the deep and blue East Sea,
South, a sea of many islands,
West, the deep Yellow Sea.
Food in the seas on three sides,
Our treasure of all species of fish.

Mighty Mount Baekdu stands on the North,
Providing water to the Rivers of Amrok and Tuman,
Flowing into seas east and west,
Marking a clear border with the Soviets.
Mount Kumgang shines bright in the center,
A preserve for the world, pride of Korea.
Mount Halla rises above the blue South Sea,
A landmark for fishermen at sea.

Four plains of Daedong, Hangang, Geumgang, and Jeonju
give our people food and clothing.
Four mines of Woonsan, Soonan, Gaecheon, and Jaeryung
give us the treasures of the Earth.
Four cities of Kyungsung, Pyongyang, Daegu, and Kaesung
shine over the land.
Four ports of Busan, Wonsan, Mokpo, and Incheon
welcome foreign ships.
Railroads spread out from Kyungsung,
Connecting the two main lines, Kyung-Eui and Kyung-Bu.
Branch lines Kyung-Won and Honam run north and south,
Covering the peninsula.

Our cities tell us our history.
Pyongyang, 2,000-year-old city of Dangun,
Kaesung, capital of Koryo,
Kyungsung, 500-year-old capital of Chosun,
Kyungju, 2,000 years of Shilla's culture
shines, origin of Pak Hyukkosai,
Chungchong has Buyo, the historic capital of Paekche.

Sons of Korea pioneering the future,
The waves of civilization wash against our shores.
Come out of the hills,
and march forward in strength
to the world of the future!

Stubborn Child Who Never Gives Up

My father was not good at collecting debts, but if he borrowed money, he would honor the pledge to repay, even if it meant selling the family cow or even removing one of the pillars from our home and selling it at the market. He always said, "You can't change the truth with trickery. Anything that is true will not be dominated by a small trick. Anything that is the result of trickery won't go more than a few years before it is exposed."

My father was large in stature. He was so strong that he had no difficulty walking up a flight of stairs carrying a bag of rice on his shoulders. The fact that at age ninety I'm still able to travel around the world and carry on my work is a result of the physical strength I inherited from my father.

My mother, whose favorite Christian hymn was "Higher Ground," was also quite a strong woman. I take after her not only for her wide forehead and round face but for her straightforward and high-spirited personality. I have a stubborn streak, and there is no doubt I am my mother's child. When I was a child, I had the nickname "all-day crier." I earned this nickname because once I started to cry, I wouldn't stop for the entire day. When I cried, it would be so loud that people would think something terrible had happened. People sleeping in bed would come outside to see what was going on. Also, I didn't just cry sitting still. I would jump around the room, accidentally injuring myself, even bleeding, and creating an uproar. I had this kind of intense personality even when I was young.

Once my mind was made up, I would never back down, not even if it meant breaking a bone in my body. Of course, this was all before I became mature. When my mother would scold me for doing something wrong, I would talk back to her, saying, "No. Absolutely not!" All I had to do was say I was wrong, but I would rather have died than let those words out of my mouth.

My mother, though, had quite a strong personality as well. She would strike me, and say, "You think you can get away with not answering your parent?" Once, she struck me so hard I was knocked down. Even after I got up, I wouldn't give in to her. She just stood in front of me, crying loudly. Even then, I wouldn't say I was wrong.

My competitive spirit was as strong as my stubbornness. I couldn't stand to lose in any situation. The adults in the village would say, "Osan's Little Tiny Eyes, once he decides to do something, he does it."

I don't remember how old I was when this happened: A boy gave me a bloody nose and ran away. For a month after that, I would go to his house every day and stand there, waiting for him to come out. The village adults were amazed to see me persist until finally his parents apologized to me. They even gave me a container full of rice cakes. This doesn't mean I was always trying to win with stubborn persistence. I also was physically much larger and stronger than other children my age. No child could beat me in arm wrestling. I once lost a wrestling match to a boy three years older than I was, and it made me so angry that I couldn't sit still. I went to a nearby mountain, stripped some bark from an acacia tree, and for the next six months I worked out on this tree every evening to become strong enough to defeat that child. At the end of six months, I challenged him to a rematch and managed to beat him.

Each generation in our family has had many children. I had one older brother, three older sisters, and three younger sisters. I actually had four other siblings who were born after Hyo Seon, the youngest sister, but they died at an early age. All in all, my mother gave birth to thirteen children, but five did not survive. Her heart must have been deeply tormented. Mother suffered a great deal to raise so many children in circumstances that were far from plentiful. As a child I had many siblings. If these siblings got together with our first and second cousins, we could do anything. Much time has passed, however, and now I feel as though I am the only one remaining in the world.

I once visited North Korea for a short while, in 1991. I went to my hometown for the first time in forty-eight years and found that my mother and most of my siblings had passed away. Only one older sister and one younger sister remained. My older sister, who had been like a mother to me when I was a child, had become a grandmother of more than seventy years. My younger sister was older than sixty, and her face was covered with wrinkles.

When we were young, I teased my younger sister a lot. I would shout, "Hey, Hyo Seon, you're going to marry a guy with one eye." And she would come back with, "What did you say? What makes you think you know that, Brother?" Then she would run up behind me and tap me on the back with her tiny fists.

In the year she turned eighteen, Hyo Seon met a man with whom one of our aunts was trying to arrange her marriage. That morning she got up early, carefully combed her hair, and powdered her face. She thoroughly cleaned our home inside and out and waited for her prospective groom to arrive. "Hyo Seon," I teased her, "you must really want to get married." This made her blush, and I still remember how beautiful she looked with the redness in her face showing through the white powder.

It has been almost twenty years since my visit to North Korea. My older sister, who wept so sorrowfully to see me, has since passed away, leaving just my younger sister. It fills me with such anguish. I feel as though my heart may melt away.

I was good with my hands, and I used to make clothes for myself. When it got cold, I would quickly knit myself a cap to wear. I was better at it than the women were, and I would give knitting tips to my older sisters. I once knitted a muffler for Hyo Seon.

My hands were as big and thick as a bear's paws, but I enjoyed needlework, and I would even make my own underwear. I would take some cloth off a roll, fold it in half, cut it to the right design, hem it, sew it up, and put it on. When I made a pair of traditional Korean socks for my mother this way, she expressed how much she liked them by saying, "Well, well, I thought Second Son was just fooling around, but these fit me perfectly."

In those days it was necessary to weave cotton cloth as a part of preparations for the marriage of a son or daughter. Mother would take cotton wool and place it on a spinning wheel to make the thread. This was called *toggaengi* in the dialect of Pyongan Province. She would set the width on the loom at twenty threads and make twelve pieces of cotton cloth, thirteen pieces of cotton cloth, and so on. Each time a child would marry, cotton cloth as soft and beautiful as processed satin would be created through Mother's coarse hands. Her hands were incredibly quick. Others might weave three or four pieces of *toggaengi* fabric in a day, but Mother could weave as many as twenty. When she was in a hurry to complete the marriage preparations for one of my older sisters, she could weave an entire roll of fabric in a day. Mother had an impatient personality. Whenever she would set her mind to doing something, she would work quickly to get it done. I take after her in that way.

Since childhood, I have always enjoyed eating a wide variety of foods. As a child, I enjoyed eating corn, raw cucumber, raw potato, and raw beans. On a visit to my maternal relatives who lived about eight kilometers away from our home, I noticed something round growing in the field. I asked what it was and was told it was *jigwa*, or sweet potato. Someone dug one up and cooked it in steam for me, so I ate it. It had such a delectable taste that I took a whole basketful of them and ate them all myself. From the following year, I couldn't keep myself away from my maternal relatives' home for more than three days. I would shout out, "Mother, I'm going out for a while," run the whole distance to where they lived, and eat sweet potatoes.

Where we lived, we had what we called "potato hill" in May. May was a critical period, because if our store of potatoes was depleted before the barley was ready for harvest, people began to starve. Surviving this time was like climbing a steep mountain, so we called it potato hill.

The barley we ate then was not the tasty, flat-grained barley that we see today. The grains were hard and more cylindrical in shape, but that was all right with us. We would soak the barley in water for about two days before cooking it. When we sat down to eat, I would press down on the barley with my spoon, trying to make it stick together. It was no use, though, because when I scooped it up in my spoon, it would just scatter like so much sand. I would mix it with *gochujang* (red pepper paste) and take a mouthful. As I chewed, the grains of barley would keep coming out between my teeth, so I had to keep my mouth tightly closed.

We also used to catch and eat tree frogs. In those days in rural areas, children would be fed tree frogs when they caught the measles and their faces became thin from the weight loss. We would catch three or four of these frogs that were big and had plenty of flesh on their fat legs. We would roast them wrapped in squash leaves, and they would be very tender and tasty, just as though they had been steamed in a rice cooker. Speaking of tasty, I can't leave out sparrow and pheasant meat, either. We would cook the lovely colored eggs of mountain birds and the waterfowl that would fly over the fields making a loud, gulping call. As I roamed the hills and fields, this is how I came to understand that there was an abundance of food in the natural environment given to us by God.

Loving Nature to Learn from It

My personality was such that I had to know about every-thing that I could see. I couldn't just pass over something superficially. I would start thinking, "I wonder what the name of that mountain is. I wonder what's up there." I had to go see for myself. While still a child, I climbed to the tops of all the mountains that were in an eight-kilometer radius of our home. I went everywhere, even beyond the mountains. That way, when I saw a mountain shining in the morning sunlight, I could have an image in my mind of what was on that mountain and I could gaze at it and feel comfort. I hated even to look at places I didn't know. I had to know about everything I could see, and even what was beyond. Otherwise, my mind was so restless that I couldn't endure it.

When I went to the mountains, I would touch all the flowers and trees. I wasn't satisfied just to look at things with my eyes; I had to touch the flowers, smell them, and even put them in my mouth and chew on them. I enjoyed the fragrances, the touch, and the tastes so much that I wouldn't have minded if someone had told me to stick my nose in the brush and keep it there the whole day. I loved nature so much that anytime I went outside, I would spend the day roaming the hills and fields and forget about having to go home. When my older sisters would go into the hills to gather wild vegetables, I would lead the way up the hill and pick the plants. Thanks to this experience, I know a lot about many kinds of wild vegetables that taste good and are high in nutrition. Among them, I like *sseumbagwi*, which when put into *gochujang bibimbap*, tastes great. When you eat *sseumbagwi*, you need to put it in your mouth and hold your breath for a moment. This makes the bitter taste go away and a sweet taste emerge. That's the right way to eat it to enjoy its wonderful flavor.

I used to enjoy climbing trees as well. Mainly I climbed up and down a huge, two-hundred-year-old chestnut tree that was in our yard. I liked the view from the upper branches of that tree. I could see even beyond the entrance to the village. Once I was up there, I wouldn't want to come down. Sometimes, I would be up in the tree until late at night, and the youngest of my older sisters would come out of the house and make a fuss over how dangerous it was and try to get me to come down.

"Yong Myung, please come down," she would say. "It's late, and you need to come in and go to bed."

"If I get sleepy, I can sleep up here."

It didn't matter what she said; I wouldn't budge from my branch in the chestnut tree. Finally, she would lose her temper and shout at me, "Hey, monkey! Get down here now!"

Maybe it's because I was born in the Year of the Monkey that I enjoyed climbing trees so much. When chestnut burrs hung in clusters from the branches, I would take a broken branch and jump up and down to knock them down. I remember this being a lot of fun. I feel sorry for children these days who don't grow up in the countryside and don't experience this kind of enjoyment.

The birds flying free in the sky were also objects of my curiosity. Once in a while some particularly pretty birds would come by, and I would study everything I could about them, noticing what the male looked like and what the female looked like. There were no books back then to tell me about the various kinds of trees, shrubs, and birds, so I had to examine each myself. Often I would miss my meals because I would be hiking around the mountains looking for the places where migratory birds went.

Once I climbed up and down a tree every morning and evening for several days to check on a magpie nest. I wanted to see how a magpie lays its eggs. I finally got to witness the magpie lay its eggs, and I became friends with the bird as well. The first few times she saw me, the magpie let out a loud squawk and made a big fuss when she saw me approach. Later, though, I could get close and she would remain still.

The insects in that area were also my friends. Every year, in late summer, a clear-toned cicada would sing in the upper branches of a persimmon tree that was right outside my room. Each summer, I would be grateful when the loud, irritating sounds of the other types of cicada that made noise all summer would suddenly stop and be replaced by the song of the clear-toned cicada. Its song let me know that the humid summer season would soon pass, with the cool autumn to follow.

Their sound went something like this: "sulu sulululululu!" Whenever I would hear the clear-toned cicada sing like this, I would look up into the persimmon tree and think, "Of course, as long as it's going to sing, it has to sing from a high place so that everyone in the village can hear it and be glad. Who could hear it if it went into a pit and sang?"

I soon realized that both the summer cicadas and the clear-toned cicadas were making sounds for love. Whether they were singing, "mem

mem mem" or "sulu sulu," they were making sounds in order to attract their mates. Once I realized this, I couldn't help but laugh every time I heard an insect singing. "Oh, you want love, do you?" I would say. "Go ahead and sing, and find yourself a good mate." Gradually I learned how to be friends with everything in nature in a way that we could share our hearts with each other.

The Yellow Sea coast was only about four kilometers from our home. It was near enough that I could easily see it from any high place near our home. There was a series of water pools along the path to the sea, and a creek flowed between them. I would often dig around one of those pools smelling of stale water to catch eel and freshwater mud crab. I would poke around in all sorts of places to catch different kinds of water life, so I came to know where each kind lived. Eels, by nature, do not like to be visible, so they hide their long bodies in crab holes and other similar places. Often, though, they can't quite fit all their body into the hole, so the end of their tail remains sticking out. I could easily catch them, simply by grabbing the tail and pulling the eel out of its hole. If we had company in our home and they wanted to eat steamed eel, then it was nothing for me to run the five-kilometer round trip to the water pools and bring back about five eels. During summer vacations, I would often catch more than forty eels in a day.

But there was one chore I didn't like doing. This was to feed the cow. Often, when my father would tell me to feed the cow, I would take it to the meadow of the neighboring village, where I would tie it up and run away. But after a while, I would start to worry about the cow. When I looked back, I could see it was still there, right where I had tied it. It just stayed there half the day, mooing and waiting for someone to come feed it. Hearing the cow mooing in the distance, I would feel sorry for it

and think, "That cow! What am I going to do with it?" Maybe you can imagine how I felt to ignore the cow's mooing. Still, when I would go back to it late in the evening, it wouldn't be angry or try to gore me with its horns. Instead it seemed happy to see me. This made me realize that a person's perspective on a major objective in life should be like that of a cow. Bide your time with patience, and something good will come to you.

There was a dog in our home that I loved very much. It was so smart that when it came time for me to come home from school, it would run to meet me when I was still a long distance from home. Whenever it saw me, it acted happy. I would always pet it with my right hand. So, even if it happened to be on my left side, it would go around to my right side and rub its face against me, begging to be petted. Then I would take my right hand and pet it on its head and back. If I didn't, the dog would whine and run circles around me as I walked down the road. "You rascal," I would say. "You know about love, don't you? Do you like love?"

Animals know about love. Have you ever seen a mother hen sitting on her eggs until they hatch? The hen will keep her eyes open and stamp her foot on the ground so no one can go near her. I would go in and out of the chicken coop, knowing it would make the hen angry. When I would go into the coop, the hen would straighten her neck and try to threaten me. Instead of backing away, I would also act in a threatening manner toward the hen. After I went into the coop a few times, the hen would just pretend not to see me. But she would keep herself bristled up and her claws long and sharp. She looked like she wanted to swoosh over and attack me, but she couldn't move because of the eggs. So she just sat there in anguish. I would go near and touch her feathers, but she wouldn't budge.

It seemed that she was determined not to move from that spot until her eggs had hatched, even if it meant letting someone pluck all the feathers from her bosom. Because she is so steadfastly attached to her eggs through love, the hen has an authority that keeps even the rooster from doing whatever he wants. The hen commands complete authority over everything under heaven, as if to say, "I don't care who you are. You had better not disturb these eggs!"

There is also a demonstration of love when a pig gives birth to piglets. I followed a mother pig around so I could watch her give birth to her litter. At the moment of birth, the mother pig gives a push with a loud grunt and a piglet slips out onto the ground. The pig lets out another loud grunt and a second piglet comes out. It is similar with cats and dogs. It made me very happy to see these little baby animals that hadn't even opened their eyes come into the world. I couldn't help but laugh with joy.

On the other hand, it gave me much anguish to witness the death of an animal. There was a slaughterhouse near the village. Once a cow was inside the slaughterhouse, a butcher would appear out of nowhere and strike the cow with an iron hammer about the size of a person's forearm. The cow would fall over. In the next moment, it would be stripped of its hide and its legs would be cut off. Life hangs on so desperately that the stumps remaining on the cow after its legs were cut off would continue to quiver. It brought tears to my eyes to watch this, and I cried out loud.

From when I was a child, I have had a certain peculiarity. I could know things that others didn't, as if I had some natural paranormal ability. If I said it was going to rain, then it would rain. I might be sitting in our home and say, "The old man Mr. So-and-So in the next village doesn't feel well today." And it would always be so. From the time I was eight I was well known as a champion matchmaker. I only had to see photographs of a prospective bride and groom and I could tell everything. If I said, "This marriage is bad," and they went ahead and married anyway, they would inevitably break up later. I'm still doing this at age ninety, and now I can tell much about a person just seeing the way he sits or the way he laughs.

If I focused my thoughts, I could tell what my older sisters were doing at a particular moment. So, although my older sisters liked me, they also feared me. They felt that I knew all their secrets.

It may seem like I have some incredible paranormal power, but actually it isn't anything to be surprised about. Even ants, which we often think of as insignificant creatures, can tell when the rainy season is coming, and they go to where they can stay dry. People in tune with nature should be able to tell what is ahead for them. It's not such a difficult thing.

You can tell which way the wind is going to blow by carefully examining a magpie's nest. A magpie will put the entrance to its nest on the opposite side from the direction where the wind is going to blow. It will take twigs in its beak and weave them together in a complex fashion, and then pick up mud with its beak and plaster the top and bottom of the nest so that the rain doesn't get in. It arranges the ends of the twigs so that they all face the same direction. Like a gutter on a roof, this makes the rain flow toward one place. Even magpies have such wisdom to help them survive, so wouldn't it be natural for people to have this ability as well?

If I were at a cow market with my father, I might say, "Father, don't buy this cow. A good cow should look good on the nape of its neck and have strong front hooves. It should have firm buttocks and back. This cow isn't like that." Sure enough, that cow would not sell. My father would say, "How do you know all this?" and I would reply, "I've known that since I was in Mother's womb." Of course, I wasn't serious. If you love cows, you can tell a lot about them.

The most powerful force in the world is love. And the most fearful thing is a mind and body united. If you quiet yourself and focus your mind, there is a place deep down where the mind is able to settle. You need to let your mind go to that place. When you put your mind in that place and go to sleep, then when you awaken you will be extremely sensitive. That is the moment when you should turn away all extraneous thoughts and focus your consciousness. Then you will be able to communicate with everything.

If you don't believe me, try it right now. Each life form in the world seeks to connect itself with that which gives it the most love. So if you have something that you don't truly love, then your possession or dominion is false and you will be forced to give it up.

Talking about the
Universe with the Insects

S pending time in the forest cleanses the mind. The sound of leaves rustling in the wind, the sound of the wind blowing through the reeds, the sound of frogs croaking in the ponds: All you can hear are the sounds of nature; no extraneous thoughts enter the mind. If you empty your mind and receive nature into your entire being, there is no separation between you and nature. Nature comes into you, and you become completely one with nature. In the moment that the boundary between you and nature disappears, you feel a profound sense of joy. Then nature becomes you, and you become nature.

I have always treasured such experiences in my life. Even now, I close my eyes and enter a state in which I am one with nature. Some refer to this as *anātman*, or "not-self," but to me it is more than that, because nature enters and settles into the place that has been made empty. While in that state, I listen to the sounds that nature hands to me—the sounds of the pine trees, the sounds of the bugs—and we become friends. I could go to a village and know, without meeting anyone, the disposition of the minds of the people living there. I would go into the fields of the village and spend the night there, then listen to what the crops in the fields would tell me. I could see whether the crops were sad or happy and that would tell me the kind of people who lived there.

The reason I could be in jail in South Korea and the United States, and even North Korea, and not feel lonely and isolated is that even in jail I could hear the sound of the wind blowing and talk to the bugs that were there with me.

You may ask, "What do you talk about with bugs?" Even the smallest grain of sand contains the principles of the world, and even a speck of dust floating in the air contains the harmony of the universe. Everything around us was given birth through a combination of forces so complex we cannot even imagine it. These forces are closely related to each other. Nothing in the universe was conceived outside the heart of God. The movement of just one leaf holds within it the breathing of the universe.

From childhood, I have had the gift of being able to resonate with the sounds of nature as I roam around the hills and meadows. Nature creates a single harmony and produces a sound that is magnificent and beautiful. No one tries to show off, and no one is ignored; there is just a supreme harmony. Whenever I found myself in difficulty, nature comforted me; whenever I collapsed in despair, it raised me back up.

Children these days are raised in urban areas and don't have opportunities to become familiar with nature, but developing sensitivity to nature is actually more important than developing our knowledge. What is the purpose of providing a university education to a child who cannot feel nature in his bosom and whose sensitivities are dull? The person separated from nature can gather book knowledge here and there and then easily become an individualistic person who worships material goods.

We need to feel the difference between the sound of spring rain falling like a soft whisper and that of the autumn rain falling with pops and crackles. It is only the person who enjoys resonance with nature who can be said to have a true character. A dandelion blooming by the side of the road is more precious than all the gold in the world.

We need to have a heart that knows how to love nature and love people. Anyone who cannot love nature or love people is not capable of loving God. Everything in creation embodies God at the level of symbol, and human beings are substantial beings created in the image of God. Only a person who can love nature can love God.

I did not spend all my time roaming the hills and meadows and playing. I also worked hard helping my older brother run the farm. On a farm there are many tasks that must be done during a particular season. The rice paddies and fields need to be plowed. Rice seedlings need to be transplanted, and weeds need to be pulled. When one is pulling weeds, the most difficult task is to weed a field of millet. After the seeds are planted, the furrows need to be weeded at least three times, and this is backbreaking work. When we were finished, we couldn't straighten our backs for a while.

Sweet potatoes don't taste very good if they are planted in clay. They need to be planted in a mixture of one-third clay and two-thirds sand if they are going to produce the best tasting sweet potatoes. For corn, human excrement was the best fertilizer, so I would take my hands and break up all the solid excrement into small pieces. By helping out on the farm, I learned what was needed to make beans grow well, what kind of soil was best for soybeans, and what soil was best for red beans. I am a farmer's farmer.

Pyongan Province was one of the earlier places in Korea to accept

Christian culture. One noticeable influence was that the farmland was already arranged in straight lines in the 1930s and 1940s. To transplant rice seedlings, we would take a pole with twelve equally spaced markings to indicate where the rows would go and lay it across the width of the paddy. Then two people would move along the pole, each planting six rows of seedlings.

Later, when I came to the southern part of Korea, I saw that they would put a string across the paddy and have dozens of people splashing around in there. It seemed like a very inefficient way of doing it. I would spread my legs to twice the width of my shoulders so I could plant the seedlings more quickly. During the rice planting season, I was able to earn enough money to at least cover my own tuition.

Ardent Student

When I turned ten, my father had me attend a traditional school in our village, where an old man taught Chinese classics. At this school, all we had to do was memorize one booklet each day. I would focus myself and complete the memorization in a half-hour. If I could stand in front of the schoolmaster and recite that day's lesson, then I was finished for the day. If the schoolmaster dozed off in the early afternoon, I would leave the school and go into the hills and meadows. The more time I spent in the hills, the more I knew where to find edible plants. Eventually, I was eating enough of these plants that I could go without lunch, and I stopped eating lunch at home.

At school, we read the *Analects* of Confucius and the works of Mencius, and we were taught Chinese characters. I excelled at writing, and by the time I was twelve the schoolmaster had me making the model characters that other students would learn from. Actually, I wanted to attend a formal school, not the traditional village school. I felt I shouldn't be just memorizing Confucius and Mencius when others were building airplanes. This was April, and my father had already paid my full year's tuition in advance. Even though I knew this, I decided to quit the village school and worked to convince my father to send me to a formal school. I worked on convincing my grandfather and even my uncle. To transfer into elementary school, I had to take an exam. To study for this exam, I had to attend a preparatory school. I convinced one of my younger cousins to go with me, and we both entered the Wonbong, a private school to help us prepare for the exam to transfer into elementary school.

The next year, when I was fourteen, I passed the exam and transferred into the third grade at Osan School. I had a late start, but I studied hard and was able to skip the fifth grade. Osan School was eight kilometers from our home, but I never missed a day or was ever late for school. Each time I would climb a hill in the road, a group of students would be waiting for me. I would walk so quickly, though, that they would have a hard time keeping up. This is how I traveled that mountain road that was rumored to be a place where tigers sometimes appeared.

The Osan School was a nationalist school established by Seung Hoon Lee, who was active in the independence movement. Not only was the Japanese language not taught, but students were actually forbidden to speak Japanese. I had a different opinion on this. I felt that we had to know our enemy if we were to defeat him. I took another transfer exam and entered the fourth grade of the Jeongju Public Normal School. In public schools, all classes were conducted in Japanese, so I memorized *katakana* and *hiragana* the night before my first day of class. (*Katakana* and *hiragana* are the two different scripts used for writing the Japanese language.) I didn't know any Japanese, so I took all the textbooks from grades one through four and memorized them over the course of two weeks. This enabled me to start understanding the language.

By the time I graduated from grammar school, I was fluent in Japanese. On the day of my graduation, I volunteered to give a speech before a gathering of all the important people in Jeongju. Normally in that situation, the student is expected to speak about his gratitude for the support received from his teachers and the school. Instead, I referred to each of my teachers by name and critiqued them, pointing out problems in the way the school was run. I also spoke on our time in history and the kind of determination that people in responsible positions should have. I gave this rather critical speech entirely in Japanese.

"Japanese people should pack their bags as soon as possible and go back to Japan," I said. "This land was handed down to us by our ancestors, and all the future generations of our people must live here."

I said these things in front of the chief of police, the county chief, and town mayor. I was taking after the spirit of Great-Uncle Yoon Guk Moon and saying things that no one else dared say. The audience was shocked. When I left the stage, I could see people's faces had turned pale.

Nothing happened to me that day, but there were problems later on. From that day, the Japanese police marked me as a person to be tracked and began watching me, making a nuisance of themselves. Later, when I was trying to go to Japan to continue my studies, the chief of police refused to place his stamp on a form that I needed, and this caused me some trouble. He regarded me as a dangerous person who should not be allowed to travel to Japan. I had a big argument with him and finally convinced him to put his stamp on the form. Only then could I go to Japan.

CHAPTER TWO

MY HEART FLOWS
WITH A RIVER
OF TEARS

Between Fear and Inspiration

As I grew older and more mature, I became preoccupied with the question, "What will I be when I grow up?" I enjoyed observing and studying nature, so I gave some thought to becoming a scientist. However, I changed my mind after I saw the tragedy of how people were plundered by the Japanese colonial authorities. They suffered so much that they could not even feed themselves. It didn't seem that becoming a scientist, even if it led to my winning a Nobel Prize, would be a way for me to wipe away the tears of suffering people.

I wanted to become a person who could take away the tears that flowed from people's eyes and the sorrow that was in their hearts. When I was lying in the forest listening to the songs of the birds, I would think, "The world needs to be made as warm and tender as those songs. I should become someone who makes people's lives as fragrant as flowers." I didn't know what career I should pursue to accomplish that, but I became convinced that I should be a person who could give happiness to people.

When I was ten our family converted to Christianity by the grace of Great-Uncle Yoon Guk Moon, who was a minister and led a fervent life of faith. From then on, I attended church faithfully, without ever missing a week. If I arrived at service even a little late, I would be so ashamed that I could not even raise my face. I don't know what I could have understood at such a young age to inspire me to be this way, but God was already a huge presence in my life. I was spending more and more time wrestling with questions dealing with life and death, and the suffering and sorrows of human existence.

When I was twelve, I witnessed my great-grandfather's grave being moved. Normally, only adults in the clan would be allowed to attend such an occasion, but I wanted very much to see for myself what happened to people after they died. I eventually persuaded my parents to allow me to come along. When the grave was dug up and I saw his remains, I was overcome with shock and fear. While the adults opened the grave with solemn ceremony, all I saw was a scrawny skeleton. There was no trace of the features my father and mother had described to me. There was only the hideous sight of white bones.

It took me a while to get over the shock of seeing my great-grandfather's bones. I said to myself, "Great-Grandfather must have looked just like us. Does this mean my parents, too, will turn into just a bunch of white bones after they die? Is this what will happen to me when I die? Everyone dies, but after we die, do we just lie there unable to think about anything?" I couldn't get these questions out of my head.

Around that same time, a number of strange events occurred in our home. I have a vivid memory of one in particular. Each time our family wove cloth, we would take the snippets of thread from the loom and save them in an earthenware jar until we had enough to make a bolt of cloth. The cloth we made from these snippets, called *yejang*, was used to make ceremonial clothes used when a child in the family married. One night, these snippets were found scattered all over the branches of an old chestnut tree in a neighboring village. They made the tree look like it had turned white. We couldn't understand who would have taken the snippets from the jar and carried them all the way to the chestnut tree, which was quite a distance from our home, and then spread them all over the tree. It didn't seem like something that could be done by human hands, and it frightened everyone in the village.

When I was sixteen, we experienced the tragedy of having five of my younger siblings die in a single year. No words could describe the heartbreak of our parents in losing five of their thirteen children in such a short time. Death seemed to spread. Other clan members lost their livestock. One family's cow suddenly died, though it had been in perfect health. At another home, several horses died, one after another. At a third home, seven pigs died in one night.

The suffering of one family seemed connected to the suffering of the nation and of the world. I was increasingly troubled to see the wretched situation of the Korean people under Japan's tyrannical rule. People didn't have enough to eat. They were sometimes forced to take grass, tree bark, and whatever else they could find, and boil these for food. There seemed to be no end to wars around the world.

Then one day I read an article in a newspaper about the suicide of a middle-school student who was the same age as I. "Why did he die?" I asked myself. "What would drive a person to kill himself at such a young age?" I was devastated by this news, as if it had happened to someone who had been close to me. With the newspaper open to that article, I wept aloud for three days and nights. The tears kept coming, and I couldn't make them stop.

I couldn't comprehend the series of strange events, or the fact that tragic events were happening to good people. Seeing the bones of my great-grandfather had inspired me to start asking questions about life and death, and the series of unusual events in and around our home caused me to hang on to religion. The word of God I was hearing in church, however, was not sufficient by itself to give me the clear answers I was seeking. To relieve the frustrations in my heart, I naturally began to immerse myself in prayer.

"Who am I? Where did I come from? What is the purpose of life? What happens to people when they die? Is there a world of the eternal soul? Does God really exist? Is God really all-powerful? If He is, why does He just stand by and watch the sorrows of the world? If God created this world, did He also create the suffering that is in the world? What will bring an end to Korea's tragic occupation by Japan? What is the meaning of the suffering of the Korean people? Why do human beings hate each other, fight, and start wars?" My heart was filled with these serious and fundamental questions. No one could easily answer them for me, so my only option was to pray. Prayer helped me to find solace. Whenever I laid out the anguishing problems in my heart to God, all my suffering and sorrow vanished and my heart felt at ease. I began spending more and more time in prayer, to the point that, eventually, I began praying through the night all the time. As a result, I had a rare and precious experience in which God answered my prayers. That day will always remain as the most cherished memory of my life—a day I can never forget.

It was the night before Easter in the year I turned sixteen. I was on Mount Myodu praying all night and begging God in tears for answers. Why had He created a world so filled with sorrow and despair? Why was the all-knowing and all-powerful God leaving the world in such pain? What should I do for my tragic homeland? I wept in tears as I asked these questions repeatedly. Early Easter morning, after I had spent the entire night in prayer, Jesus appeared before me. He appeared in an instant, like a gust of wind, and said to me, "God is in great sorrow because of the pain of humankind. You must take on a special mission on earth having to do with Heaven's work."

That morning, I saw clearly the sorrowful face of Jesus. I heard his voice clearly. The experience of witnessing the manifestation of Jesus caused my body to shake violently, like a quaking aspen's leaves trembling in a strong breeze. I was simultaneously overcome with fear so great I felt I might die and gratitude so profound I felt I might explode. Jesus spoke clearly about the work I would have to do. His words were extraordinary, having to do with saving humanity from its suffering and bringing joy to God.

My initial response was, "I can't do this. How can I do this? Why would you even give me a mission of such paramount importance?" I was truly afraid. I wanted somehow to avoid this mission, and I clung to the hem of his clothing and wept inconsolably.

The More It Hurts,
the More You Should Love

I was thrown into extreme confusion. I couldn't open my heart to my parents and share my huge secret with them. But neither could I just keep it to myself. I was at a loss over what to do. What was clear was that I had received a special mission from Heaven.

It was such a huge and tremendous responsibility. I shuddered in fear to think that I might not be able to handle it on my own. I clung to prayer even more than before, in an attempt to quiet my confused heart. But even this had no effect. No matter how much I tried, I could not free myself for even a moment from the memory of having met Jesus. My encounter with Jesus changed my life completely. His sorrowful expression was etched into my heart as if it had been branded there, and I could not think of anything else. From that day on, I immersed myself completely in the word of God. At times, I was surrounded by endless darkness and filled with such pain that it was difficult to breathe. At other times, my heart was filled with joy, as though I were watching the morning sun rise above the horizon. In an effort to quiet my heart and my tears, I composed the following poem:

CROWN OF GLORY

When I doubt people, I feel pain.
When I judge people, it is unbearable.
When I hate people, there is no value to my existence.

Yet if I believe, I am deceived.
If I love, I am betrayed.
Suffering and grieving tonight, my head in my hands,
Am I wrong?

Yes I am wrong.
Even though we are deceived, still believe.
Though we are betrayed, still forgive.
Love completely, even those who hate you.

Wipe your tears away and welcome with a smile
Those who know nothing but deceit,
And those who betray without regret.

O, Master, the pain of loving.
Look at my hands.
Place your hand on my chest.
My heart is bursting, such agony.

But when I loved those who acted against me,
I brought victory.
If you have done the same things,
I will give you the Crown of Glory.

I experienced a series of days like these that led me into a deeper and deeper world of prayer. I embraced new words of truth that Jesus was giving me directly and let myself be completely captivated by God. I began to live an entirely different life. I had many things to think about, and I gradually became a boy of few words.

Anyone who follows the path of God must pursue his goal with his whole heart and total dedication. It requires a steadfastness of purpose. I am stubborn by birth, so I have always had plenty of tenacity. I used this God-given tenacity to overcome difficulties and follow the way that was given me. Anytime I began to waver, I steadied myself by remembering: "I received God's word directly." It was not easy to choose this course, because it would require me to sacrifice the rest of my youth. At times, I felt I would rather avoid the path.

A wise person will place hope in the future and continue to move forward, no matter how difficult it may be. A foolish person, on the other hand, will throw away his future for the sake of immediate happiness. I, too, at times held foolish thoughts when I was still very young, but in the end I chose the path of the wise person. I gladly offered up my life in order to pursue the way God desired. I could not have run away if I tried; this was the only way I could have chosen. So why did God call me? Even now, at ninety years of age, I wonder every day why God called me. Of all the people in the world, why did He choose me? It wasn't because I had a particularly good appearance, or outstanding character, or deep conviction. I was just an unremarkable, stubborn, and foolish young boy. If God saw something in me, it must have been a sincere heart that sought Him with tears of love. Whatever the time or place, love is most important. God was searching for a person who would live with a heart of love and who, when faced with suffering, could cut off its effects with love. I was a boy in a rural village with nothing to show for myself. Even now, I insist uncompromisingly on sacrificing my life to live for God's love and nothing else.

There was nothing I could know on my own, so I took all my questions to God. I asked, "God, do You really exist?" and that was how I came to know that He did, in fact, exist. I asked, "God, do You have any cherished desires?" and this was how I came to know that He, too, had cherished desires. I asked Him, "God, do You need me?" and this was how I discovered that He had use for me.

On those days when my prayers and dedication connected to Heaven, Jesus appeared to me without fail and conveyed special messages. If I was earnest in my desire to know something, Jesus would appear with a gentle expression and give me answers of truth. His words were always on the mark, and they struck deep into my bosom like sharp arrows. These were not mere words; they were revelations about the creation of the universe that opened the door to a new world. When Jesus spoke, it seemed like a soft breeze, but I took his words to heart and prayed with an earnestness strong enough to uproot a tree. Gradually, I came into a new realization about God's purpose in creating the universe, and His principles of creation.

During the summer of that year, I went on a pilgrimage around the country. I had no money. I would go to homes and ask to be fed. If I was lucky, I caught a ride on a truck. This was how I visited every corner of the country. Everywhere I went, I saw that my homeland was a crucible of tears. There was no end to the sorrowful sighs of suffering from hungry people. Their woeful lamentations turned to tears that flowed like a river.

"This wretched history must end as quickly as possible," I told myself. "Our people must not be left to suffer in sorrow and despair. Somehow,

I need to find a way to go to Japan and to America so that I can let the world know the greatness of the Korean people."

Through this pilgrimage, I was able to redouble my determination toward my future work.

As I clenched my two fists, my mind became totally focused, and I could see clearly the path I had to follow in my life: "I absolutely will save our people, and bring God's peace on this earth."

A Knife Not Sharpened Grows Dull

After completing grammar school, I moved to Seoul and lived alone in the Heuksok-Dong neighborhood while attending the Kyeongsung School of Commerce and Technology.

The winter in Seoul was extremely cold. It was normal for the temperature to fall to minus twenty degrees Celsius, and when it did, the Han River would freeze over. The house where I lived was on a ridge, and there was no running water. We drew our water from a well that was so deep it took more than ten arm-lengths of rope for the pail to reach the water below. The rope kept breaking, so I made a chain and attached it to the pail. Each time I brought water up, though, my hands would freeze to the chain and I could only keep them warm by blowing on them.

To fight the cold, I used my knitting talents. I made a sweater, thick socks, a cap, and gloves. The hat was so stylish that when I wore it around town some people would think I was a woman.

I never heated my room, even on the coldest winter days, mainly because I didn't have the money to do so. I also felt that having a roof over my head when I slept meant that I was living in luxury compared to homeless people forced to find ways to keep themselves warm on the streets. One day, it was so cold I slept while holding a lightbulb against my body under the quilt, like a hot water bottle. During the night, I burned myself on the hot bulb, causing some skin to peel. Even now, when someone mentions Seoul, the first thing that comes to mind is how cold it was back then.

My meals consisted of a bowl of rice and never more than one side dish, whereas average Korean meals include up to twelve side dishes. It was always one meal, one dish. One side dish was enough. Even today, because of the habit I formed while living alone, I don't need many side dishes at my meals. I prefer to have just one side dish that is prepared well. When I see a meal that has been prepared with many side dishes, it only seems troublesome to me. I never ate lunch while attending school in Seoul. I became accustomed to eating just two meals a day while roaming around the hills as a child. I continued this lifestyle until I was nearly thirty.

My time in Seoul gave me a good understanding of how much work goes into managing a household.

I returned to Heuksok-Dong in the 1980s and was surprised to find the house where I once lived still standing. The room where I lived and the courtyard where I used to hang my laundry were still there. I was sad to see, though, that the well where I had to blow on my hands while pulling up pails of water was gone.

During my time in Heuksok-Dong, I adopted for myself the motto, "Before seeking to dominate the universe, first perfect your ability to dominate yourself." This means that to have the strength to save the nation and the world, I first had to train my own body. I trained myself through prayer and meditation and through sports and exercise programs. As a result, I would not be swayed by hunger or any other emotion or desire of the physical body. Even when I ate a meal, I would say, "Rice, I want you to become the fertilizer for the work that I am preparing myself to do." I learned boxing, soccer, and self-defense techniques. Because of this, although I have gained some weight since I was young, I still have the flexibility of a young person.

Kyeongsung School of Commerce and Technology had a policy that the students would take turns cleaning their own classrooms. In my class, I decided to clean the classroom every day by myself. I did not do this as some kind of punishment. It was an expression of my desire that welled up naturally from within to love the school more than anyone else. In the beginning, others would try to help, but they could see I didn't appreciate this and preferred to do it alone. Eventually my classmates decided, "Go ahead. Do it by yourself." And so the cleaning became my job.

I was an unusually quiet student. Unlike my classmates, I didn't engage in idle chatter, and I would often go an entire day without speaking a word. This may have been the reason that, although I never engaged in physical violence, my classmates treated me with respect and were careful how they acted in my presence. If I went to the toilet and there was a line of students waiting their turn, they would immediately let me go first. If someone had a problem, I was frequently the one they sought out for advice.

I was very persistent in asking questions during class, and there were more than a few teachers who were stumped by my questions. For example, when we were learning a new formula in mathematics or physics class, I would ask, "Who made this formula? Please explain it to us step by step so that I can understand it exactly," and refused to back down until I got clear answers. I was relentless with my teachers, digging deeper and deeper. I couldn't accept any principle in the world until I had taken it apart and figured it out for myself. I found myself wishing I had been the person to first discover such a beautiful formula. The stubborn character that had made me cry all night as a little boy was making its appearance in my studies as well. Just as when I prayed, I poured myself completely into my studies and invested my full sincerity and dedication.

Any task we do requires sincerity and dedication, and not just for a day or two. It needs to be a continuous process. A knife used once and never sharpened turns dull. The same is true with sincerity and dedication. We need to continue our efforts on a daily basis with the thought that we are sharpening our blade daily. Whatever the task, if we continue the effort in this way, we eventually reach a mystical state. If you pick up a paintbrush and focus your sincerity and dedication on your hand and say to yourself, "A great artist will come and help me," and concentrate your mind, you can create a wonderful painting that will inspire the world.

I dedicated myself to learning how to speak faster and more ac-curately than anyone else. I would go into a small room where no one could hear me and practice tongue twisters out loud. I practiced pouring out what I wanted to say very quickly. Eventually, I was able to say ten words in the time that it took others to say just one. Even now, though I am old, I can speak very quickly. Some say that I speak so quickly that they have difficulty understanding me, but my heart is in such a hurry that I cannot bear to speak slowly. My mind is full of things I want to say. How can I slow down?

In that sense, I am very much like my grandfather, who enjoyed talking with people. Grandfather could go three or four hours talking to people in our home's guest room, explaining to them his views on the events of the day. I am the same way. When I am with people and there is good communication of heart, I completely lose track of time, and I don't know if night is falling or if the sun is rising. The words in my heart form an unstoppable flow. When I am like this, I don't want to eat; I just want to talk. It's difficult for the people who are listening, and beads of sweat begin to appear on their foreheads. Sweat is running down my face, too, as I continue talking, and they dare not ask to excuse themselves and leave. We often end up staying up all night together.

A Key to Unlock a Great Secret

Just as I had climbed all the mountain peaks around my hometown, I explored every corner of Seoul. In those days, there was a streetcar line that ran from one end of the city to another. The price of a ticket was just five *jeon* (one *jeon* is the equivalent of a penny), but I didn't want to spend that money and would walk all the way into the center of the city. On hot summer days, I would be dripping with sweat as I walked, and on frigid winter days I would walk almost at a run, as if piercing my way through the bitter arctic wind. I walked so quickly that I could go from Heuksok-Dong, across the Han River, to the Hwa Shin Department Store on Jong Ro in just forty-five minutes. Most people would take an hour and a half, so you can imagine how quickly I was walking.

I saved the price of a streetcar ticket and gave the money to people who needed it more than I did. It was such a small amount it was embarrassing to give it, but I gave it with a heart that desired to give a fortune. I gave it with a prayer that this money would be a seed for the person to receive many blessings. Every April, my family would send me money for tuition. But I couldn't stand by and watch people around me who were in financial difficulty, so the money wouldn't even last to May. Once, when I was on my way to school, I came across a person who was so sick he seemed about to die. I felt so bad for him I couldn't pass him by. I carried him on my back to a hospital about a kilometer and a quarter away. I had the money I intended to use to pay my tuition, so I paid the bill. However, once I paid the hospital, I had nothing left. In the following days, the school repeatedly demanded I pay my tuition. My friends felt sorry for me and took up a collection for me. I can never forget the friends who helped me through that situation.

The giving and receiving of help is a relationship that is matched in heaven. You might not realize it at the time, but thinking back later, you may understand, "Oh, so that's why God sent me there at that time!" So if a person who needs your help suddenly appears before you, you should realize that Heaven sent you to that person to help him, and then do your best. If Heaven wants you to give the person ten units of help, it won't do if you only give him five. If Heaven says to give him ten, you should give him a hundred. When helping someone, you should be ready, if necessary, to empty your wallet.

In Seoul, I came across *baram ddok,* a fluffy "air-filled" rice cake, for the first time in my life. These are colorful rice cakes made in a beautiful design. When I first saw one, I was amazed at how wonderful they looked. When I bit into one, however, I discovered they had no filling, only air. They just collapsed in my mouth.

This made me realize something about Seoul at that time. Seoul was just like an air-filled rice cake. I understood why people in Seoul were often thought of as misers by other Koreans. On the surface, Seoul seemed like a world filled with rich and important people. In reality, though, it was full of poor people. Many beggars, clothed only in rags, lived under the Han River Bridge. I visited them, cut their hair for them, and shared my heart with them. Poor people have many tears. They have a lot of sorrow pent up in their hearts. I would just say a few words to someone, and he would break down in tears. Sometimes, one of them would hand me rice he had been given as he begged. He would hand it to me with hands caked in dirt. I never refused the food. I received it with a joyful heart.

I attended church every Sunday in my hometown, and I continued this practice in Seoul. Mainly, I attended the Myungsudae Jesus Church located in Heuksok-Dong and the Seobinggo Pentecostal Church that held services on the opposite shore of the Han River. On cold winter days, as I was walking across the frozen river to Seobinggo-Dong, the ice would make crackling sounds under my feet.

At church I served as a Sunday School teacher. The children always enjoyed my interesting lessons. I am no longer as adept at telling jokes as I was when I was young, but back then I could tell funny stories. When I wept, they wept with me, and when I laughed, they laughed along with me. I was so popular with them that they would follow me around wherever I went.

Behind Myungsudae is Mount Seodal, also known as Mount Darma. I would often climb up on a large boulder on Mount Darma and spend the night in prayer. In hot weather and in cold, I immersed myself in prayer without missing a night. Once I entered into prayer, I would weep, and my nose would start to run. I would pray for hours over words I had received from God. His words were like coded messages, and I felt I needed to immerse myself even more deeply in prayer. Thinking back on it now, I realize that even then God had placed in my hands the key that unlocked the door to secrets. However, I wasn't able to open the door, because my prayers were insufficient. I was so preoccupied that when I ate my meals, it didn't feel as though I were eating.

At bedtime, I would close my eyes, but I couldn't fall asleep. Other students rooming in the same house didn't realize I was going up on the hill to pray. They must have felt I was somehow different, though, because they related to me with respect. Generally, we got along well, making each other laugh by telling funny stories.

I can relate well with anyone. If an old woman comes to me, I can be her friend. If children come, I can play with them. You can have communication of heart with anyone by relating to them with love.

Mrs. Gi Wan Lee became close to me after she was inspired by my prayers during early morning services at the church. We maintained our friendship for more than fifty years, until she left this world at age eighty. Her younger sister, Mrs. Gi Bong Lee, was always busy managing the rooming house, but she related to me with warmth. She would say she didn't feel right unless she could find something to do for me. She would try to give me extra side dishes for my meals. I didn't talk much and wasn't much fun, so I don't know why she would want to treat me so well. Sometime later, when the Japanese colonial police were holding me in the Kyeonggi Province Police Station, she brought me clothes and food. Even now it warms my heart to think of her.

There was also a Mrs. Song who ran a small store near my rooming house. She helped me a lot during this time. She would say that anyone who lives away from his hometown is always hungry, and she would bring me items from her store that she had not been able to sell. It was a small store, and she barely made enough money to support herself, but she always took care of me with a kind heart.

One day, we held a service on a sandy stretch by the Han River. When it came time for lunch, everyone found a place to sit down and eat. I was in the habit of not eating lunch and didn't feel comfortable sitting there doing nothing while others ate. I quietly walked away from the group and found a place to sit on a pile of rocks. Mrs. Song saw me there and brought me two pieces of bread and some flavored ice. How grateful I felt! These were just one *jeon* apiece, and only four jeon in total, but I have never been able to forget the gratitude I felt in that moment.

I always remember when someone helps me, no matter how small it may be. Even now that I am ninety years old, I can recite from memory all the times that people helped me and what they did for me. I can never forget the people who did not hesitate to put themselves to great trouble on my behalf and generously gave me their blessings.

If I receive a favor, it is important to me that I repay it. If I cannot meet the person who did this for me, it is important for me to remember that person in my heart. I need to live with the sincere thought that I will repay the person by helping someone else.

Like a Fireball Burning Hot

After graduating from the Kyeongsung Institute in 1942, I traveled to Japan to continue my studies. I went because I felt that I needed to have exact knowledge about Japan. On the train to Busan, I couldn't stop the tears from flowing. I covered myself with my coat and cried out loud. My nose ran and my face swelled up, I cried so much. It grieved me to think that I was leaving my country behind as it suffered under the yoke of colonial rule. I looked out the window as I wept, and I could see that the hills and rivers were weeping even more sorrowfully than I was. I saw with my own eyes the tears flowing from the grass and trees. Upon seeing this vision, I said, "I promise to the hills and streams of my homeland that I will return, carrying with me the liberation of my homeland. So don't cry, but wait for me."

I boarded the Busan-to-Shimonoseki ferry at two o'clock in the morning on April 1. There was a strong wind that night, but I could not leave the deck. I stayed there watching as the lights of Busan became more and more distant. I stayed on deck until morning. On arriving in Tokyo, I entered Waseda Koutou Kougakko, a technical engineering school affiliated with Waseda University. I studied in the Electrical Engineering Department. I chose electrical engineering because I felt I could not establish a new religious philosophy without knowing modern engineering.

The invisible world of mathematics has something in common with religion. To do something great, a person needs to excel in powers of reasoning. Perhaps because of my large head, I was good at mathematics that others found difficult, and I enjoyed studying it. My head was so large it was difficult for me to find hats that fit. I had to go to the factory twice to have a hat tailor-made for me. The size of my head may also have something to do with my ability to focus on something and finish relatively quickly what might take others several years to complete.

During my studies in Japan, I peppered my teachers with questions, just as I had in Korea. Once I began asking questions, I would continue and continue. Some teachers would pretend not to see me and simply ignore me when I asked, "What do you think about this?" If I had any doubts about something, I couldn't be satisfied until I had pursued the matter all the way to the root. I wasn't deliberately trying to embarrass my teachers. I felt that if I were going to study a subject I should study it completely.

On my desk in the boarding house, I always had three Bibles lying open side by side. One was in Korean, one in Japanese, and one in English. I would read the same passages in three languages again and again. Each time I read a passage, I would underline verses and make notes in the margins until the pages of my Bibles became stained with black ink and difficult to read.

Soon after school began, I attended an event held by the Association of Korean Students to welcome new students from our country. There I sang a song from our homeland with great fervor, showing everyone my love for my country. The Japanese police were in attendance, and this was a time when Koreans were expected to assimilate themselves into Japanese culture. Nonetheless, I sang the Korean song with pride. Duk Mun Eom, who had entered the Department of Architectural

Engineering that year, was deeply moved to hear me sing this song, and we became lifelong friends.

During this time, Korean students who were enrolled in various schools in the Tokyo area had formed an underground independence movement. This was only natural, as our homeland was groaning in agony under Japanese colonial rule.

The movement grew in response to what the Japanese called "the Great East Asian War (1937–1945). As the war intensified, Tokyo began conscripting Korean students as "student soldiers" and sending them to the front. The work of the underground independence movement was spurred on by such moves. We had extensive debates on what to do about Hirohito, the Japanese emperor. I took on a major position in the movement. It involved working in close relationship with the Republic of Korea Provisional Government, located in Shanghai and headed by Kim Gu. My responsibilities in this position could have required me to give up my life. I did not hesitate, though, because I felt that, if I died, it would have been for a righteous cause.

There was a police station beside Waseda University. The Japanese police got wind of my work and kept a sharp eye on me. The police always knew when I was about to return home to Korea during school vacation and would follow me to the dock to make sure I left. I cannot even remember the number of times I was taken into custody by the police, beaten, tortured, and locked in a cell. Even under the worst torture, however, I refused to give them the information they sought.

The more they beat me, the bolder I became. Once I had a fight on the Yotsugawa Bridge with police who were chasing me. I ripped out a piece of the bridge railing and used it as a weapon in the fight. In those days, I was a ball of fire.

Befriending Laborers by
Sharing Their Suffering

Just as I had done in Seoul, I made it a point to go everywhere in Tokyo. When my friends would go to places such as Nikko to see the
beautiful scenery, I would prefer to stay behind and walk through
all the neighborhoods of Tokyo. I found that it was a city that looked
fancy on the outside but was actually filled with impoverished people.
Again I gave all the money I received from home to the poor people.

Back then everyone in Japan was hungry too. Among the Korean
students there were many who were in financial difficulty. When I received my allotment of meal tickets each month I would give them all
away to students who couldn't afford them and told them, "Eat. Eat all
you want." I didn't worry about earning money. I could go anywhere and
work as a day laborer and be fed. I enjoyed earning money and using
the money to help pay the tuition of students who didn't have money.
Helping others and giving them food to eat filled me with energy.

After I had given away all the money I had, I would work as a
deliveryman using a bicycle-drawn cart. I went to every district of
Tokyo with that cart. Once, in Ginza, with its dazzling lights, I was
carrying a telephone pole on my cart and it turned over in the middle

of an intersection. Everyone around ran for their lives. Because of these kinds of experiences I still know the geography of Tokyo like the back of my hand.

I was a laborer among laborers and a friend to laborers. Just like the laborers who smelled of sweat, I would go to the work sites and work until the sweat was pouring down my body. They were my brothers, and I didn't mind the terrible smells. I shared sleeping quilts with them that were so filthy that black lice crawled across them in a line formation. I didn't hesitate to grasp hands that were caked with dirt. Their sweat mixed with grime was filled with an irresistible warmth of heart. It was their warm hearts that I found so attractive.

Primarily I worked as a laborer at the Kawasaki steel mill and shipyard. In the shipyard there were barges used to haul coal. We would form teams of three laborers each and work until one o'clock in the morning to fill a barge with one hundred twenty tons of coal. We Koreans could do in one night what it took the Japanese three days to accomplish.

There were people at some work sites who extorted the blood and sweat of the laborers. Often these were the foremen who directly managed the laborers. They would take thirty percent of the money earned by the laborers they managed and keep it for themselves. The laborers were powerless to do anything about this. The foremen would exploit the weak but curry favor with those who were strong. I became so angry with one foreman that I finally went to him with two friends and demanded that he pay the workers their full wages.

"If you make someone work, then pay him exactly what he is owed," I told him.

He still refused, so we went to him a second day and even a third. We were determined to keep up the pressure until he relented. Finally

I kicked him and he even fell down. I usually am a quiet and peaceable person, but when I become angry the stubborn character of my younger years comes back.

The Kawasaki steel mill had vats used to store sulfuric acid. Workers would clean these by going into them and making the raw material flow out. The fumes from the sulfuric acid were extremely toxic, and a person could not remain inside for more than fifteen minutes. Even in such deplorable working conditions, the workers risked their lives in order to have food to eat. Food was that precious.

I was always hungry. I was careful, though, to never eat a meal for my own sake. I felt there needed to be a specific reason for me to eat a meal. So as I would sit down to each meal I would ask myself if my hunger was worthy. "Did I really work hard? Did I work for myself, or for a public purpose?" I would face a bowl of rice and tell it, "I am eating you so that I can do tasks that are more glorious and more for the public good than what I did yesterday." Then the rice would smile back at me with its approval. In those instances, the time spent eating a meal was mystical and joyful. When I didn't feel qualified to talk this way, I would skip the meal no matter how hungry I might be. As a result, there were not many days when I would have even two meals.

I didn't limit myself to two meals a day because I had a small appetite. In fact, once I began to eat there was no limit to the amount I could consume. I once ate eleven large bowls of udon (noodles) in one sitting. Another time I ate seven bowls of a dish consisting of chicken and a fried egg over rice. Despite this appetite I kept up my custom of not eating lunch and limiting myself to two meals a day until I was more than thirty years old.

The sensation of hunger is a type of nostalgia. I knew very well about the nostalgia of hunger, but I believed it was the least I could do to sacrifice one meal a day for the sake of the world. I also never allowed myself to wear new clothes. No matter how cold it might get, I would not heat my room. When it was extremely cold I used a newspaper to cover myself; it felt as warm as a quilt made of silk. I am very familiar with the value of a sheet of newspaper.

At times I would simply go live for a while in an area of Shinagawa where poor people lived. I slept with them, using rags for cover. On warm sunny days I picked lice from their hair and ate rice with them. There were many prostitutes on the streets of Shinagawa. I would listen to them tell me about themselves, and I became their best friend without ever drinking a drop of liquor. Some people claim they need to be drunk in order to speak candidly about what is on their mind, but that is just an excuse. When these women realized that I was sincere in my sympathy for them, even without drinking any liquor, they opened their hearts to me and told me their troubles.

I worked in many different jobs during my studies in Japan. I was a janitor in an office building. I wrote letters for illiterate people. I worked at various job sites and was a foreman. I was a fortune teller. When I needed money quickly, I wrote calligraphy and sold it. I never fell behind in my studies, however. I believed that all these things were part of my training process. I did all sorts of jobs and met all sorts of people. In the process I learned a lot about people. Because I had this experience I can now take one look at a person and have a good idea of what the person does for a living and whether he is a good person. I don't have to weigh various thoughts in my head, because my body will tell me first.

I still believe that to develop good character a person needs to experience many difficulties before turning thirty. People need to go down into the crucible of despair at the bottom of human existence and experience what that is like. People need to discover new possibilities in the midst of hell. It is only when climbing out of the depths of despair and making a new determination that we can be reborn as people able to pioneer a new future.

We should not look only in one direction. We should look at both those who are in a higher position and those lower. We should know to look east, west, south, and north. To live a successful life depends on how well we see with our mind's eye. To see well with the mind's eye we must have many different experiences and remember them. Even in the most difficult situations we should maintain our composure, demonstrate warmth toward others, be self-reliant, and adapt well to any circumstance.

A person of good character must be accustomed to rising to a high position and then quickly falling to a low position. Most people are afraid of falling from a high position, so they do everything they can to preserve it. However, water that does not flow becomes stagnant. A person who rises to a high position must be able to go back down and wait for the time to come up again. When the opportunity comes, he can rise to an even higher position than before. This is the type of person who can acquire a greatness that is admired by many people and is a great leader. These are the experiences that a person should have before turning thirty.

Today I tell young people to experience everything they can in the world. They need to directly or indirectly experience everything in the world, as if they were devouring an encyclopedia. It is only then that they can form their own identity. A person's self-identity is his clear subjective nature. Once a person has the confidence to say, "I can go all around the country, and I will never come across a person who is capable of defeating me," then he is ready to take on any task and have the confidence to accomplish it successfully. When a person lives life in this way, he will be successful. Success is assured. This is the conclusion I arrived at while living as a beggar in Tokyo.

I shared meals and slept with laborers in Tokyo, shared the grief of hunger with beggars, learned the hard life, and earned my doctorate in the philosophy of suffering. Only then was I able to understand God's will as He works to bring salvation to humanity. It is important to become the king of suffering before age thirty. The way to gain the glory of the Kingdom of Heaven is to become a king of suffering.

The Calm Sea of the Heart

Japan's situation in the war became increasingly desperate. In the urgent need to replenish the shrinking ranks of its military, it began giving early graduation to students and sending them to the war front. For this reason, I, too, graduated six months early.

Once my graduation date was set for September 30, 1943, I sent a telegram to my family saying, "Will return on *Konron Maru*," giving the name of the ship I was scheduled to board in Shimonoseki for Busan. However, on the day I was to leave Tokyo for the trip back to Korea, I had a strange experience in which my feet stuck to the ground, preventing me from moving. As hard as I tried, I could not pick my feet up off the ground to go to the train at Tokyo station.

I told myself, "It must be that Heaven doesn't want me to board that ship." So I decided to stay in Japan a while longer and went with my friends to climb Mount Fuji. When I returned to Tokyo a few days later, I found the country in an uproar over news that the *Konron Maru*, the ship I was supposed to be on, had been sunk on its way to Busan. I was told that more than five hundred people, including many university students, had been killed. *Konron Maru* was a large ship in which Japan took great pride, but it had been sunk by an American torpedo.

When my mother heard the news that the ship her son was scheduled to board had been sunk, she immediately ran out of the house without even thinking to put on her shoes. She ran barefoot eight kilometers to the train station and went directly to Busan. When she arrived at the Maritime Police Station in Busan, she discovered my name was not on the passenger manifest. The boarding house in Tokyo, however, told her that I had packed my bags and left. This put her in total confusion and agony. She just kept calling my name, not even realizing that she had large splinters in her bare feet.

I can easily imagine how she must have been beside herself with worry that something might have happened to her son. I can understand my mother's heart, but from the day I chose to follow God's path I became a terrible son to her. I couldn't afford to let myself be tied down by personal emotions. So I had not sent word that I had not boarded the ship that had been sunk, even though I knew she would be deeply concerned for my safety.

Upon finally returning to Korea, I found nothing had changed. Japan's tyrannical rule was becoming worse by the day. The entire land was soaked in blood and tears. I returned to Heuksok-Dong in Seoul and attended the Myungsudae Church. I kept detailed diaries of all the new realizations that I had each day. On days when I had a great number of such realizations, I would fill an entire diary. I was receiving answers to many of the questions that I had struggled with over the years. It was as if my years of prayers and search for truth were being answered. It happened in a short time, as if a ball of fire were passing through me.

During this time I had the realization, "The relationship between God and mankind is that of a father and his children, and God is deeply saddened to see their suffering." In this moment all the secrets of the universe were resolved in my mind. Suddenly, it was as if someone had turned on a movie projector. Everything that had happened since the time humankind broke God's commandment played out clearly before my eyes. Hot tears flowed continuously from my eyes. I fell to my knees and bowed my head to the floor. For the longest time I couldn't get up. Just as when my father carried me home on his back when I was a child, I laid my body down in God's lap and let the tears flow. Nine years after my encounter with Jesus, my eyes had finally been opened to the true love of God.

God created Adam and Eve and sent them into this world to be fruitful, to multiply, and to bring about a world of peace where they would live. But they could not follow God's timetable. They committed fornication and bore two sons, Cain and Abel. The children who were born from the Fall did not trust each other and brought about an incident where one brother murdered the other. The peace of this world was shattered, sin covered the world, and God's sorrow began. Then humankind committed another terrible sin by killing Jesus, the Messiah. So the suffering that humanity experiences today is a process of atonement that it must pass through as God's sorrow continues.

Jesus appeared to me when I was a boy of sixteen because he wanted me to know the root of the original sin that humankind had committed and to bring about a world of peace where sin and the Fall would no longer exist. I received God's serious instructions to atone for the sins of humanity and bring about the world of peace that God had originally created. The world of peace that is God's desire is not someplace we go to after death. God wants this world, where we live now, to be the completely peaceful and happy world that He created in the beginning. God certainly did not send Adam and Eve into the world for them to suffer. I had to let the world know this incredible truth.

Having discovered the secrets of the creation of the universe, I felt my heart become like a calm ocean. My heart was filled with the word of God. It felt as though it might explode, and my face was always shining with joy.

"Please Don't Die"

I continued to devote myself to prayer, and I came to feel intuitively that the time had come for me to marry. Because I had decided to follow God's path, everything about my life had to be done in accordance with God's will. Once I came to know something through prayer, I had no choice but to follow. So I went to one of my aunts who had much experience in arranging marriages and asked her to introduce me to a suitable wife. This is how I met Seon Gil Choi, the daughter of a prominent Christian family in Jeongju.

She was a well-raised woman from an upright family. She had attended only elementary school, but her character was so strong and her Christian faith so deep that she had been imprisoned at age sixteen for refusing to comply with a Japanese colonial requirement that all Koreans worship at Shinto shrines. I was told that I was the twenty-fourth man to be considered as her groom, so it seems she was very selective about whom she would marry.

Once I returned to Seoul, however, I forgot completely I had even met the woman. My plan after completing my studies in Japan had been to travel to Hailar, China, a city on the border between China, the Soviet Union, and Mongolia.

My school in Tokyo had arranged a job for me with the Manchuria Electric Company, and my plan was to work in Hailar for about three years while learning Russian, Chinese, and Mongolian. Just as I had earlier sought out a school that would teach me Japanese so that I could win over the Japanese, I wanted to go to this border city and learn a number of foreign languages as a way of preparing myself for the future.

It was becoming increasingly clear, however, that Japan was heading for defeat in the war. I decided that it would be better for me not to go to Manchuria. So I stopped by a branch office of the Manchuria Electric Company in Andong (present-day Dandong) and submitted paperwork to cancel my job placement. I then headed for my hometown.

When I arrived, I found that the aunt whom I had asked to arrange my marriage was in great distress. Apparently, the woman I had met was refusing to consider anyone other than me as her partner and was causing great trouble for her family. My aunt took me by the arm and led me to the Choi family home.

I explained to Seon Gil Choi clearly about the kind of life I intended to lead. "Even if we marry now, you should be prepared to live without me for at least seven years," I told her.

"Why should I do that?" she responded.

I told her, "I have a task that is more important than family life right now. In fact, my reason for getting married has to do with my ability to carry out God's providence. Our marriage needs to develop beyond the family to the point where we can love the nation and all humanity. Now that you know that this is my intention, do you truly want to marry me?"

She responded with a firm voice: "It doesn't matter to me. After I met you, I dreamed of a field of flowers in the moonlight. I am certain that you are my spouse sent from heaven. I can endure any difficulty."

I was still concerned, and I pressed her several times. Each time she sought to set my mind at ease, saying, "I am willing to do anything, as long as I am able to marry you. Don't worry about anything."

My future father-in-law suddenly passed away a week before our scheduled wedding date, so our wedding was delayed. We were finally able to hold our ceremony on May 4, 1944. Normally May is a time for beautiful spring days, but on our wedding day it rained heavily. Rev. Ho Bin Lee of the Jesus Church officiated. Later, after Korea's liberation from Japan, Reverend Lee would go to South Korea and establish an ecumenical seminary called the Jungang Seminary.

My wife and I began our married life in my boarding room in Heuksok-Dong. I truly loved her and took such good care of her that the mistress of the boarding house would say, "Oh my, you must really love her, since you treat her as if you were handling an egg."

I got a job at the Kyeongsung branch of the Kashima Gumi Construction Company in Yongsan in order to support our family while I also carried out church work. Then, one day in October, the Japanese police suddenly stormed into our home.

"Do you know so-and-so of Waseda University?" they demanded. Without even giving me a chance to reply, they pulled me out of the house and took me to the Kyeonggi Province Police Station. I was being detained because one of my friends had been arrested for being a communist and had mentioned my name to his interrogators.

Once inside the police station, I was immediately subjected to torture. "You're a member of the Communist Party, aren't you? Weren't you working with that rascal while you were studying in Japan? Don't even bother trying to deny it. All we have to do is put in a call to Tokyo Police Headquarters and they will tell us everything. You can give us the list of party members or die like a dog."

They beat me with a table and broke all four of its legs against my body, but I refused to give them the names of the people who had worked with me in Japan.

The Japanese police then went to where I was living with my wife, turned it upside down, and discovered my diaries. They brought the diaries to me and went through them page by page, demanding I tell them about the names they found. I denied everything, even though I knew they might kill me for my silence. The police stomped on me mercilessly with their spiked military boots until my body was as limp as if I were dead. Then they hung me from the ceiling and swung me back and forth. Like a slab of meat hanging in a butcher shop, I swung this way and that as they pushed me with a stick. Soon, blood filled my mouth and began dripping onto the cement floor below me. Each time I lost consciousness they would pour a bucket of water over me. As soon as I regained consciousness the torture would begin again.

They held my nose and stuck the spout of a teakettle into my mouth, forcing me to swallow water. When my stomach became bloated with water they laid me face-up on the floor, looking like a frog, and began stomping on my abdomen with their military boots. The water would be forced up my esophagus, and I would vomit until everything turned black. On the days after I had been tortured this way my esophagus felt as though it were on fire. The pain was so great I could not bear to swallow a single mouthful of soup. I had no energy and would just lie face down on the floor, completely unable to move.

The war was coming to an end, and the Japanese police were desperate. They tortured me in ways words cannot describe. I endured, though, and never gave them the names of any of my friends. Even as I was slipping in and out of consciousness, I made sure not to give them what they wanted. Finally tiring of torturing me, the Japanese police sent for my mother. When she arrived my legs were so swollen that I couldn't stand on my own. Two policemen had to put my arms over their shoulders and help me walk to the visiting room.

My mother had tears in her eyes even before she set eyes on me. "Endure just a little longer," she said. "I will somehow get you a lawyer. Please endure, and don't die before then."

My mother saw how my face was covered with blood, and she pleaded with me. "It doesn't matter how much good you are trying to do," she said. "It's more important that you keep yourself alive. No matter what happens, don't die."

I felt sorry for her. I would have liked to call out, "Mother," embrace her, and cry out loud with her. I couldn't do that, though, because I knew perfectly well why the Japanese police had brought her there. My mother kept pleading with me not to die, but all I could do in return was blink my badly swollen and bloodied eyes.

During the four months I was held in the Kyeonggi Province Police Station, Mrs. Gi Bong Lee, the mistress of the boarding house, kept me supplied with food and clothing. She wept every time she visited me. I would comfort her, saying, "Endure a little longer. This era is coming to an end soon. Japan will be defeated shortly. Please don't cry." These were not empty words. This is the faith God gave me.

As soon as the police released me in February of the following year, I took all my diaries that had been stacked in the boarding house to the bank of the Han River. There I burned them so they would not cause any further trouble to my friends. If I had not done this, I knew the diaries could eventually be used by the police to harm others. My body did not recover easily from the torture. I had blood in my feces for quite a while. Mrs. Lee, the boarding house mistress, and her sister helped me to nurse my body back to health with great sincerity and dedication.

Finally, on August 15, 1945, Korea was liberated from Japan. This was the day every Korean had been waiting for. It was a day of tremendous emotion. Shouts of "Mansei!" and people waving the *Taegukgi* (the national flag for the whole of Korea) covered the entire peninsula.

I could not join in the festivities, however. My heart was deadly serious because I could foresee the terrible calamity that was about to befall the Korean peninsula. I went alone into a small room and immersed myself in prayer. Soon after that, my fears were realized. Although liberated from Japanese rule, our homeland was cut in two at the 38th parallel. In the North, a communist regime that denied the existence of God came to power.

A Command That Must Be Obeyed

Immediately following liberation, our country was in indescribable chaos. Daily necessities were difficult to come by, even for people with money. We ran out of rice in our home, so I set out for Paekchon, Hwanghae Province, a community north of Seoul and just south of the 38th parallel, to pick up some rice that had been purchased previously. On my way, though, I received a revelation that said: "Go across the 38th parallel! Find the people of God who are in the North." I immediately crossed the 38th parallel and headed for Pyongyang.

It had been only a month since our first son was born. I was concerned for my wife. I knew she would be anxiously waiting for me, but there was no time for me to return home before going north. God's commands are very serious, and they must be followed without reservation or hesitation. I took nothing with me except for the Bible that I had read dozens of times and had filled with underlined notes to myself in tiny letters the size of sesame seeds.

Refugees were already streaming south to escape communist rule. In particular, the Communist Party's rejection of religion meant that many Christians were heading south in search of the freedom to worship. The communists branded religion as the opiate of the people and insisted that no one could practice religion. This was where I went following the call from Heaven. No minister would want to go into such a place, but I went there with my own two feet.

As the number of refugees heading south increased, the North began to tighten its border security. It was not easy for me to get across the 38th parallel. During the time it took me to walk forty-eight kilometers to the border and until my arrival in Pyongyang, I never questioned why I had to go such a difficult course.

I arrived in Pyongyang on June 6. Christianity had set down its roots so deeply in this city that it was known as "the Jerusalem of the East." During their occupation, the Japanese had tried in several ways to suppress Christianity. They forced citizens to worship at Shinto shrines and even had them bow in the direction of the imperial palace in Tokyo, where the emperor lived. After arriving in Pyongyang, I began my evangelical work in the home of Choi Seob Rah, who lived in the Kyeongchang Ri neighborhood near Pyongyang's West Gate.

I began by taking care of the children in the neighborhood. I would tell them children's stories that illustrated Bible verses. They were children, but I spoke to them in the polite form of speech normally reserved for adults and did my best to take care of them. At the same time, I held out hope that someone would come to hear the new message that I had to convey. There were days when I would watch the front gate the whole day, hoping that someone would come.

Soon, people with sincere faith began coming to see me. I would speak to them through the night, teaching them the new message. It didn't matter who came. It could be a three-year-old child or a blind old woman with a bent back. I treated them all with love and respect. I bowed down in front of them and served them as though they had come from heaven. Even if my guests were old men and women, I would share with them late into the night.

I never said to myself, "Oh, I hate it when such old people come." Everyone is precious. Whether it is a man or woman, young or old, everyone has the same precious value.

People listened to this twenty-six-year-old young man talk to them about the Letter to the Romans and the Book of Revelation. What they heard was different from what they had heard elsewhere, so gradually people hungry for the truth began to gather.

One young man would come every day and listen to me speak but would then leave without saying a word. This was Won Pil Kim. He became the first member of my spiritual family. He had graduated from Pyongyang Normal School and was working as a teacher. We took turns preparing the rice for meals, and this was how we formed the relationship of spiritual master and disciple.

Once I began lecturing on the Bible, I could not stop until members of the congregation excused themselves. I preached with such passion that I would sweat all over my body. Sometimes I would take a break and go into a separate room where I was alone, take off my shirt, and wring the sweat out of it. It was like this not just during the summer but even in the cold of winter. That was how much energy I poured into my teaching.

For services, everyone dressed in clean white clothing. We sang the same hymns dozens of times in repetition, making it a very passionate service. Members of the congregation would be so moved and inspired that we would all begin to weep. People called us "the weeping church." When services ended, members of the congregation testified about the grace they had received during the service. During these testimonies we felt intoxicated by grace. It was as though our bodies were floating up to heaven.

Many people in our church had spiritual experiences. Some would go into trances, some would prophesy, some would speak in tongues, some would interpret. Sometimes a person who did not belong to our church would be in the congregation. Another congregant would go up to him with eyes closed and tap him on the shoulder. Then that person would suddenly begin praying a tearful prayer of repentance. In such instances, the hot fire of the Holy Spirit would pass through our gathering. When the Holy Spirit did its work, people were cured of chronic illnesses, as thoroughly as though they had never existed. A rumor began to circulate that someone had eaten some of my left-over rice and been cured of an abdominal condition. People began to say, "The food at that church has medicinal effects," and many people began to wait for me to finish eating, hoping to eat any rice I might leave.

As such spiritual phenomena became known, our congregation grew, and soon we had so many people that we could not close the doors. Grandmother Seung Do Ji and Grandmother Se Hyun Ok came to the church because they each had a dream in which they were told, "A young spiritual teacher has come from the South and is now across from Mansudae (the central square of Pyongyang) so go meet him." No one evangelized them. They simply came to the address they were given in their dreams. When they arrived they were happy to see that I was the person they had heard about in their dreams. I only had to see their faces to understand why they had come. When I answered their questions, without first asking them what they wanted to know, they were beside themselves with joy and surprise.

I taught the word of God through stories about my own experiences. Perhaps for this reason, many people found they were able to receive clear answers to questions that they could never get answered before. Some believers from large churches in the city converted to our church after hearing me preach. In one instance, fifteen core members of the Jangsujae Church, the most prominent church in Pyongyang, came to our church as a group, causing members of the elders' board of that church to lodge a strong protest against us.

Mrs. In Ju Kim's father-in-law was a well-known elder in Pyongyang. The family home was directly adjacent to the church that her father-in-law attended. Yet instead of attending that church, she secretly attended ours. To leave her home without her in-laws knowing, she would go to the back of the house, climb up onto one of the large earthenware jars, and then climb over the fence. She did this when she was pregnant, and the fence she climbed was two or three times the height of a normal person. It took courage for her to do that. Eventually, she received severe persecution from her father-in-law. I would know when this was happening. On days when I would feel a strong pain in my heart, I would send someone to Mrs. Kim's home. As they stood outside her home they could hear her being beaten severely by her father-in-law. He would beat her so severely that she would shed tears of blood. She would say later, though, that the knowledge that our members were standing outside the gate praying for her would take away her pain.

"Teacher, how did you know I was being beaten?" she would later ask me. "When our members are at the gate, my pain goes away, and my father-in-law finds that it takes much more energy for him to beat me. Why is that?"

Her in-laws beat her and even tied her to a post, but they still could not stop her from coming to our church. Finally, her family members came to our church and started beating me. They tore my clothing and made my face swell up, but I never struck them back. I knew that doing so would only make the situation even more difficult for Mrs. Kim.

As more people from large churches around Pyongyang began attending our services, the ministers of these established churches became jealous and complained about us to the police. The communist authorities considered religion to be a thorn in their side and were looking for excuses to suppress it. They jumped on the opportunity given to them by these ministers and took me into custody. On August 11, 1946, I was charged with coming from the South for the purpose of espionage, and was imprisoned in the Daedong Security Station in Pyongyang. I was falsely accused of being sent to the North by South Korean President Syngman Rhee as part of an attempt to take over the North.

They even brought in a Soviet interrogator, but they could not establish that I had committed any crime. Finally, after three months, they found me not guilty and released me, but by this time my body was in terrible shape. I had lost so much blood while being tortured that my life was in grave danger. The members of my church took me in and cared for me. They saved my life without expecting anything in return.

Once I recovered I resumed my evangelical work. Within a year our congregation had become quite large. The established churches would not leave us alone. More and more members of their congregations began attending our services.

Finally, some eighty ministers took action by writing letters to the police. On February 22, 1948, I was again taken into custody by the communist authorities. I was charged with being a spy for Syngman

Rhee and disturbing the social order. I was taken away in handcuffs. Three days later, my head was shaved and I was placed in a prison cell. I still remember how it felt to watch my hair, which I had grown during the time I was leading the church, fall to the floor. I also remember the face of the man, a Mr. Lee, who cut my hair.

In prison, the authorities beat me endlessly and demanded that I confess my crimes. I endured, though. Even as I was vomiting blood and seemed on the verge of death, I never let myself lose consciousness. Sometimes the pain would be so great I would bend over at the waist. Without thinking, I found myself praying, "God, save me." In the next moment, though, I caught myself and prayed with confidence, "God, don't worry about me. Sun Myung Moon is not dead yet. I won't let myself die in such a miserable way as this."

I was right. It was not yet time for me to die. There was a mountain of tasks before me that I had to accomplish. I had a mission. I was not someone so weak as to be beaten into submission by something as trivial as torture.

Each time I collapsed from the torture I would endure by telling myself, "I am being beaten for the sake of the Korean people. I am shedding tears as a way of shouldering the pain of our people." When the torture was so severe that it took me to the verge of losing consciousness, I would invariably hear the voice of God. In the moments when my life seemed about to end, God would appear to me. My body still carries several scars that I received then. The flesh that was gouged from my body and the blood that was lost have been replaced, but the pain of that experience remains with me in these scars. I have often looked at these scars and told myself, "Because you carry these scars, you must succeed."

I was scheduled to go to trial on April 3, the fortieth day of my imprisonment. This was delayed by four days, however, and my trial was held on April 7. Many of the most famous ministers in North Korea came to the courtroom and accused me of all manner of crimes. The Communist Party also scorned me, saying religion was the opiate of the people. Members of our congregation stood to one side and wept sorrowfully. They wept as though their child or husband had passed away.

I did not shed tears, however. I had members who would weep for me with such sorrow that they were engulfed in grief, so I did not feel lonely as I traveled Heaven's path. I was not facing misfortune, so I felt I should not weep. As I left the courthouse after my sentencing, I raised my shackled hands and shook them as a sign to our members. The shackles made a clanging sound that sounded to me like bells. That day I was taken to the Pyongyang prison.

I did not fear life in prison. It was not as if this were the first time for me. Also, there was a hierarchy among the prisoners in each cell, and I was quite good at becoming friends with the head prisoner at the top of this hierarchy. All I had to do was exchange a few words and any head prisoner would quickly become my friend. When we have a heart of love we can open anyone's heart.

After I had been in the cell, sitting in the farthest corner, for a few days, the head prisoner moved me to a higher position. I wanted to sit in a tiny corner next to the toilet, but he kept insisting that I move to a higher position in the cell. No matter how much I refused, he insisted.

After making friends with the head prisoner, I looked carefully at each person in the cell. A person's face tells everything about him. "Oh, your face is this way, so you must be this way." "Your face is such a way, so you must have such a trait."

The prisoners were surprised to find how much I could tell them about themselves simply by reading their facial features. In their minds they didn't like the fact that a person they were seeing for the first time was able to tell so much about them, but they had to acknowledge that I was describing them correctly. I was able to open my heart and share with everyone, so in prison, too, I had friends. I became friends with a murderer. It was an unjust imprisonment for me, but it was a meaningful period of training. Any period of trial in this world has important meaning.

In prison even the lice can be friends. It was extremely cold in the prison. Lice would crawl in single file along the seams of our prison clothes. When we took the lice and put them together, they would attach themselves to each other and become like a tiny round ball. We would roll these, similar to the way horsedung beetles roll balls of dung, and the lice would do everything they could to stay together. Lice have a character of digging in, and they would put their heads together so that only their back ends were sticking out. We had a lot of fun in the cell watching this.

No one likes lice or fleas. In prison, though, even lice and fleas become important partners for conversation. The moment you set your eyes on a bedbug or flea, some realization flashes in your mind, and it is important that you not let this pass without notice. We never know when, or through what means, God will speak to us. So we need to be mindful to examine carefully even things like bedbugs and fleas.

A Grain of Rice Is Greater Than the Earth

On May 20, three months after being placed in Pyongyang prison, I was moved to Heungnam prison. I felt indignation and also shamed before Heaven. I was tied to a thief so I could not escape. We were taken by vehicle on a route that took seventeen hours. As I looked out the window a powerful feeling of grief welled up inside me. It seemed incredible to me that I would have to travel this winding road along rivers and through valleys as a prisoner.

Heungnam prison was a concentration camp for special laborers working in the Heungnam Nitrogen Fertilizer Factory. During the next two years and five months I underwent hard compulsory labor. Compulsory labor was a practice that North Korea learned from the Soviet Union. The Soviet government could not simply kill members of the bourgeoisie and other people who were not communists, because the world was watching and they needed to be mindful of world opinion. So it came up with the punishment of compulsory labor. People who were exploited in this way were forced to continue working until they died of exhaustion.

North Korean communists copied the Soviet system and sentenced all prisoners to three years of compulsory labor. In reality, the prisoners would usually die from the labor before their terms were up.

Our days began at 4:30 in the morning. We were made to line up in formation on the field, and our bodies and clothing were inspected for contraband items. We took off all our clothing, and each item was thoroughly inspected. Each piece of clothing would be beaten for so long that even the last speck of dust would not remain. The entire process took at least two hours. Heungnam was on the seacoast, and in the winter the wind was as painful as a knife as it cut into our naked bodies.

When the inspection was over we would be fed an awful meal. Then we would walk four kilometers to the fertilizer factory. We were marched four abreast, were made to hold the hand of the person next to us, and could not even hold our heads up. Guards armed with rifles and pistols surrounded us. Anyone who caused his row to start falling behind, or failed to hold on to the hand of the person next to him, was beaten severely for trying to escape.

In winter the snow would be deeper than a person's height. On cold winter mornings when we were marched through snow as deep as we were tall, my head would start feeling as though it were spinning. The frozen road was extremely slippery, and the cold wind blew so ferociously it made the hair on our heads stand up straight. We had no energy, even after eating breakfast, and our knees kept collapsing beneath us. Still we had to make our way to the job site, even if it meant dragging our exhausted legs along the way. As I made my way along this road that took us to the edge of consciousness, I kept reminding myself that I belonged to Heaven.

At the factory there was a mound of a substance that we referred to as "ammonia." In reality, it probably was ammonium sulfate, a common form of fertilizer. It would come in by conveyor belt and looked like a white waterfall as it fell off the belt onto the mound below. It was quite hot when it first came off the belt, and fumes rose from it even in the middle of winter. Quickly it would cool and become as solid as ice.

Our job was to dig the fertilizer out of the mound with shovels and put it into straw bags. We referred to this mound that was over twenty meters high as "the fertilizer mountain." Eight to nine hundred people were digging away at the fertilizer in a large space, making it appear as though we were trying to cut the mountain in half.

We were organized in teams of ten, and each team was responsible to fill and load thirteen hundred bags a day. So each person had to fill one hundred thirty bags. If a team failed to meet its quota, its meal rations were cut in half. Everyone worked as if his life depended on making the quota.

To help us carry the bags of fertilizer as efficiently as possible, we made needles out of steel wire and used these to tie the bags after they had been filled. We would put a piece of wire on a rail track that ran along the floor of the factory. The wire was flattened by having one of the small rail cars used for hauling materials run over it, and then it could be used as a needle.

To open holes in the bags, we used shards of glass that we got by breaking the factory windows. The guards must have felt sorry to see their prisoners working under harsh conditions because they never stopped us from breaking the windows. Once I broke a tooth while trying to cut a piece of wire. Even now you can see that one of my front teeth is broken. This remains with me as an unforgettable memento from Heungnam prison.

Everyone grew thin under the pressure of hard labor. I was the exception. I was able to maintain my weight at around seventy-two kilos, making me an object of envy for the other prisoners. I always excelled in physical strength. On one occasion, though, I became extremely ill with symptoms similar to tuberculosis. I had these symptoms for nearly a month. However, I did not miss even a day of work at the factory. I knew that if I were absent other prisoners would be held responsible for my share of the work.

People called me "the man like a steel rod" because of my strength. I could endure even the most difficult work. Prison and compulsory labor were not such a big problem for me. No matter how fierce the beating or terrible the environment, a person can endure if he carries a definite purpose in his heart.

Prisoners were also exposed to sulfuric acid, which was used in the manufacture of ammonium sulfate. When I worked at the Kawasaki steel mill in Japan I witnessed several instances in which a person cleaning vats used to store sulfuric acid had died from the effects of acid poisoning. The situation in Heungnam was far worse. Exposure to sulfuric acid was so harmful that it would cause hair loss and sores on our skin that oozed liquid. Most people who worked in the factory would begin vomiting blood and die after about six months. We would wear rubber pieces on our fingers for protection, but the acid would quickly wear through these. The acid fumes would also eat through our clothes, making them useless, and our skin would break and bleed. In some cases, the bone would become visible. We had to continue working without so much as a day's rest, even when our sores were bleeding and oozing pus.

Our meal rations consisted of less rice than it took to fill two small bowls. There were no side dishes, but we were given a soup that was radish greens in saltwater. The soup was so salty it made our throats burn, but the rice was so hard we couldn't eat it without washing it down with the soup. No one ever left even a single drop of the soup. When we received our bowl of rice, prisoners would put all the rice into their mouths at once. Having eaten their own rice, they would look around, stretching their necks sometimes, to watch how the others ate. Sometimes someone would put his spoon in someone else's soup bowl, and there would be a fight.

One minister who was with me in Heungnam once said to me, "Let me have just one bean, and I will give you two cows after we get out of here." People were so desperate that if a prisoner died at mealtime, the others would dig out any rice still in his mouth and eat it themselves.

The pain of hunger can only be known by those who have experienced it. When a person is hungry, a mere grain of rice becomes very precious. Even now, it makes me tense just to think of Heungnam. It's hard to believe that a single grain of rice can give such stimulation to the body, but when you are hungry you have such a longing for food that it makes you cry. When a person has a full stomach the world seems big, but to a hungry person a grain of rice is bigger than the earth. A grain of rice takes on enormous value to someone who is hungry.

Beginning with my first day in prison I made it a habit to take half of my ration of rice and give it to my fellow prisoners, keeping only half for myself. I trained myself this way for three weeks and then ate the whole ration. This made me think that I was eating enough rice for two people, which made it easier to endure the hunger.

Life in that prison was so terrible that it cannot even be imagined by someone who did not experience it. Half the prisoners would die within a year, so almost every day we had to watch as dead bodies were carried out the back gate in a wooden box. We would work so hard, and our only hope for leaving was as a dead body in that wooden casket. Even for a merciless and cruel regime, what they did to us clearly went beyond all boundaries of inhumanity. All those bags of fertilizer filled with the tears and grief of the prisoners were loaded onto ships and taken to the Soviet Union.

Heungnam Prison in the Snow

The most valued possession in prison after food was a needle and thread. Our clothes would wear out and be torn during the hard labor, but it was difficult to get a needle and thread to mend them. After a while prisoners began to look like beggars in rags. It was very important to mend the holes in our clothes in order to block, even a little, the cold winter winds. A small piece of cloth found lying on the road was extremely valuable. Even if the cloth were covered with cow dung, the prisoners would fight each other to try to pick it up.

Once as I was carrying the bags of fertilizer I discovered a needle stuck in one of the bags. It must have been left there accidentally when the bag was made. From that time on, I became the tailor of Heungnam prison. It was such a joy to find that needle. Every day I mended pants and knee breeches for other prisoners.

Even in the middle of winter it was so hot inside the fertilizer factory that we would sweat. So you can imagine how unbearable it was during the summer. Not even once, however, did I roll up my pants and let my shins show. Even during the hottest part of the summer I kept my pant legs tied in the traditional Korean fashion. Others would take off their pants and work in their underwear, but I kept myself properly dressed.

When we finished work our bodies would be covered with sweat and fertilizer dust, and most prisoners would take off their clothes and wash themselves in the filthy water that flowed from the factory. I, however, never washed myself where others could see my body. Instead, I would save half of the single cup of water we were rationed each day, then get up early in the morning while the others still slept to wipe myself off with a small piece of cloth dipped in that half-cup of water. I considered my body to be precious, and I didn't want to casually expose it to others. I also used this time early in the morning to focus my spirit and pray.

The prison cell held thirty-six people, and I took a small corner next to the toilet. In this space no one would step over me, but nobody wanted this space. We called it a toilet, but actually it was only a small earthenware jar without even a lid. Fluid would overflow from the toilet in the summer, and it would freeze in the winter. There is no describing the putrid smell that came from it. The prisoners often experienced diarrhea because of the salty soup and hard rice balls that we ate every day.

I would be sitting by the toilet and hear someone say, "Oh, my stomach." The person would make his way to the toilet in quick short steps. As soon as he exposed his bottom, the diarrhea would come shooting out. Because I was next to the toilet I was often splashed. Even during the night, when everyone was asleep, sometimes someone would have abdominal pain. When I heard people yelping in pain as they were being stepped on, I would know that someone was making his way to the toilet and I would get up and press myself against the corner. If I was asleep and did not hear him coming, I would suffer the consequences. Still I kept the spot by the toilet as my own for the entire time. In order to endure this impossible situation, I even tried to think of these sights and sounds as some form of art.

"Why do you choose to stay there?" other prisoners would ask. I would answer, "This is where I feel most comfortable." I wasn't just saying this. This was, indeed, the place where my heart felt most at ease.

My prisoner number was 596. People called me "Number five nine six." On nights when I couldn't sleep, I would stare at the ceiling and repeat this number to myself over and over. (5 is *oh*, 9 is *guh*, and 6 is *ryuk*.) If I said it quickly, it sounded very much like *eogul*, a Korean word used to describe the feeling of injustice. I truly had been imprisoned unjustly.

The Communist Party initiated *dokbohoi*, or meetings where newspapers, books, or other policy materials were read aloud, as a way of studying and learning communist propaganda. Also, we had to write letters of gratitude to North Korean President Kim Il Sung. The Security Detachment kept a close watch on our every move. Every day we were told to write letters of gratitude saying what we had learned, but I never wrote even a single page of these.

We were supposed to write something like this: "Our Father Kim Il Sung, out of his love for us, gives us food to eat each day, gives us meals with meat, and lets us lead such a wonderful life. I am so grateful." I could not write anything of the sort. Even if I were looking death in the face, I could not submit such letters to the atheistic Communist Party. Instead of writing them I worked ten times harder than the others in order to survive in the prison. The only way I could get away with not writing these letters was if I were the number one prisoner. Because of this effort I became the best prisoner and even received an award from a Communist Party official.

My mother visited me many times while I was in prison. There was no direct transportation from Jeongju to Heungnam. She had to take a train to Seoul, where she would change to a train on the Seoul to Wonsan line. The trip would take her more than twenty grueling hours.

Before starting out she would go to great trouble to prepare *misutkaru* (cooked rice powder) for me so that her son, who had been imprisoned in the prime of his life, would have something to eat. To make this powder she would gather rice from our relatives and even the distant relatives of my older sisters' husbands. When she came to the prison visiting room and saw me standing on the other side of the glass, she would immediately begin to shed tears. She was a strong woman, but the sight of her son undergoing such suffering made her weak.

My mother handed me the pair of silk trousers I had worn on my wedding day. The prison uniform I was wearing had become threadbare, and my skin showed through the material. However, instead of wearing the silk trousers, I gave them to another prisoner. As for the *misutkaru* that she had gone into debt to prepare, I gave it all away right there as she watched. My mother had invested her full heart and dedication into preparing clothing and food for her son, and she was heartbroken to see me giving away these things, without keeping anything for myself.

"Mother," I said to her, "I am not just the son of some man named Moon. Before I am a son of the Moon clan, I am a son of the Republic of Korea. And even before that I am a son of the world, and a son of heaven and earth. I think it is right for me to love those things first, and only after that follow your words and love you. I am not the son of some small-minded person. Please conduct yourself in a manner befitting your son."

My words were as cold as ice to her, and it hurt so much for me to watch her weep that I felt as though my heart would be torn apart. I missed her so much that sometimes I would wake up in the middle of the night thinking of her, but this was all the more reason for me not to succumb to my emotions. I was a person doing the work of God. It was more important for me to clothe just one more person a little more warmly and to fill his stomach with a little more food than it was for me to be concerned about my personal relationship with my mother.

Even while in prison I enjoyed taking whatever time I could find to talk with people. There were always people around me who wanted to listen to what I had to say. Even in the hunger and cold of prison life there was warmth in sharing with people with whom I had an affinity of heart. The relationships formed in Heungnam left me with twelve people who were both compatriots and as close as family to me, with whom I could spend the rest of my life. Among them was a famous minister who had served as president of the Association of Christian Churches in Korea's five northern provinces. These were people with whom I shared intense emotions in situations where our lives were on the line, and this made them closer to me than my own flesh and blood. Their being there gave my prison experience meaning.

I would pray three times each day for the people who had helped me and for the members of my congregation in Pyongyang, calling out each one by name. When I did I always felt that I needed to repay a thousand-fold the people who would slip me a handful of food they had hidden in their clothing.

U.N. Forces Open the Prison Gate

The Korean War had begun while I was imprisoned in Heungnam. Three days after it started, the South Korean military lost the capital of Seoul and retreated farther south. Then sixteen nations, with the United States in the lead, formed a United Nations force and intervened in the war. U.S. forces landed at Incheon and pushed toward Wonsan, a major industrial city in North Korea.

It was only natural for the Heungnam prison and factory to be targets for U.S. aerial bombing operations. When the bombing began, the prison guards would leave the prisoners and take refuge in bomb shelters. They weren't concerned whether we lived or died. One day Jesus appeared right before me with a tearful face. This gave me a strong premonition, so I shouted, "Everyone stay within twelve meters of me!" Soon after that a huge bomb exploded near us. Those prisoners who had stayed close to me, as I told them, survived.

As the bombing became more intense, guards began executing prisoners. They called out the prisoners' numbers and told them to come with three days' food rations and a shovel. The prisoners assumed they were being moved to another prison, but in reality they were marched into the mountains, made to dig a hole, and then killed and buried there. Prisoners were being called out in the order of the length of their sentences, with those with the longest sentences being called first. I realized that my turn would come the next day.

The night before my scheduled execution the bombs fell like rain in the monsoon season. It was October 13, 1950, and the U.S. forces, having succeeded in the Incheon landing, had come up the peninsula to take Pyongyang and were now pressing against Heungnam. The U.S. military attacked Heungnam with full force that night, with B-29 bombers in the lead. The bombing was so intense that it seemed all of Heungnam had been turned into a sea of fire. The high walls around the prison began to fall, and the guards ran for their lives. Finally the gate of the prison that had kept us in that place opened. At around two o'clock in the morning on the next day, I walked calmly out of Heungnam prison with dignity.

I had been imprisoned for two years and eight months in Heungnam and Pyongyang, so I was a terrible sight. My underwear and outerwear were in tatters. Dressed in those rags, instead of going to my hometown, I headed to Pyongyang with a group of people who had followed me in prison. Some chose to come with me instead of going in search of their wives and children. I could imagine how my mother must be crying every day out of concern for my welfare, but it was more important that I look after the members of my congregation in Pyongyang.

On the way to Pyongyang we could see clearly how North Korea had prepared for this war. Major cities were all connected by two-lane roads that could be used for military purposes in an emergency. Many of the bridges had been constructed with enough cement to let them withstand the weight of thirty-ton tanks. The fertilizer that the prisoners in Heungnam prison had sacrificed their lives to put into bags was sent to the Soviet Union in exchange for outdated but still lethal weaponry that was then deployed along the 38th parallel.

As soon as I arrived in Pyongyang I went in search of the members who were with me before my incarceration. I needed to find out where they were and what their situation was. They had been scattered by the war, but I felt responsible to find them and help them figure out a way to carry on their lives. I didn't know where they might be living, so my only option was to search the city of Pyongyang from one corner to the other.

After a week of searching I found only three or four people. I had saved some powdered rice I received while still in prison, so I mixed it with water to make rice cake to share with them. On the trip from Heungnam I had staved off my hunger with one or two potatoes that were frozen solid. I had not touched the rice powder. It made me feel full just to watch them eagerly eat the rice cake.

I stayed in Pyongyang for forty days looking for anyone I could think of, whether young or old. In the end I never did find out what happened to most of them. But they have never been erased from my heart.

On the night of December 2, I began walking south. Won Pil Kim and I followed a long line of refugees that extended about twelve kilometers. We even took with us a man who could not walk properly. He had been among those who followed me in Heungnam prison. His family name was Pak. He had been released before me. When I found him in his home, all the other members of his family had left for the South. He was alone in the house with a broken leg. I placed him on a bicycle and took him with me.

The North Korean army had already recaptured the flat roads for military use, so we traveled across frozen rice paddies, heading south as quickly as we could. The Chinese army was not far behind us, but it was difficult for us to move quickly when we had someone with us who could not walk. Half the time the road was so bad that I carried him on my back and someone else pushed the empty bicycle along. He kept saying he didn't want to be a burden to me and tried several times to take his own life. I convinced him to go on, sometimes scolding him loudly, and we stayed together until the end.

We were refugees on the run who still had to eat. We went into homes whose inhabitants had headed south before us and searched for rice or any other food that might have been left behind. We boiled anything we found, whether it was rice, barley, or potatoes. We were barely able to stay alive this way. There were no rice bowls and we had to use pieces of wood as chopsticks, but the food tasted good. The Bible says, "Blessed are the poor," doesn't it? We could eat anything that made our stomachs growl with satisfaction. Even a humble piece of barley cake tasted so good that we would not have felt jealous of a king's meal. No matter how hungry I was, I always made sure to stop eating before the others. This way they could eat a little more themselves.

After walking a long distance, we were approaching the northern bank of the Imjin River. Somehow I felt it was important that we cross the river quickly and that we didn't have a moment to spare. I felt strongly that we had to get over this obstacle for us to stay alive. I pushed Won Pil Kim mercilessly. Won Pil was young and he would fall asleep as we walked, but I kept forcing him on and pulling the bicycle. We covered thirty-two kilometers that night and reached the bank of the Imjin River. Fortunately, the river was frozen solid. We followed some refugees in front of us across the river. A long line of refugees stretched out behind us. As soon as we had crossed the river, however, the U.N. forces closed the crossing and stopped letting people across.

Had we arrived at the river even a few minutes later, we would not have been able to cross.

After we had crossed, Won Pil Kim looked back at the road we had come on and asked, "How did you know the river crossing was about to be closed?"

"Somehow I just knew," I said. "This kind of thing happens often to anyone who takes the path of Heaven. People often don't know that salvation is just beyond the next obstacle. We didn't have a single moment to waste, and if necessary I would have grabbed you by the scruff of the neck and pulled you across."

Won Pil Kim seemed moved by my words, but my heart was uneasy. When we arrived at the point where the 38th parallel divided the peninsula in two, I placed one foot in South Korea and one foot in North Korea and began to pray.

"For now, we are pushed southward like this, but soon I will return to the North. I will gather the forces of the free world behind me to liberate North Korea and unite North and South."

This was how I had prayed during the entire time we walked along with the refugees.

CHAPTER THREE

INTERNAL RICHES THROUGH STRUGGLES AND SUFFERING

"You Are My Spiritual Teacher"

After crossing the Imjin River, we traveled by way of Seoul, Wonju, and Kyungju to Busan. We arrived finally on January 27, 1951. Busan was filled with refugees from the North. It felt like the whole country had gathered there. Any accommodation fit to live in was already occupied. Our tiny place had barely enough room to sit. Our only option was to go into the woods at night, keeping warm as best we could, and then return to the city by day to look for food.

My hair, which was kept short during my prison time, had now grown back. My trousers, mended from the inside with cotton from a sleeping quilt, had become threadbare. My clothes were saturated so fully with an oily grime that raindrops in heavy rain were not absorbed into the cloth but simply rolled off.

Almost nothing was left of the soles of my shoes, although the upper part was mostly still there. I might as well have been walking barefoot. The fact was simply that I was the lowest of the low, a beggar among beggars. There was no work to be had, and we had no money in our pockets. The only way we could eat was to beg.

Yet even while begging for food, I maintained my dignity. If someone refused to help, I would say in a clear and confident voice, "Listen. If you do not help people like us who are in need, you will have great difficulties if you hope to receive blessings in the future!" People would give when faced with such thoughts. We took the food we gathered this way to a flat area where we all could sit together. Dozens of people like us ate in such places. We had nothing and even had to beg for food, but a warm friendship always flowed among us.

Once in the middle of a day like this, suddenly I heard someone shout, "Look here! How long has it been?"

I turned to see standing before me Duk Mun Eom, a friend from my days in Japan. Duk Mun Eom had become my friend for life back then after having been so moved by a patriotic song I sang. Today he is one of Korea's most prominent architects, having designed the Sejong Cultural Center and the Lotte Hotel.

"Let's go," he said, as he embraced me in my wretched clothes. "Let's go to my home."

By that time, Duk Mun Eom had married. He lived together with his family in a single room. To make room for me, he hung a quilt down the middle of that room, dividing it, with one side for me. On the other he slept with his wife and two young children.

"Now," he said, "tell me about your life lately. I always wondered where you were and what you might be doing. We were close friends," he said, "but you have always been more than a friend to me. Did you know that I always held you in great respect?"

Up to that point, I had never shared my heart candidly with any of my friends. In Japan, I went so far as to hide the fact that I often read the Bible. If someone came into my room when I was reading, I would quickly put the Bible away. But in the home of Duk Mun Eom, I shared my story for the first time. I spoke throughout the night. I told him of my encounter with God, crossing the 38th parallel, starting a church, and surviving Heungnam prison. My story took a full three days to tell. When I finished, Duk Mun Eom stood and knelt down before me in a full ceremonial bow.

"What are you doing?" I asked in shock and surprise. I grabbed his hand and tried to stop him, but it was no use. I could not.

"From this moment on," said Duk Mun Eom, "you are my great spiritual teacher. This bow is my greeting to you as my teacher, so please accept it."

He has been with me ever since, both as my friend and as my disciple. Soon after this, I found a job on Pier 4 in Busan harbor. I worked only at night. With my pay, I bought bean porridge at Choryang Station. The hot porridge was sold with a rag wrapped around the container to keep it hot. I always held the porridge container against my body for more than an hour before eating it. This helped to warm my body, which froze from working throughout the long, cold night.

I found lodging in a shelter for laborers located in the Choryang neighborhood. My room was so small that I could not lie down, even diagonally, without my feet pressing against the wall. But this was the room where I sharpened a pencil and solemnly wrote the first draft of *Wolli Wonbon* (the original version of the *Divine Principle*). I was financially destitute, but this was of no importance to me. Even living in a slum, there is nothing a determined soul cannot do. All we need is the will.

Won Pil Kim had just turned twenty. He did all sorts of jobs. He worked in a restaurant and brought home the scorched rice that couldn't be served to customers. We ate this together. Because of his gift for drawing, he soon got a job with the U.S. military as a painter.

Eventually, he and I climbed up to Beomnetgol in Beomil-Dong and built a house. Because this area was near a cemetery, there was nothing nearby except a rocky ravine. We had no land we could call our own, so we leveled a section of the steep slope and built a home there. We didn't even have a shovel! We borrowed a small shovel from someone's kitchen and returned it before the owner realized it was missing. Won Pil Kim and I broke rocks, dug the earth, and carried up gravel. We mixed mud and straw to make bricks, then stacked them up to make the walls. We got some empty ration boxes from an American base, flattened them out, and used them as the roof. We laid down a sheet of black plastic for the floor.

Even simple huts are built better than this. Ours was built against a boulder, so a big piece of rock stuck up in the middle of the room. Our only possessions were the small desk that sat behind that rock and Won Pil Kim's easel. When it rained, a spring would bubble up inside our room. How romantic to hear the sound of the water flowing beneath us where we sat! In the morning, after sleeping in this unheated room with a leaking roof and water still flowing below, we would arise with runny noses. Even so, we still were happy for our small space where we could lie down and put our minds at ease. The surroundings were miserable, but we were filled with hope from living on the path of God's will.

Each morning, when Won Pil Kim went to work at the American base, I accompanied him to the bottom of the hill. When he returned home in the evening, I went out to welcome him home. The remainder of my time I spent writing the *Wolli Wonbon*. Our room always had plenty of sharpened pencils. Even when there was no rice in the rice jar, we always had pencils.

Won Pil Kim helped in many ways, both materially and spiritually. Through this I could concentrate on my writing. Even when exhausted from a full day's work, he followed me around, looking for ways to help. I was getting so little sleep those days that I could fall asleep anywhere. Sometimes I even fell asleep on the toilet. Won Pil Kim followed me to the toilet to make sure I was all right.

But that was not all. He wanted so much to contribute even a little to the book I was writing. He began to draw portraits for American soldiers, and in this way he earned money to keep me supplied with pencils. At the time, it was popular among American soldiers to have a portrait drawn of their wife or girlfriend before returning to America. Won Pil Kim glued sheets of silk on wooden frames, painted the portraits, and sold them for four dollars each.

I felt grateful for his dedication. I sat beside him when he painted and did all I could to help him. While he was away at his job on the American base, I would put the glue on the silk, cut the wood for frames, and put them together. Before he came home, I washed his brushes and bought the paints he needed. After coming home, he would take a 4B pencil and draw the portrait. At first, he was drawing only one or two, but soon word of his work spread. He became so well known among the soldiers that he was drawing twenty and thirty at a time. It got to where our home was filled with portraits, and we had trouble finding room to sleep at night.

As the workload increased, I started to do more than just help on the sidelines. Won Pil drew outlines of the faces, and I colored the lips and clothing. From the money we earned together, we bought pencils and drawing materials and spent the rest for witnessing. It is important to record God's words in writing, but even more important is to tell people about His will.

The Crazy, Handsome Man by the Well

When we built the mud-walled house and began the church in Beomnetgol, there were only three people to hear me preach. For me, however, I was not talking to just those three people. I thought to myself, "Though they cannot be seen, I am preaching to thousands, even tens of thousands." I envisioned as I preached that all humanity was in attendance. These three people sat before me while I conveyed the words of the *Principle* in a loud, booming voice.

There was a well in front of our house. Soon a rumor began to spread among those who came to take water from that well that a crazy man lived in the house with mud walls. They fetched their water and peered into this ramshackle mud house to see a man in wretched clothing speaking like he was shouting commands to the whole world. It is only natural that people began to whisper among themselves. I preached that heaven and earth would be turned upside down and Korea would unite the world.

Rumors about me soon spread beyond those using the well to those at the bottom of the hill. Perhaps these rumors are what brought people coming out of curiosity to see the crazy man living next to the well.

Among these curious ones were students from a nearby seminary, as well as a group of professors from the prestigious Ewha Womans University. The rumors became embellished to say that I was a handsome man with good stature, so middle-aged women began to climb the hill to see me, as a way to pass the time.

On the day I finished writing *Wolli Wonbon*, I put my pencil down and prayed, "The moment has come for me to evangelize. Please send me the saints to whom I may give witness." After this, I then went out to the well. It was May 10, late spring. I was wearing traditional Korean trousers with cotton lining and an old jacket, sweating in the heat. I caught sight of a young woman wiping the sweat from her brow as she struggled up the hill toward the well.

I spoke to her, saying, "God has been giving you tremendous love for the past seven years." She jumped backward in surprise. It had been seven years since she had decided to dedicate her life to God.

"My name is Hyun Shil Kang," she said. "I am an evangelist at the Beom Cheon Church that sits in the neighborhood at the bottom of this hill. I heard there is a crazy man living here, so I have come here to witness to him."

This was how she greeted me. I invited her into our house. She looked around the squalid room, making plain how very strange she found it. Eventually, her eyes settled on my desk, "Why do you have so many pencils?" she asked.

"Until this morning," I replied, "I was writing a book that reveals the principles of the universe. I think God has sent you here so that you can learn about these principles from me."

"What principles? I am here because I heard there is a crazy man living here who needs to be witnessed to."

I handed her a cushion to sit on, and I sat down as well. The spring water made its trickling sound as it flowed beneath us.

"In the future, Korea will play its role at the pinnacle of the world," I said. "People will regret that they could not be born as Koreans." She clearly thought I was speaking nonsense.

"Just as Elijah appeared in the person of John the Baptist," I continued, "Jesus will come in the flesh to Korea."

This made her angry.

"I'm sure Jesus will have better places to come than a place so wretched as Korea," she retorted.

Then she said, "Have you ever read the Book of Revelation? I have ..."

I interrupted her mid-sentence, saying, "You want to say you have studied at the Goryo Theological Seminary?"

"How did you know that?" she demanded.

"Do you think I would have waited for you without knowing even that about you? You said you came here to witness to me. Please, then, teach me."

Hyun Shil Kang was clearly knowledgeable in theology. She quoted Bible texts to me one after another in an effort to attack my views. She continued to challenge me strongly as I kept responding to each of her challenges with answers in a strong and clear voice. Our debate continued so long that it began to grow dark, so I stood up and cooked dinner. The only thing we had besides rice was some overripe *kimchi*. (*Kimchi* is cabbage fermented with spicy red peppers or other ingredients common to Korean cuisine.) Nevertheless, we sat there with the sound of water trickling below and shared this food before resuming our debate.

She came back the next day and the day after that, each time to continue our debate. In the end, she chose to devote her life to the principles I teach.

Later that year, on a windy November day, my wife showed up at the door of the Beomnetgol hut. There standing with her was a seven-year-old boy, my son, who was born the year I left home. I had left that day simply to go pick up some rice, but went to Pyongyang instead. The years had passed, and now he had grown into a young boy. I could not bring myself to look him in the eye, nor could I reach out to stroke his face and embrace him in joy. I just stood there like a stone statue, frozen in place, speechless.

My wife did not have to say a word. I felt the pain and suffering this poor mother and child had to experience in the midst of war. Even before this visit, I knew where they were living and what their situation was, but I was not yet at the point where I could take care of my family. I knew this, and I had asked her several times, just as before our marriage, "Please trust me and wait just a little longer."

When the time was right, I planned to go get them. But in this situation, as they stood in the door, the right time had not yet come. The hut, our church, was small and shabby. A number of members ate there and lived there with me to study God's word. I could not bring my family there.

My wife took a look around the hut, expressed great disappointment, and turned to leave. She and my son set off back down the steep path.

A Church with No Denomination

oreans have a saying that a person insulted by others lives a long time. If I were to live in proportion to the number of insults I've received, I could live another hundred years. Also, my stomach has been filled not with food but with insults, so you could say that my stomach is the most full of anyone's. People from the established churches who had opposed me and thrown stones at me when I started a church in Pyongyang resumed their persecution, this time in Busan. Even before we had properly begun our church, they set out to give us trouble. Words like "heretic" and "pseudo" were placed in front of my name so often that they seemed to become part of my name. Indeed, the name Sun Myung Moon came to be synonymous with heresy and pseudo-religion. It's hard to even hear my name mentioned without these words.

By 1953, the persecution had become extreme. We closed the hut in Busan and moved first to Daegu and then to Seoul. In May of the following year, we rented a house in Seoul's Bukhak-Dong neighborhood, located near Jangchoongdan Park, and hung out a sign that read "Holy Spirit Association for the Unification of World Christianity."

We chose this name to signify that we belonged to no denomination, and we certainly had no plans to create a new one. *World Christianity* refers to all of Christianity worldwide and both past and present. *Unification* reveals our purpose of oneness, and *Holy Spirit* is used to denote harmony between the spiritual and physical worlds built on the love of the father-son relationship at the center. Our name is meant to say, "The spiritual world, centering on God, is with us."

In particular, unification represents my purpose to bring about God's ideal world. Unification is not union. Union is when two things come together. Unification is when two become one. "Unification Church" became our commonly known name later, but it was given to us by others. In the beginning, university students referred to us as "the Seoul Church."

I do not like using the word *kyohoi* in its common usage to mean church. But I like its meaning from the original Chinese characters. *Kyo* means "to teach," and *hoi* means "gathering." The Korean word means, literally, "gathering for teaching." The word for religion, *jongkyo*, is composed of two Chinese characters meaning "central" and "teaching," respectively.

When the word *church* means a gathering where spiritual fundamentals are taught, it has a good meaning. But the meaning of the word *kyohoi* does not provide any reason for people to share with each other. People in general do not use the word *kyohoi* with that meaning.

I did not want to place ourselves in this separatist type of category. My hope was for the rise of a church without a denomination. True religion tries to save the nation, even if it must sacrifice itself. It tries to save the world, even at the cost of sacrificing the nation. And it tries to save all humanity, even if it means sacrificing the world. In this understanding, there can never be a time when the denomination takes precedence.

It was necessary to hang out a church sign, but in my heart I was ready to take it down at any time. As soon as a person hangs a sign that says "church," he is making a distinction between church and not church. Taking something that is one and dividing it into two is not right. This was not my dream. It is not the path I chose to travel. If I need to take down that sign to save the nation or the world, I am ready to do so at any time.

Our sign hung near the front entrance. It would have looked better if we had hung it someplace high, but the eaves on the house came down very low, giving us no good spot to place a sign. In the end, we hung it about as high as the height of a child. In fact, some children in the neighborhood took down our sign, played with it, and broke it in two. Because of its historical significance, we could not throw it away. We attached the two pieces back together with wire and nailed it more securely to the front. Perhaps because our sign was treated with such disrespect, our church also received humiliating treatment beyond description.

The eaves were so low that people had to duck their heads in order to pass through the entrance. The room was about two and a half meters square, and it was so cramped that when six of us would pray we might bump foreheads with each other. People in the neighborhood laughed at our sign. They made fun of us, asking what kind of world unification we dreamt of in that tiny little house that "you have to crawl to get into." They didn't try to find out why we had chosen such a name. They simply looked at us as if we were crazy.

This did not bother us, however. In Busan, we had begged for food to sustain ourselves, and now we had a room in which to hold services. We had nothing to fear. For a suit, I took a pair of U.S. Army fatigues and dyed them black. I wore these with black rubber shoes. Even if others sought to belittle us, in our hearts we were more dignified than anyone.

People who attended called one another *shikku*, or family member. We were intoxicated with love. Anyone who came there could see what I was doing and hear what I was saying. We were connected by an invisible cord of love that let us communicate with God. A woman would be at home preparing rice and suddenly run off to the church. Someone else would say she was going to change into a new dress and then run off to the church in her old dress with holes in it. If a woman's in-laws shaved her hair to keep her from going to the church, she would come with her bald head.

As our members increased, we began to evangelize on university campuses. In the 1950s, university students were highly regarded as intellectuals in Korean society. We began by working near the gates of Ewha Womans University and Yonsei University. Soon a sizable number of students were spending time at our church.

Professor Yoon Young Yang, who taught music at Ewha, and Professor Choong Hwa Han, who was the dormitory master, came to our church. Many students also came, but they did not come just one or two at a time. Dozens came, and their numbers grew rapidly. This surprised the established churches and us as well.

Within two months after we began our campus evangelical work, our congregation exploded in size, primarily with students from Ewha and Yonsei. The rate of growth was incredible. It was as if a spring breeze had blown through and changed the hearts of the students all in a moment. Dozens of Ewha students packed up their belongings and moved out of the dormitory. This happened on a single day. If someone tried to stop them, they would say, "Why? Why are you trying to stop me? If you want to stop me, you'll have to kill me. Kill me!" They even came out by climbing the walls around the building. I tried to stop them, but it was no use. They did not want to be in their clean school; they wanted to be in our little church that smelled of dirty feet. There was nothing anyone could do about it.

Finally Dean Hwal Ran Kim (Helen Kim) sent Professor Young Oon Kim of the Department of Religious Social Welfare to our church. Professor Kim had studied theology in Canada and was a theologian in whom Ewha held great hope for the future. Dean Kim chose Professor Kim because her specialty was theology, and she assumed she could develop a definitive critique of our theology that could be used to finally stop this influx of students. But a week after meeting me, this special representative, Professor Kim, joined our church and became one of our most enthusiastic members. This gave us even more credibility among the other professors and students at Ewha. Our membership numbers snowballed.

The situation grew out of control, and established churches resumed their accusations that we were stealing their members. This seemed unfair to me. I never told anyone to listen to my sermons or attend our church. If I chased people out the front door, they would come in the back. If I locked the doors, they would climb over the fence. I was powerless to stop them. The people most perplexed by this were the administrators of Yonsei and Ewha, who in turn were supported by Christian foundations. They could not stand by and do nothing as their students and faculty went swarming to some other religious group.

Two Universities Expel
Students and Professors

Yonsei University and Ewha Womans University were embroiled in crisis and finally chose a measure that had never been used before and has never been used since. Ewha fired five professors, including Professor Young Oon Kim, and expelled fourteen students. The expelled students included five in the graduating class. Yonsei also fired one professor and expelled two students.

The school chaplain of Ewha tried advising the students, "You can attend that church after you graduate. That way, no harm will come to the school." But it was of no use. It had the opposite effect.

The expelled students protested vehemently. "There are many atheists in our school," they said. "And we even have the children of traditional shamans attending our school. How can the school justify expelling us and following the hypocrisy of this double standard?"

The school, however, stood fast. It simply repeated its position: "We are a private school and a Christian school. We have the right to expel any student we choose."

When the media got word of the incident, one newspaper carried an editorial titled, "Expulsion Is Wrong in a Country with Religious

Freedom." This situation soon became a topic for debate among the general public.

Ewha, since it was supported by a Christian foundation in Canada, was concerned that its support would be cut if it became known that large numbers of its students attended a church declared to be heretical. In those days, Ewha held chapel three times a week, took attendance, and submitted these attendance records to mission headquarters.

After the students were expelled and the professors fired, public opinion began to turn in our favor. Ewha, in an effort to counter this trend, began a campaign of false rumors too vile to repeat. Unfortunately, as is so often the case, the more vile the rumor, the more people revel in believing and repeating it as true. These false rumors began to feed on themselves, and soon they took on a life of their own. Our church suffered from this for more than a year.

I did not want the problem to grow out of control like this. I did not want to cause problems. I tried to convince the students and professors to lead simple, quiet lives of faith. I explained that there was no need for them to leave the dormitories and cause such public trouble. But they were adamant. "Why do you tell us not to come here?" they asked. "We wish to receive the same grace as everyone else." In the end, they were forced to leave their schools. I was not comfortable with this.

After being forced from their schools, the students went as a group to a prayer hall on Mount Samgak on the outskirts of Seoul. They went to seek comfort for their wounded hearts. They had been kicked out of their schools, their families were angry with them, and their friends no longer wished to meet them. They had no place to go. They fasted and spent their entire time praying with such emotion that their eyes filled with tears and their noses ran. Soon, some began to speak in tongues.

It is true that God appears when we are on the edge of despair and desperation. The students who were expelled from their schools and cast out by their families and society found God in the prayer hall on Mount Samgak.

I went to Mount Samgak and gave food and comfort to the students who had become emaciated from fasting.

"It is bad enough that you've been unjustly expelled," I explained. "Please do not fast also. If your conscience is clear over what you have done, then being insulted for it is not dishonorable. Do not be discouraged, but wait for your time."

Five of those students who were seniors later transferred into Sookmyung Women's University. But the damage was already done.

This incident played a decisive role and was the turning point in gaining me a profoundly negative reputation. Newspaper reports began to read as if all the evil acts committed by various religions were done by us. People who at first reacted to the rumors with "Could it be true?" now began to say, "It's true."

It hurt to be subjected to such unfair treatment. The injustice was so intense that it made me angry. I wanted to shout out in rebuttal, but I did not speak out or attempt to fight. We had too much else to accomplish and had no time to waste in fighting.

I believed that such misunderstandings and hatred would dissolve with time and that we should not use our energy to be overly concerned about them. I pretended not to hear people who said, "Sun Myung Moon should be struck by lightning," or the Christian ministers who prayed for my death.

But instead of dying down, the rumors grew ever more outrageous with each passing day. It felt as if the whole world had united in pointing fingers of accusation at me. Even in the heat of the Heungnam fertilizer factory, I refused to let others see even my shins, yet now rumors had it that I danced naked in our church. Soon people who came to our church for the first time looked at me with eyes that seemed to say, "Are you the one who takes off his clothes and dances?"

I knew better than anyone that it would take time for such misunderstandings to go away, so I never tried to argue with them, saying, "I'm not like that." We cannot know someone without meeting the person, yet there were so many who did not hesitate to curse me without ever having met me. I knew it was useless to battle against such people, so I endured in silence.

The Yonsei-Ewha incident forced our church to the brink of destruction. The image of "pseudo-religion," or "cult," became inseparably identified with my name, and all established churches joined together to call for the government to prosecute me.

On July 4, 1955, the police raided our church and took me and four members — Won Pil Kim, Hyo Young Eu, Hyo Min Eu, and Hyo Won Eu — into custody. Ministers and elders of the established churches joined hands with secular authorities in writing letters calling for our church to be closed. These four members, who had been with me from the beginning, were forced to stay in prison with me.

The matter did not end there. The police investigated my background and came up with a charge of draft evasion. But this, too, was egregious. By the time I escaped the North Korean death camp to head south, I was already beyond the age of compulsory military service. Still they charged me with draft evasion.

New Buds Grow on Scorched Branches

Tthe detectives of the Special Intelligence Section of the Office of
Public Order who raided our church and took me into custody
brought me to the Chung Bu Police Station. I was outraged to
be charged with draft evasion but said nothing. I had a mouth to speak,
but I was never given the chance to say a word.

Some saw my silence in the face of unjust treatment and called me
"spineless." I endured this sort of name-calling in silence as well, believing that this too must be a path that had been given to me. If this was
the path I must follow to reach my objective, then there was nothing I
could do about it. Because I followed such a clear path, I could not be
defeated. The more I was attacked, the more care I took to act more
honorably than anyone.

Once I made this decision in my heart, the police had no control over me.
When the detective was writing his report, I was guiding him how to write it.

"Why don't you include this content," I would say. "And up here, you
need to write it this way." He did as I said. Each phrase that I told him
to write was correct, but when the detective put them all together, he
found that they led him to the opposite conclusion from what he had
intended. He became angry and tore up the report.

On July 13, 1955, on the sixth day of incarceration in Chung Bu Police Station, I was placed in prison once again. This time, it was the Seodaemun prison in Seoul. I was shackled, but I was neither ashamed nor sorrowful. Life in prison was no obstacle for me. It might have served as a motivation to stimulate a heart of great anger, but it never blocked my path. For me, it was a way to gather additional capital for my future activities. I overcame life in prison by telling myself, "I am not someone to die in prison. I cannot die. This is only a springboard for me to take a great leap toward the world of liberation."

It is the rule in the world, and the law of heaven, that that which is evil will fall and that which is good will rise up. Even if I must go into a dung heap, I will not fail if I maintain a pure heart. As I was being led away in shackles, some women passed by, looked at me askance, and twisted their faces in disapproval. They exuded the feeling that I was grotesque even to look at, because they believed I was the leader of a sex cult. But I was neither afraid nor ashamed. Even if filthy words were used to harass me and our church, I would not be shaken.

Of course, I had normal feelings. Outwardly, I maintained my dignity, but there were many times when I felt stifled and sorrowful to the marrow of my bones. Each time I felt my heart weaken, I endured by telling myself, "I am not someone to just die in prison. I will stand again. I am certain of this." I redoubled my determination, saying, "I am taking all the pain into myself. I am carrying the entire burden for our church."

One could easily expect that my imprisonment would mean the end of our church, with all members going their separate ways. Instead, members came to visit me every day. In some cases, they even fought over who would come to see me first. Visitations were allowed only after 8 a.m., but members would line up and wait outside the prison gate from early in the morning. The more people cursed me, and the more bitter my situation became, the more people would line up to visit me, encourage me, and shed tears for me.

I did not even greet them with great emotion. In fact, I would rebuff them, saying things like: "Why do you come and make such a fuss?" Still, they followed me in tears. This was their expression of faith and love. They were not attached to me because I knew how to speak smoothly or eloquently. They liked me because they knew about the love that lay deep in my heart. Our members recognized my true heart. I will never be able to forget the ones who followed me even as I was forced to stand shackled in court. I will always remember their expressions as they sobbed to see me sitting at the defendant's table.

The guards at the prison were amazed. "How does this man make those people become so crazy?" they wondered when they saw our members flock to the prison. "He is not their husband, and none of them is his wife. He's not their son. How can they be so devoted to him?"

In at least one case, a guard commented, "We heard that Moon was a dictator and exploited people, but it is so clear that this is not true." This guard became a member and followed our way.

Finally, after I was three months in bondage, the court found me not guilty and I was released. On the day of my release, the chief warden and all the prison section chiefs gave me a formal sendoff. Within three months, all became part of our Unification family. The reason their hearts turned toward me was simple. Once they could see me up close, they realized I was not at all the person portrayed by the rumors they'd heard. As it turned out, the false rumors circulating in society actually helped our evangelical efforts.

When I had been led away by the police, all media and society had made a huge fuss. But when I was found not guilty and released, they were silent. The only report on my not-guilty verdict and release was a three-line story in an inconspicuous corner of the newspaper that read, "Reverend Moon not guilty, released." The vile rumors that had put the whole country in an uproar had all been false, but this information was completely buried. Our members protested, saying, "Reverend Moon, this is unjust. It makes us so angry, we can't stand it." They wept in front of me, but I remained silent and quieted them.

I never forgot the pain I experienced when harassed and subjected to all those false accusations. I endured, even when so many people stood against me that I felt like there was no place left for me to stand in all of Korea. The sorrow I felt from this time has remained with me in a corner of my heart.

I might be a tree that is buffeted by the wind and rain and scorched by fire, but I would never be a tree that burns and dies. Even a branch that has been scorched will have new buds when the spring comes. If I continue on my way with humility and strong conviction, the day will surely come when the world will understand the value of what I do.

We Are Trained by Our Wounds

People rejected the new expression of truth I preached, calling it heresy. Jesus, born in the land of Judaism, likewise was accused of heresy and was thus crucified. By comparison, my persecution was not nearly as painful or unjust. I could endure any amount of pain placed on my body. The charge of heresy against our church, however, was most unjust and more difficult for me.

Some theologians who studied our church in its early days described our teachings as original and systematic. Some were prepared to accept them. This means that the magnitude of the heresy controversy surrounding our church was based on more than just theology. It had more to do with issues of power.

Most of our members had attended other churches before joining our church. This was a big reason our church was treated as an enemy by established churches. When Professor Yoon Young Yang, one of the Ewha professors, joined our church, she was taken to the police station to be interrogated. There she discovered that some eighty Christian ministers had written letters to the authorities criticizing our church. It was not the case that we had done something wrong. Rather, we were seen as posing a threat to the power of certain people and institutions.

It was their vague feelings of fear and their extreme factionalism that drove them in their efforts to suppress our church.

People from many religious groups were attracted to our church and its new teachings. I would say to our members, "Why did you come here? Go back to your churches," and almost threaten them as I tried to chase them away. But they would soon return. The people who flocked to see me would not listen to anyone. They wouldn't listen to their teachers or their parents. They wanted to hear me speak. I wasn't paying them or feeding them, but they believed in what I taught and kept coming to me.

The reason was that I opened a way for them to resolve their frustrations. Before I knew the truth, I, too, was frustrated. I was frustrated when I looked up to heaven and when I looked at the people around me. This is why I could understand the frustrations of the people who came to our church. They had questions about life, and they could not find answers. The word of God I conveyed answered their questions with clarity. Young people who sought me out found answers in the words I spoke. They wanted to come to our church and join me on my spiritual journey, no matter how difficult it might be.

I am the person who finds the way and opens it. I guide people along the path to heal broken families and rebuild the society, nation, and world so that we can finally return to God. People who come to me understand this. They want to go with me in search of God. How can people find fault with this? All we were doing was going in search of God, and for this we were subjected to all manner of persecution and criticism.

Unfortunately, during the period when our church was involved in the heresy controversy, my wife made matters even more difficult for me. After our meeting in Busan, she and her relatives began to demand that either I quit the church immediately and start life with her and our son or else give her a divorce. They even came to Seodaemun prison during my incarceration there to put the divorce papers before me, demanding I place my stamp on them. I know how important marriage is in the effort to establish God's peaceful world, so I endured their demands in silence.

She also subjected members of our church to horrible abuse. Personally I could endure. I did not mind her insults and reckless treatment of me, but it was difficult for me to stand by and watch her offensive behavior toward our members. She stormed into our church at all hours to curse our members, destroy church property, and take items that belonged to the church. She even threw water containing human feces at members. When she came, it was impossible for us to hold worship services. In the end, as soon as I came out of Seodaemun prison, I acceded to the demands of her family and placed my stamp on the divorce document. I was pushed into a divorce against my own principles.

When I think of my former wife today, my heart goes out to her. The influence of her own family, which was strongly Christian, and the leadership of Korea's established churches had much to do with her behaving the way she did. She was so clear and firm in her commitment before we married. The way she changed gives us a lesson on how much we need to fear the power of social prejudice and established concepts.

I experienced both the sorrow of divorce and the pain of being branded a heretic. But I did not bend. These were things I had to endure on my path to redeem the original sin of humanity, the things I had to endure to move forward on the path toward God's Kingdom. It is darkest before the dawn. I overcame the darkness by clinging to God and praying to Him. Other than the fleeting moments that I would spend in sleep, all my available time was spent in prayer.

A Sincere Heart Is Most Important

I reemerged into the world after three months, having been found not guilty. I realized more than ever that I owed a tremendous debt to God. To repay this debt, I searched for a place where our church could start again. I did not, however, pray by saying, "God, build us a church." I never complained about, or felt ashamed of, the small and humble church building we were using up until that time. I was grateful to have a place to pray. I never wished for a large or comfortable space.

Nevertheless, we needed a place where our members could gather and offer services, so we took out a loan of two million won and purchased a house in poor repair on a hillside in Cheongpa-Dong. It was one of many houses categorized then as "enemy property," meaning that it had been vacant since being abandoned by Japanese who left Korea at the time of our nation's liberation. It was a small house with only about sixty-five square meters of floor space. It was at the end of a long and narrow alleyway. Approaching the house was like going through a long, dark tunnel. All the pillars and walls were covered with dirt, which made us wonder what had been going on there before we arrived. I worked with the young people of our church for four days with a lye solution to scrub off all the dirt.

After our move to the Cheongpa-Dong church, I could hardly sleep. I would sit on the floor of the main bedroom crouched over in prayer until three or four in the morning. I might take a nap until five, but then I would get up and start the day's activities. I continued this lifestyle for seven years. Even though I was getting only one or two hours of sleep a day, I never felt sleepy during the day. My eyes shone brightly, like the morning star. I never felt tired.

My mind was so full of things to do that I did not even want to waste time eating. Instead of having people take time to set a table for my meals, I ate on the floor and crouched over my food to eat it. "Pour out your dedication! Pour it out, even if you are sleepy! Pour it out until you are exhausted!" I kept repeating these phrases to myself. I prayed in the midst of continued opposition and false accusations with the thought that I was planting seeds that would someday reap a bountiful harvest. If the harvest could not be reaped in Korea, then I was confident that it would be reaped elsewhere in the world.

A year after my release from prison, our church had four hundred members. As I prayed, I would call out their names one by one. Their faces would pass through my mind even before I called their names. Some would be crying, some laughing. In my prayers, I could tell how each person was doing, including whether they were suffering from illness.

Sometimes, as I called out their names in prayer, I would get an inspiration that a particular person would come to the church that day. The person would come, without fail. When I would go to someone who had appeared sick to me in my prayer and ask, "Are you sick?" the person would confirm it. Members were amazed that I would know without being told that they were sick. Each time they asked, "How do you do that?" I would answer with a simple smile.

Something similar happened as we were preparing for a Holy Blessing Ceremony. Before the ceremony, I asked every bride and groom candidate whether they had maintained their chastity. When I asked one particular groom candidate, he answered in a loud voice that he had remained pure. I asked him a second time, and he again assured me he had. I asked him a third time, and again he gave the same answer.

I looked at him straight in the eye and said, "You did your military service in Hwacheon, Kangwon Province, didn't you?" This time he answered "Yes" in a voice filled with fear.

"You received some time off, and as you were coming to Seoul you stopped at an inn, didn't you? And that night you had illicit sex with a woman wearing a red skirt. I know exactly what you did. Why do you lie?"

I became angry at the man and chased him out of the Blessing ceremony venue. If a person keeps his heart's eyes open, he can see even what is hidden.

Some were attracted to our church more because of such paranormal phenomena than because of the teachings. Many people think that spiritual powers are most important. The phenomena often called miracles, however, tend to confuse people in the society at large. A faith that relies on unexplained or miraculous occurrences is not a healthy faith. All sin must be restored through redemption. It cannot be done by relying on spiritual powers. As our church began to mature, I stopped talking to members about the things that I was seeing with my heart's eyes.

Membership continued to grow. Whether I faced dozens of people or hundreds, I acted the same way, as if there were only one. I would listen whenever a person wanted to tell me about his or her personal situation. Whether it was an old woman or a young man, I would listen with dedication, as if this were the only person I had to deal with. Each member would say, "No one in Korea listens to what I have to say as well as Reverend Moon." A grandmother might start by telling me how she got married and eventually tell me about her husband's illnesses.

I enjoy listening to other people talk about themselves. When people open up to me and talk about themselves, I don't even realize the passing of time. I listen to them for ten, even twenty, hours. People who want to talk have a sense of urgency. They are looking for solutions to their problems. So I feel I need to listen to them with my full dedication. That is the way to love their life and repay the debt I owe for my life. The most important thing is to think of life as precious. In the same way that I listened with sincerity to what others had to say, I also shared with them my sincere heart with fervor, and I would pray for them in tears.

How often I prayed with tears through the night! Tears saturated the floor boards where I prayed, with no chance to dry.

Later, while I was in the United States, I received word that church members were planning to remodel the Cheongpa-Dong church. With great urgency I sent a telegram telling them to stop work on the church building immediately. Yes, this church embodies an irrecoverable period in my personal history, but more important than that, it testifies directly to the history of our church. No matter how wonderfully it might have been refurbished, what good could come of it if our history were destroyed? What matters is not some beautiful exterior but the secret life of tears that dwells within that building. It may not be up to a certain standard, but it embodies a tradition, and therein lies its value. People who cannot respect their own tradition are destined to fail.

There is history carved into the pillars of the Cheongpa-Dong church.

When I look at a particular pillar, I am reminded of a time when I clung to that pillar and wept over a particular matter. To see that pillar where I wept makes me weep again. To see a door frame that is a little crooked reminds me of the past. Now, though, the old floor boards are all gone. The floor boards where I bent over in prayer and shed so many tears are gone, and the traces of those tears are also gone. What I need are the memories of that pain. It doesn't matter if the external style or appearance is old. Much time has passed, and now we have many churches that are well built. But for me, I would rather go to the small house on the hill in Cheongpa-Dong and pray. I feel more comfortable there.

I have lived my entire life praying and preaching, but even now I tremble when I stand before a group of people. This is because to stand in such a position and speak about public matters can mean that many lives will be saved or that many will be lost. It is a matter of utmost importance to me that I can lead the people who hear my words onto the path of life. These are the moments when I draw a clear line on the crossroads between life and death.

Even now, I do not organize my sermons in advance. I am concerned that doing so might allow my own private objectives to enter into the content. With such preparation I may be able to show off how much knowledge I have stored in my head but not pour out my earnest and passionate heart. During this time, before I appeared in public, I always offered my dedication by spending at least ten hours in prayer. This is the way I set my roots down deeply. Even if the leaves on a mighty tree are a little bug-eaten, the tree remains healthy if its roots are deep. My words may be a little awkward at times, but everything will be all right so long as a sincere heart is there.

In the early time of our church I wore an old U.S. military jacket and fatigues dyed black and preached with such fervor that I dripped with sweat and tears. Not a day went by without my weeping out loud. My heart would fill with emotion, and tears would pour from my eyes and stream down my face. Those were times my spirit seemed on the verge of leaving my body. I felt as though I were on the verge of death. My clothes were soaked with sweat, and beads of sweat rolled down from my head.

In the days of the Cheongpa-Dong church, everyone went through difficult times, but Hyo Won Eu endured particular difficulty. He suffered an illness in his lungs, and although it was difficult for him, still he lectured our church's teachings eighteen hours a day for three years and eight months. We could not afford to eat well. We ate barley instead of rice and sustained ourselves with two meals a day. Our only side dish was raw *kimchi* that was left to ferment for only one night.

Hyo Won Eu liked to eat small salted shrimp. He placed a container of these small shrimp in one corner of the room, and once in a while he would go over with a pair of chopsticks and eat a few. That was how he endured through those difficult days. It pained my heart to see Hyo Won Eu lying exhausted on the floor, hungry and tired. I wanted to give him salted conch, but this was much too expensive for us in those days. It still pains me to think of how hard he worked, trying to record my words that flowed like a waterfall, even as he was ill.

Aided by the hard work and sacrifice of members, the church grew steadily. The Sunghwa Students Association was formed for middle and high school students. They were inspired to take the lunches their mothers prepared for them and give them up so our pioneer missionaries could eat. On their own initiative, the students created a list to take turns providing their lunches in this way. The evangelists who had to eat the lunch of the student knew that the student would be missing lunch that day and going hungry, and so they would eat the lunch in tears. The students' expression of dedication was even more impressive than the lunch itself, and we all redoubled our determination to accomplish the will of God, even if we had to sacrifice our lives.

Though times were difficult, we sent missionaries out to many parts of the country. Despite the members' humble desire, the cascade of vile rumors made it difficult for them to feel open to say they were from the Unification Church. They would go into neighborhoods and clean streets and help out in homes that needed it. In the evenings, our missionaries would hold literacy classes and tell people about the word of God. They would serve people in this way for several months and build up trust. As a result, our church continued to grow. I have not forgotten these members who, though they wanted very much to go to college, chose instead to remain with me and dedicate themselves to the work of the church.

CHAPTER FOUR

LAUNCHING OUR GLOBAL MISSION

Following God's Path with
No Thought for My Life

As soon as I was released from Seodaemun prison, I went to the Gabsa Buddhist temple on Mount Gyeryoung in Choongcheong Province. I needed to heal the wounds from my torture in Seodaemun prison. Also, I needed a forest where I could pray and think about the future of our church. This was not long after the end of the Korean War, and just finding enough food to survive was often a difficult task. Despite such short-term difficulties, however, it was important that I make plans for the longer term. We still did not have a church large enough to hold all our members for service, but I felt it was important to spend some time looking out into the distant future.

Following the collapse of Japanese colonial rule and the liberation of Korea in 1945, the two countries had not established diplomatic relations. Japan had not recognized the government in Seoul, and Korea considered Japan an enemy country. My belief was that, when the situation of the world was considered, it was important for the two countries to resume contacts. A number of attempts were made to send a missionary to Japan, but these were unsuccessful. In the end, it was Bong Choon Choi who accomplished this task.

In 1958, I called Bong Choon Choi to meet me on the mountain behind the Gabsa temple. "You need to go immediately to Japan," I said. "You will not be able to return to Korea until you have succeeded."

"Yes!" he replied, without hesitation.

We then sang the Korean Christian hymn whose words begin:

Called of God, we honor the call;

Lord, we'll go wherever you say.

We came down the mountain together in high spirits. He never asked how he was supposed to support himself in Japan or how he was supposed to begin his activities there. Bong Choon Choi was that kind of audacious man. Travel to Japan was not allowed for most Koreans. His only option was to try to enter Japan even without a visa. He would need to endure many things.

Bong Choon Choi did not even know if he could enter Japan, but he was prepared, if necessary, to lay down his life. Until I could hear that he had safely crossed the strait to Japan, I put aside all other work and sat praying in a small room in the church. I didn't eat or sleep. We even had to take out a loan of 1.5 million won to send him. We had many members who had nothing to eat, but evangelizing Japan was so important that everything else had to be put aside.

Unfortunately, Bong Choon Choi was arrested as soon as he arrived in Japan. He was placed in prison, first in Hiroshima and later in Yamaguchi, until he could be deported back to Korea. While in prison he decided he would rather die than be sent back, and so he began to fast. During his fast, he developed a fever. The Japanese authorities decided to place him in a hospital and delay his deportation until his health could be restored. While in the hospital, he managed to escape from custody.

After such efforts made at the risk of his life over a year and a half, Bong Choon Choi established the church in Japan in October 1959. Korea and Japan would not establish diplomatic relations for another six years. In fact Korea, because the painful memory of suffering under Japan's colonial rule was still quite fresh, was rebuffing any suggestion that it open contacts with Japan.

I had our missionary smuggle himself into this enemy country for the sake of Korea's future. Instead of refusing all contact, Korea needed to evangelize Japan so that it would be in the position to be the senior partner in the bilateral relationship. Korea was impoverished materially, so it needed to open a channel to the Japanese leadership, get Japan on its side, and then link itself to the United States. I envisioned that this was how Korea could survive.

As a result of the successful effort to send a missionary to Japan, owing to Bong Choon Choi's sacrifice, an exceptional youth leader named Osami Kuboki joined the church, together with a group of young people who followed him. The Japanese church became securely established as a result of their work.

We sent missionaries to America in the following year. There was no visa trouble this time. They were able to receive passports and visas before leaving. In securing the passports, we were aided by some cabinet ministers of the Liberal Party who had played a part in having me imprisoned in the Seodaemun prison. Previously, they had opposed us, but now they were helping us.

The United States in those days seemed like a very far-off country. Some of our church members opposed the idea of sending missionaries there, saying it was more important to grow our foundation in Korea first. I convinced the members of its importance, however, saying that unless America's crisis could be resolved, Korea would be destroyed, too. In January 1959, we sent Young Oon Kim, one of the professors who had been fired by Ewha Womans University. Then in September of that year, we sent David S.C. Kim. The work they began in America was aimed at the entire world.

Money Earned Honorably,
Used Prayerfully

Funds accumulated through business operations are sacred. For business profits to be sacred, however, it is important not to lie or to take excessive profit. When conducting business, we must always be honest, and we should never take a profit of more than thirty percent. Money earned in this honorable manner must, of course, be spent prayerfully. It must be spent with a clear purpose and intent. This is the principle of business management that I have promoted throughout my life. I believe the purpose of business is not simply to make money. It is also to support the missionary work, which is the work of God.

One reason I worked to create funds for missionary work through business was that I did not want to take money from our members for this purpose. No matter how lofty the purpose might be, sending missionaries overseas could not be accomplished just by wishing it. It required funds. These funds should be earned in the name of the church. Funds for missionary work had to be earned in an honorable way. Only then could we be proud of everything we did.

As I looked at various options for making money, postage stamps caught my eye. In those days, I was suggesting to members that they write to each other at least three times a month. Mailing a letter cost forty won, but I suggested that they not simply place one forty-won stamp on their letters. Instead, I suggested they use forty one-won stamps. We took the canceled postage stamps from these letters, sold them to collectors, and managed to make 1 million won in the first year. Seeing that used postage stamps, which seemed insignificant, could bring in big money, the members continued this work for seven years. We also sold black-and-white photographs of famous places or popular entertainment personalities that we had hand-colored with paint. This business also contributed significantly to the operation of our church activities.

As the church grew, postage stamps and painted photographs were no longer enough to generate the funds we needed for our missionary work. We needed to take our business to a higher level if we were to send missionaries all over the world.

In 1962, before the Korean government re-denominated the currency, a lathe that the Japanese had been using but then abandoned in 1945 was purchased for 720,000 won. Following re-denomination, it was worth 72,000 won. Korean currency was pegged to the U.S. dollar, then at 125 won per dollar, so the official value of the investment was $576. We placed this lathe in the coal briquette storage room of the house, abandoned by the Japanese, that we were using as our church. We hung a sign outside that read "Tongil Industries."

"To you, this lathe may seem insignificant," I explained. "You may wonder what kind of business we are going to do by installing one piece of old and used machinery. This machine that you see here, however, will be multiplied before long to become seven thousand—and even seventy thousand—lathes, and the company will develop along with

Korea's defense and automobile industries. This machine that we installed today will surely be a cornerstone for building our country's automobile industry. Have faith. Have the conviction that this will surely happen."

This was what I said to those then gathered in front of the coal briquette storage room. It was a humble beginning, but our purpose was lofty and great. They responded to my call and worked with dedication. As a result, in 1963 we were able to start another business on a somewhat larger scale. This involved building a fishing boat. The boat was launched at a pier in the Manseok-Dong section of Incheon and christened *Cheon Seung Ho*, meaning "Victory of Heaven." Some two hundred people attended the ceremony where this fishing boat was sent out onto the ocean.

Water is the source of life. We were all born from our mothers' womb. Inside the womb is water, so we were all born from water. I launched the boat with the belief that, in a similar way to how we receive life from water, we need to go out onto the ocean and pass through a series of trials there in order to become capable of surviving the trials we will face on land.

Cheon Seung Ho was an exceptional boat. It sailed throughout the Yellow Sea and caught many fish. The reaction of many, though, was that we had enough to do on land and that there was no need for us to be going out onto the ocean and catching fish. I sensed, however, that the world was about to enter an oceanic era. The launching of *Cheon Seung Ho* was a small, but precious, first step in opening that era. I was already picturing in my mind the vast ocean with boats larger and faster than *Cheon Seung Ho*.

Power of Dance Moves the World

We were not a rich church. We were a poor church started by people who couldn't afford enough food to keep themselves well fed. We didn't have the fancy church buildings that other churches had, and we ate barley when others ate rice. We saved our money a little at a time and then shared that money with people who were poorer than us. Our missionaries slept in unheated rooms by laying their sleeping quilts on the bare cement floors. When mealtime came, it was common for them to stave off their hunger by eating a few cooked potatoes. In every case, we did our best not to spend money on ourselves.

In 1963, we used the money we had saved this way to select seventeen children and form a children's dance troupe called the Little Angels. Korea in those days had very little in the way of cultural performances. We had nothing that we ourselves could watch and enjoy, let alone something to show people in other countries. Everyone was too busy trying to survive to remember what Korean dance was like or even the fact that we had a cultural heritage extending back five thousand years.

My plan was to have these seventeen children learn how to dance and then send them out into the world. Many foreigners knew about

Korea only as a poor country that had fought a terrible war. I wanted to show them the beautiful dances of Korea so that they would realize that the Korean people are a people of culture. We could insist all we wanted that we were a people of culture with a five-thousand-year tradition, but no one would believe us if we had nothing to show them.

Our dances, with dancers dressed in beautiful, full-length *hanboks*, gently twirling around, are a wonderful cultural heritage that can give a new experience to Westerners who are accustomed to watching dancers jump around with bare legs. (A *hanbok* is a traditional Korean dress.) Our dances are imbued with the sorrowful history of the Korean people. The movements of Korean dance — in which dancers keep their heads slightly bowed and move carefully so as not to draw undue attention to themselves — were created by the Korean people, whose long history has been filled with grief.

As the dancer raises one foot wrapped in white *beoseon*, the traditional Korean leggings, and puts it forward to take a single step, she turns her head gently and raises her hand. As I watch, the gentle subtlety of her movements seems to melt away all the worries and frustrations in my heart. There is no attempt to move the audience with a lot of words spoken in a booming voice. Instead, each dance move, performed with great gentleness and subtlety, moves the heart of the audience. This is the power of art. It allows people who don't understand each other's language to communicate. It lets people who don't know about each other's history understand each other's heart.

In particular, the innocent facial expressions and bright smiles of the children would be certain to completely wipe away the dark image of a country that had only recently been at war. I created this dance troupe to introduce the dances from our country's five-thousand-year history, especially to people in the United States, which was the most advanced country in the world at that time.

The society around us, however, heaped criticism on us. Before even seeing the Little Angels dance, they began to criticize. "The women of the Unification Church dance day and night," went their outrageous criticism, "and now it looks like they've given birth to children who also dance."

No such rumors could shake my resolve, however. I was confident of showing the world what Korean dance was like. I wanted to let the people who accused us of having danced naked see the beautiful, gentle movements of dancers stepping lightly in their *beoseon* leggings. These were not wild dances with twisting and turning without rhythm. They were gentle dances by innocent dancers clothed in the traditional dress of our country.

Angels Open a Path
through a Dark Forest

There are two things we must leave our descendants when we die. One is tradition, and the other is education. A people without tradition will fail. Tradition is the soul that allows a people to continue; a people without a soul cannot survive. The second thing of importance is education. A people will also fail if it does not educate its descendants. Education gives us the power to live with new knowledge and objectives. Through education, people acquire wisdom for living. Anyone who cannot read will be ignorant, but once educated, a person will know how to use his wisdom in the world to manage his own life.

Education helps us understand the principles by which the world operates. To open up a new future, we need, on the one hand, to pass on to our descendants the tradition that has been handed down to us over thousands of years and, on the other, to also supply them with education concerning new things. When tradition and new knowledge are appropriately integrated in our lives, they give birth to an original culture. Tradition and education are both important, and it is impossible to say which takes priority over the other. The wisdom to integrate the two also comes to us through education.

At the same time that I founded the dance troupe, I also founded the Little Angels School of the Arts (later renamed Sunhwa Arts School). The purpose in founding this school was to spread our ideals to the world through the arts. The issue of whether we had the ability to manage a school was of secondary importance. I first put my plan into action. If the purpose is clear and good, then it should be put into action quickly. I wanted to educate children to love heaven, love their country, and love humanity.

I wrote my motto for the school as a piece of calligraphy that said in Chinese characters, "Love Heaven, Love Humanity, Love Country." Someone asked me then, "Why do you put 'Love Country' at the end, when you say your purpose is to show Korea's unique culture to the world?"

I answered him, saying, "If a person loves heaven and loves humanity, he has already loved his country. Loving the country has already been accomplished in the process."

If a Korean can cause the world to respect him, then he has already accomplished the purpose of letting the world know about Korea. The Little Angels went to many countries and demonstrated the excellence of Korean culture, but they never made any nationalistic claims about their country. The image of Korea as a country of great culture and tradition was planted deeply in the minds of the people who saw their performances and gave them their applause. In that sense, the Little Angels did more than anyone to publicize Korea to the world and practice love for their country. It gives me great satisfaction every time I see the performances by Su Mi Jo and Young Ok Shin, graduates of Sunhwa Arts School who have gone on to become world-renowned vocalists, and by Julia Moon and Sue Jin Kang, who are among the best ballerinas in the world.

Since 1965, when they held their first overseas performance in the United States, the Little Angels have been introducing Korea's beautiful tradition all over the world. They were invited by the British royal family to perform in the presence of Queen Elizabeth II. They were invited to take part in the bicentennial celebration in the United States, where they performed at the John F. Kennedy Center for the Performing Arts. They gave a special performance for U.S. President Richard Nixon, and they took part in the cultural and performing arts festival that was part of the Seoul Olympic Games. The Little Angels are known around the world as cultural ambassadors for peace.

The following is something that happened in 1990, when I visited Moscow. The Little Angels gave a performance on the night before I was to leave the Soviet Union, after having met President Mikhail Gorbachev. Korea's little girls stood in the center of Moscow, the center of communism. After performing Korean dances dressed in their *hanboks*, the Little Angels sang Russian folk songs with their beautiful voices. Shouts of "Encore!" from the audience made it impossible for them to leave the stage. In the end, they completely exhausted their repertoire of songs.

First Lady Raisa Gorbachev was seated in the audience. South Korea and the Soviet Union had not yet established diplomatic relations, and it was very unusual for the first lady to attend a cultural performance from such a country. However, Mrs. Gorbachev sat in the front row and applauded enthusiastically throughout the program. After the performance, she came backstage and handed the troupe flowers. She repeatedly praised the greatness of Korean culture, saying, "The Little Angels are truly angels of peace. I did not know that South Korea had such beautiful traditional culture. During the entire performance, it was as if I were dreaming a dream about my own childhood." Mrs. Gorbachev embraced each member of the troupe and kissed them on the cheek, saying, "My Little Angels!"

In 1998, the Little Angels visited Pyongyang as the first purely private, nongovernmental cultural exchange program and gave three performances there. They danced the cute "Little Groom Dance" and the colorful "Fan Dance." The eyes of the North Koreans watching the performance were filled with tears. The image of a woman sobbing uncontrollably was captured in the lens of a newspaper photographer. Yong Soon Kim, chairman of North Korea's Asia-Pacific Peace Commission, praised the Little Angels after their performance, saying, "They have opened a narrow path through the dark forest."

That was exactly what the Little Angels had done. They demonstrated for the first time that Koreans from North and South, who had turned their backs on each other for such a long time, were capable of coming together in one place and watching each other's performances. People often think that politics moves the world, but that is not the case. It is culture and art that move the world. It is emotion, not reason, that strikes people in the innermost part of their hearts. When hearts change and are able to receive new things, ideologies and social regimes change as a result. The Little Angels did more than just advertise our traditional culture to the world. They created narrow paths between worlds completely different from each other.

Each time I meet the Little Angels, I tell them, "You must have beautiful hearts to perform beautiful dances. You must have beautiful hearts to have beautiful faces." True beauty is a beauty that wells up from within us. The Little Angels have been able to move the hearts of people throughout the world, because the beauty of Korea's tradition and spiritual culture are imbued in their dances. So the applause for the Little Angels is actually applause for Korea's traditional culture.

World Tour

From childhood, my mind has always yearned for faraway places. In my hometown, I would climb a mountain and long for the sea. When I arrived in Seoul, I wanted to go to Japan. I have always dreamed of going to places larger than where I was.

In 1965, I embarked on my first trip around the world. My suitcase was filled with soil and stones from Korea. My plan was that, as I traveled around the world, I would plant Korea's soil and stones in each country to signify Korea's linkage to the world. For ten months, I toured forty countries, including Japan, the United States, and the nations of Europe. On the day I left Seoul, hundreds of our members came in buses to see me off, and they filled the departure lounge at Gimpo Airport. In those days, going overseas was a significant event. Our members thronged to the airport on that January day with a cold strong wind blowing out of the northwest. No one had told them to do this. They did as their hearts told them. I received their hearts with deep gratitude.

At that time, we were carrying out mission work in ten countries, and it was my plan to increase that to forty countries within two years. It was to lay the foundation for this that I decided to visit forty countries on my trip. My first stop was Japan. I received a tremendous welcome there, where Bong Choon Choi had risked his life to start our mission.

I put the following question to the Japanese members: "Are you 'of Japan,' or have you transcended the state of being 'of Japan'?"

I continued: "God doesn't want that which is 'of Japan.' He doesn't need that which is 'of Japan.' He needs people who transcend Japan. You need to go beyond the limitations of Japan to become Japanese people who love the world, if you are to be people who can be used by God." It may not have been easy for them to hear this, but I made myself very clear.

My second destination was the United States. I entered the country through the airport in San Francisco, where I was met by our missionaries. From there, we toured the entire country. During the time I was touring America, I felt strongly, "This is the country that leads the whole world. The new culture that will be created in the future must rise up with America as its foundation." I set a plan then to purchase a facility for workshops in the United States that would hold five hundred people. Of course, this would not be only for Koreans. It would be an international facility that would receive people from over one hundred countries.

Fortunately, this hope was soon realized. Many countries sent people to this workshop facility, where they would study and debate about world peace for several months at a time. Race, nationality, and religion made no difference.

I believe that the world will develop better societies when people who have transcended race, nationality, and religion and hold a wide variety of opinions come together and candidly discuss world peace.

During my tour of the United States, I visited every state except Alaska and Hawaii. We rented a station wagon and drove day and night. One time when the driver looked so tired, I encouraged him, saying, "Listen, we didn't come here for sightseeing. We're here to do important work. We need to go carefully."

We didn't waste time sitting down to eat. If we had two slices of bread, a piece of sausage, and some pickles, then that was plenty of food for a meal. We ate breakfast, lunch, and dinner like this. We also slept in the car. The car was our lodging; it was our bed and our restaurant. We ate, slept, and prayed in that small car. There was nothing we couldn't do there. I had a particular purpose to accomplish, so it was easy for me to endure minor inconveniences to the physical body.

After the United States and Canada, I went to Central and South America, and then on to Europe. To my eyes, Europe was in the cultural sphere of the Vatican. It seemed to me that we could not succeed in Europe without understanding the Vatican. Even the Alps, which were supposed to be so difficult to climb, seemed of little significance in comparison to the Vatican.

I went to the Vatican, where European Catholics gather to pray, and prayed with such fervor that beads of sweat ran down my face. I prayed that Christianity, which had become divided among so many denominations and groups, could be unified quickly. God created one world, but people have divided it in ways convenient to themselves. I became more convinced than ever that these divisions must be erased and the world unified as one. From Europe, I went on to Egypt and the Middle East and completed my tour after ten months.

When I returned to Seoul, my suitcase was full of soil and stones from one hundred twenty locations in forty countries. When I planted the soil and stones I had taken from Korea, I took soil and stones from each location and brought them back to Korea. I connected Korea to these forty countries in this way to prepare for the day in the future when the world of peace would be realized centering on Korea. I began preparations to send missionaries to those forty countries.

PHOTOS FROM
MY LIFE

The home in North Korea where I was born. Originally, it had a small wing on each end, but now, only the main building remains.

Early in the morning on Easter Sunday, April 21, 1935, Jesus came to me in prayer and gave me my heavenly mission. I was sixteen years old (by the Korean way of counting). I appreciate this 1982 painting, by Shigeyoshi Watanabe, which captures well the spirit of that moment.

Ph3

Left: My grandfather Chi Guk Moon, who supported education for village youth.
Center: My great-uncle Yoon Guk Moon, the noted pastor and Korean patriot.
Right: A portrait of my mother, Kyung Gye Kim, painted in 1988, based on old photos.

Left: My student photo in 1941, the year I graduated from technical school, where I studied electrical engineering.
Right: Cooking rice with my cousin, Seung Ryong Moon (*second from left*), and friends in the late 1930s. I am on the right.

I taught Sunday School at the Myungsudae Jesus Church in Seoul in the early 1940s. I am standing in the back row (*see arrow*).

March 8, 1941. Commencement ceremony of the third graduating class of Kyeongsung School of Commerce and Technology. I am in the back row, fifth from the left (*see arrow*).

This naval vessel participated in the bombardment of Heungnam, where I had been a prisoner for nearly three years. U.N. forces, including future U.S. Army General Alexander Haig, liberated me from the prison camp with their shelling on October 14, 1950.

Above: The mud-walled hut that Won Pil Kim and I built in early 1951 out of ration cartons stood on a lonely hill by a cemetery in Busan. *Right:* I was greeted by our members after my release from Seodaemun prison in Seoul on October 4, 1955. I was indicted for "draft evasion" even though I had been in a North Korean prison camp during the war. I was declared innocent after serving three months in jail.

Teaching members in our church in Cheongpa-Dong right
after coming out of Seodaemun prison.

November 1, 1958. I am standing (*left*) with students from Ewha Womans University
and Professor Won Bok Choi (*right*), who were unjustly expelled for their faith.

Early spring 1959 in Yamok, Kyeonggi Province. I took the members to help plant rice. The farmers benefited, and for us it was training.

We often went outdoors in the Seoul area, where I would teach the members about God's providence.

Left: On April 11, 1960, Hak Ja Han and I married. She and her mother, an early disciple, escaped from North Korea during the Korean War.
Right: A nice interlude with my wife on Cheongpyeong Lake.

Even this family portrait taken in Korea on January 1, 2009, doesn't include everyone. We have 14 children, living in different parts of the world, and an ever-growing number of grandchildren and great-grandchildren.

On May 1, 1966, the 12th anniversary of the founding of the Unification Church, I signed copies of the Korean-language second edition of my teachings, the *Divine Principle*. I am on the left, with my wife.

In 1969, during my second world tour. The movement in Japan had grown enormously, and our meetings had to be held in large outdoor venues like this park in suburban Tokyo.

February 1, 1974, meeting President Richard Nixon (*left*) at the White House at the height of the Watergate controversy. For the sake of a strong, unified America, I asked Americans and the media, through newspaper ads, to "Forgive, Love and Unite."

New York's Carnegie Hall on October 1, 1973, the first stop on a 21-city speaking tour of the United States that ended January 29, 1974.

More than 1.2 million people attended the World Freedom Rally in Seoul's Yoido Plaza on June 7, 1975.

Washington Monument on September 18, 1976. As part of our U.S. Bicentennial commemorations, I declared "God's Hope for America" before an estimated crowd of 300,000. *Inset:* My interpreter, Dr. Bo Hi Pak, is on the right.

Dr. Morton Kaplan (*left*), conference chairman, offers me and my wife the appreciation of the conferees at the conclusion of the 12th International Conference on the Unity of the Sciences (ICUS) in Chicago, November 24-27, 1983. I hosted a total of 21 annual ICUS conferences. ICUS focused on the relationship between science and absolute values.

My stay in Danbury Prison in Connecticut was from July 20, 1984, through August 20, 1985. I was accused of not paying $7,500 in taxes on interest income, despite investing millions for the moral renewal of the U.S. Here (*right*) I walk in the exercise yard with Takeru Kamiyama, one of my disciples.

My wife and I officiated at the October 14, 1982, Holy Marriage Blessing at Jamsil Gymnasium in Seoul. The Blessing and the pursuit of "World Peace Through Ideal Families" is the centerpiece of my ministry. Since 1960, and as of the beginning of 2010, I have given the Blessing to more than 4 million people in ceremonies conducted with live worldwide satellite links.

On December 22, 2003, Christians, Muslims, Jews, and other faith leaders of the Middle East Peace Initiative gather in front of the Dome of the Rock in Jerusalem. Hundreds of religious and social leaders have participated in over 40 pilgrimages to promote peace in the Holy Land.

I purchased this former Christian Brothers Catholic Seminary on the Hudson River in Upstate New York in 1975 to found the Unification Theological Seminary (UTS), open to all faiths. I chose a faculty consisting of scholars from each world religion.

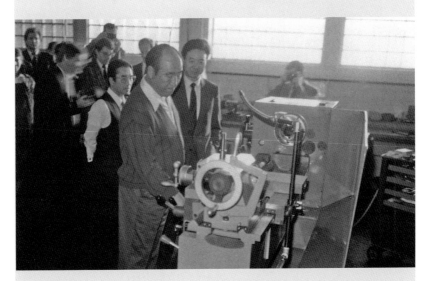

Visiting our machine shop in Germany in 1989. I have long advocated that advanced technology should be shared among all nations to promote freedom and prosperity.

August 1998, fishing for king salmon in Kodiak, Alaska. I am fourth from the left, next to my wife. Church leaders are on either side.

On June 4, 2002, soccer great Pelé (*left*) paid a courtesy visit to my residence in Hannam-Dong. Here my wife explains the World Peace Cup Soccer Tournament. I shared with Pelé the vision of promoting soccer as a way to build bridges of peace between nations.

On December 6, 1991, my wife and I traveled to Pyongyang, North Korea, at the invitation of President Kim Il Sung (*center*), and met with him in the Majeon Presidential Palace in Heungnam.

On March 24, 1994, I hosted President Mikhail Gorbachev (*right*) and First Lady Raisa at the Summit Council for World Peace in Korea. I founded the Summit Council to convene former heads of state to deliberate on solutions to conflicts.

President Leonard Kravchuk (*left*) of the Ukraine greeted me on October 20, 2005, during my 120-nation tour to inaugurate the Universal Peace Federation.

On December 1, 2005, my wife and I were welcomed by H.E. Gloria Macapagal Arroyo (*right*), president of the Philippines, at Malacañang Palace in Manila. I had been urging the U.N. to strengthen its commitment to interfaith cooperation and was gratified to see that, under her leadership, the Philippines government initiated resolutions. Then-Speaker Jose De Venecia has also encouraged me in my hope to see an interfaith deliberative body established in the U.N.

At the Manhattan Center in New York on September 23, 2007, I asked delegates from 194 nations to pledge to lay the foundation for a new "Abel" or "Peace" U.N., which seeks to fulfill the U.N.'s ideals with a structure that emphasizes living for the sake of others.

Last Plane to America

Near the end of 1971, I went to the United States again. I had certain tasks that absolutely needed to be accomplished there, but getting there was not so easy. It was not my first time to go to the United States, yet I had to wait an unusually long time to receive my visa. Some members suggested that I delay my departure, but I could not do that. It was difficult for me to explain to the members, but it was important that I leave Korea on the designated date. So I decided to go first to Japan and apply for a U.S. visa while in Japan. I was in a hurry to leave Korea.

The day of my departure was quite cold, but so many members came to see me off that they could not all get into the terminal. When it came time for me to go through the passport control desk, however, it was discovered that my passport was missing the stamp of the section chief of the Foreign Ministry's passport section. This stamp was required as proof that the government had cleared me to leave the country. Because of this, I missed the flight I had been scheduled to board.

The members who had prepared for my departure apologized profusely and suggested that I return home and wait while they tracked down the section chief and got him to place his stamp in my passport.

"No," I told them. "I will wait here at the airport. Go quickly and get the stamp."

My heart was filled with urgency. It happened to be a Sunday, so the section chief would not be at his desk. But I could not afford to let myself be concerned by such matters. In the end, our members went to the home of the section chief and had him place his stamp in my passport. So I was able to board the final flight of the day out of Korea. That night, the government declared a national state of emergency and imposed heavy restrictions on foreign travel by private citizens. I had boarded the last flight that would allow me to go to America.

I applied for a U.S. visa in Japan, but again it was refused. I discovered later what the problem was. The Korean government still had a record of my being detained by the Japanese colonial police just prior to liberation on charges of being a communist. The early 1970s was a time when communism was spreading with ferocity. By 1975, we had sent missionaries to 127 countries, but those in four communist countries were expelled. Evangelizing in communist countries in that era could result in death. I never gave up, however, and continued to send missionaries to the Soviet Union and other communist countries. Our first missionary to Czechoslovakia arrived in 1968.

Around 1980, we began to refer to our mission work in the communist countries of Eastern Europe as "Mission Butterfly." A larva must go through a long period of suffering before it can grow wings and become a butterfly, and we felt that this was similar to the suffering of our underground missionaries working in communist countries. It is a difficult process for a butterfly to come out of its cocoon, but once it has its wings, the butterfly can fly anywhere it wants. In the same way, we knew that once communism came to its demise, our missionaries would grow wings and begin to fly.

Missionary Young Oon Kim, who had gone to the United States in early 1959, toured the major universities in that country to convey God's word. In the process, she met Peter Koch, a German student at the University of California at Berkeley, and this young man decided to suspend his studies and travel by ship to Rotterdam and then start his missionary work in Germany. Missionaries to the communist countries of Asia were sent out from Japan. These missionaries had to be sent to places where their lives might be in danger without so much as a special worship service to mark their departure.

This pained me as much as having to push Bong Choon Choi to try again to smuggle himself into Japan during our final meeting in the pine forest behind the Gabsa temple. A parent who has to watch a child being punished would much rather be allowed to take the punishment himself.

I would have preferred to go out as a missionary myself. My heart was full of tears as I sent those members to places where they would be watched and possibly executed for their religious activities. Once the missionaries had left, I spent most of my time in prayer. Earnest prayers were the best thing I could do to help protect their lives. Missionary work in communist countries was dangerous work. A missionary never knew when the Communist Party might take him.

People who went as missionaries to communist countries could not even tell their parents where they were going. The parents knew well the dangers of going to such countries and would never give permission for their children to go. Gunther Werzer was discovered by the KGB and deported. In Romania, where the dictatorship of Nicolae Ceausescu was at its height of power, the secret police were constantly following and intercepting the telephone calls of our missionaries.

It was as if the missionaries had gone into the lion's den. The number of missionaries going to communist countries, however, kept growing.

Then in 1973, there was a terrible incident in Czechoslovakia where thirty of our members were taken into custody. One member, Marie Zivna, lost her life while in prison at the young age of twenty-four. She was the first martyr who died while conducting missionary work in a communist country. In the following year, another person lost his life in prison.

Each time I heard that one of our members had died in jail, my entire body froze. I could not speak or eat. I couldn't even pray. I just sat motionless for a while, unable to do anything. It was as if my body had turned to stone. If those people had never met me, or never heard what I taught, they never would have found themselves in a cold and lonely jail cell, and they never would have died the way they did. When they died, they suffered in my place. I asked myself, "Is my life worth so much that it couldn't be exchanged for theirs? How am I going to take on the responsibility for the evangelization of the communist bloc that they were bearing in my place?" I could not speak. I fell into a sorrow that seemed to have no end, as if I had been thrown into deep water.

Then I saw Marie Zivna before me in the form of a yellow butterfly. The yellow butterfly that had escaped Czechoslovakia's prison fluttered its wings as if to tell me to be strong and to stand up. By carrying on her missionary activities at the risk of her life, Marie truly had been transformed from being a caterpillar to being a beautiful butterfly.

Missionaries working in such extreme circumstances often received revelations through dreams and visions. They were isolated and could not communicate freely with others, so God gave them revelations to let them know the path they must follow. It would often happen that a missionary who had lain down to sleep for a short while would have a dream in which he was told, "Get up quickly and go someplace else." He did as he was told in the dream, only to discover later that the secret police had raided the place where he had been resting. In another instance, a member had a dream in which a person he had never seen before came to him and told him how to carry out his missionary work. Later, when he met me for the first time, he exclaimed, "You're the person I saw in my dream."

I risked my life to overthrow communism and to build God's nation, but was suspected of being a communist myself, and my application for a U.S. visa was rejected. My only choice was to submit all the materials showing my anti-communist work. In the end I barely got my visa to enter the United States.

The reason I went to all this trouble to go to America was to fight against the dark forces that had caused America's moral degradation. I left Korea to wage war on the forces of evil. At the time, all the major problems of the world — communism, drugs, corruption, and sexual decadence — were mixed together in a hellish stew. I declared, "I have come to America as a fireman and a doctor. If a house catches fire, a fireman needs to come, and if someone is sick, a doctor pays a visit." I was like a fireman who had gone to America to extinguish the fires of immorality, and like a doctor who had gone to cure America of the illness that made it lose sight of God and go to the brink of decadence.

America in the early 1970s was embroiled in the Vietnam War, and activists were protesting. It was a country seriously divided. Young people searching for meaning experimented with alcohol, drugs, and free sex, and in the process were neglecting their eternal souls. Mainstream religion, which should have provided guidance to such young people, was not performing its role. It could not help them end their aimless wandering and return to proper ways of living. The hedonistic, materialistic culture dragged many young people down, because they had no place to rest their hearts.

Soon after I arrived in the United States, I toured the country, speaking on the topics "The Future of Christianity" and "God's Hope for America." In front of large audiences, I spoke out about the weaknesses of America in a way that no one else would.

I proclaimed that America was founded on the Puritan spirit and had grown to be the strongest country in the world in just two hundred years because it received God's boundless love and blessing. I reminded the audiences that America's freedom came from God, but that America had cast God aside. "America has a great tradition," I said. "All you have to do is revive it." I went to the United States to reawaken America's spirit, to save America from destruction, and to urge the American people to repent and return to God.

Our Future Lies with the Ocean

s I toured the world, no one knew I was making plans to
develop economic foundations on a worldwide scale. As
the church grew and the number of missions increased,
the amount of funds we needed to support these activities increased
dramatically. We needed income. As I toured forty-eight states in the
United States, I gave much thought to the kinds of businesses that could
support the activities we had planned.

What came to my mind then was that Americans eat meat every day.
I checked the price of a cow. I saw that a cow that costs a small amount
in Texas could cost several hundred dollars in New York. But when I
checked the price of tuna, I discovered that one bluefin tuna cost more
than four thousand dollars. Tuna lay more than a million eggs at a time,
whereas a cow will have only one calf at a time. It was clear that catching
tuna would be a much better business endeavor than raising cattle.

One problem was that Americans did not eat much fish. The Japanese, however, were extremely fond of tuna. There were many Japanese
living in the United States then, and expensive restaurants operated by
Japanese sold raw tuna at a high price. Gradually some Americans were
learning to enjoy raw fish and started to like eating tuna.

The earth where we live is covered more by ocean than by land. The United States borders the Atlantic and Pacific Oceans and therefore has plenty of fish. Also, beyond the three-hundred-twenty-two-kilometer limit, no country has territorial claims on the ocean. Anyone can go out to catch fish. In order to start a farm or raise cattle, we would need to buy land, but there is no need for that in the ocean. All we needed was one boat, and we could go as far as necessary in order to catch fish. The ocean is filled with things to eat. Also, on the ocean surface, there is an active shipping industry. Ships carry things made in countries all over the world to be sold elsewhere. The ocean is a treasure trove that guarantees humankind a bright future. That is why I teach that those who are concerned with the future of humanity must be concerned with the oceans. When we can love and inherit the oceans, we inherit the future.

We purchased several boats in the United States. These were not the large ships that might be seen in a travel brochure, but fishing boats about ten to twelve meters in length. They could chase tuna and not have major accidents. These boats were placed in Washington, San Francisco, Tampa, and Alaska. We also purchased a ship repair facility.

We did a lot of our own research. We placed one boat in each region and measured the water temperature. We checked to see how many tuna were caught each day and placed the data on a chart. We didn't just take data that experts had created previously; our members went out on the water themselves to gather the information. The results of studies done by university-based researchers in the area were used as a reference. In addition, I went to those areas, lived there myself, and checked them out. No data were more accurate than what we gathered. We went to a lot of trouble to conduct this research, but we did not keep it to ourselves. Instead, we shared it with the fishing industry. We also developed new fishing grounds. If too many fish are caught in one area, it depletes the fish population. It is important to go to new areas. Within a short time, we had made a major impact on the U.S. fishing industry.

We entered the business of catching fish on the open sea. Our idea was that one ship would go out to sea and catch fish for at least six months without returning to port. When the ship had all the fish it could carry, a transport ship would go out to it, take its fish, and resupply it with food and fuel. The ship had large refrigeration facilities in which it could store fish for a long time. The name of our ship was *New Hope*, and it was well known for being able to catch many fish.

I took that boat out myself and caught tuna. People were often afraid of getting on boats. When I suggested to young people that they get on a boat, their first reaction was often one of fear. "I get seasick," I often heard them say. "All I have to do is get on a boat, and I start getting woozy and feel like I'm going to die." So I got on the boat first myself.

From that day, I went out on the boat almost every day for seven years. Even now, when I am ninety years old, I like to go out on the ocean whenever I have the time. Now, there are more and more young people who say they want to go out on the boats. More women also say they want to do this. With any task, if the leader does it first, the people follow. As a result, I have become well known as a tuna fisherman.

It would have been of little use, however, if we had only caught the tuna. We also needed to be able to sell it at the right price. We created a tuna-processing facility and even sold the tuna ourselves. We put the tuna in large refrigerated trucks and went out and sold them. If selling was difficult, we started our own seafood restaurants and sold the tuna directly to consumers. Once we had our own restaurants, people could not ignore us.

The United States has three of the world's four largest fishing grounds. Three-quarters of the world's fish population live in waters near the United States. Yet, the United States has relatively few commercial fishermen, and its fishing industry is extremely underdeveloped. The government has taken many measures designed to support the fishing industry, but they have not had a major effect. The government offered to sell boats at a big discount on the condition that buyers use them for three years, but few people took advantage of the opportunity. How frustrating this is!

When we started to put money into the fishing industry, it caused a stir in each port where we went. This was not surprising, since communities prospered wherever we invested. Our work, ultimately, was to pioneer new worlds. We were not simply catching fish. We were taking paths not taken by others. How exciting it is to be a pioneer!

The ocean changes constantly. They say people's minds change morning and night, but the ocean changes moment to moment. That is why the ocean is both mysterious and beautiful. The ocean embraces everything in heaven and earth. Water vapor can condense at a particular spot, form clouds, and then become rain and fall back down.

I am very fond of nature, because it never deceives. If it is high, it becomes lower; if it is low, it becomes higher. In every instance, it adjusts its height to become level. If I am sitting holding a fishing pole, it seems as though I have all the time in the world. What is there on the ocean to stand in our way? Who is there to make us hurry? We have a lot of time for ourselves. All we need to do is watch the ocean and talk with it. The longer a person spends on the ocean, the greater the spiritual aspect of his life will become. The ocean, however, can be calm one minute but then quickly change its face and send us strong waves. Waves several times the height of a person will rise up above the boat, as if to devour it. A strong wind will tear at the sail and make a fearful sound.

Think of this, though. Even when the waves have risen and a fearful wind is blowing, the fish in the water have no trouble sleeping. They give themselves over to the waves and don't resist them. This is what I learned from the fish. I decided not to be afraid, no matter how strong the waves were. I let the waves carry me. I made myself one with the boat, and we rose with the waves. Once I started doing that, my heart was never shaken, no matter what kind of waves I came up against. The ocean has been such a wonderful teacher for me in my life that I created the Ocean Challenge program to give young people the leadership training the ocean provides.

My Hope for a New American Revolution

T he initial reaction to my efforts, shown by Americans, was so cold. They questioned how a religious leader from Korea, an insignificant country that had barely survived hunger and war, could dare call on Americans to repent.

It was not just Americans who opposed me. The reaction from the Japanese Red Army, a communist group in league with international communists, was particularly strong. They were even caught by the FBI trying to sneak into the workshop center in Boston where I often stayed. There were so many attempts to harm me that my children could not attend school without the presence of bodyguards. Because of the continued threats on my life, I spoke from behind bulletproof glass for a period.

Despite such opposition, the lecture series by the small-eyed man from the Orient gathered more and more interest. People began to listen to the teachings, which were completely different from what they had heard until then. The content of the lectures dealing with the fundamental principles of the universe and seeking to reawaken the founding spirit of America was a breath of fresh air for Americans who had fallen into the hell of immorality and sloth.

Americans experienced a revolution of consciousness through

my lectures. Young people began to follow me, calling me "Father Moon" or "Reverend Moon" and cutting their shoulder-length hair and their scruffy beards. When appearances change, minds also change. So God began to enter into the hearts of young people who had been immersed in alcohol and drugs.

The lectures were attended by a variety of young people, transcending denominations. When I would interrupt my sermons to ask, "Are there any Presbyterians here?" many young people would wave their hands, saying, "Here." If I asked, "Are there any Catholics?" hands would go up again. When I asked, "How about Southern Baptists?" many people would again answer, "Me."

"Why do you come to hear me instead of going to hear a sermon in your own religious group?" I asked. "Go home and go to your own church to hear God's Word."

When I said this, the audience responded, "We want to hear Reverend Moon!"

More and more people began gathering, and even some ministers of Presbyterian and Baptist churches came, bringing with them the young people of their churches. As time went on, Reverend Moon became an icon representing a revolution of consciousness in American society.

I taught American young people how to endure difficulty. I thoroughly taught them the principle that a person must be able to rule himself before he can rule the universe. My teachings provided a new inspiration to American young people living in an age of confusion. They shouted in agreement with my message of sexual purity and true families. The reception was so enthusiastic that it made me sweat with excitement as well.

"Do you want to bear the cross of pain?" I asked them. "No one wants to go the way of the cross. Your heart may want to go that way, but your body says 'No!' Just because something is pleasing to the eye doesn't mean it is good for the heart. There are many things that look good, but an examination of their inner aspect shows them to be evil.

"If you catch yourself seeking after only things pleasing to the eye and try following that path, you must immediately stop yourself and say, 'You rascal!' Also, if you feel the desire to eat only things pleasing to the mouth, you must scold your body, saying, 'You rascal,' and block yourself. You young people are attracted to the opposite sex, aren't you? In this case, too, you must make a strong stand against such urges. If a person cannot control himself, he cannot do anything in this world. Think that if you break down, the universe will break down."

I was teaching them the motto that I had followed as a young man, which was "Before seeking to rule the universe, first perfect your ability to rule yourself." America had great wealth and had become obsessed with material goods. I stood in the midst of this materialistic culture and talked about matters of the mind and heart. The mind cannot be seen with the eye or held in the hand. Yet, we clearly are ruled by our minds. Without our minds, we are nothing. Then I talked about true love, God-centered love, which should guide the mind. I said that true freedom can be enjoyed only when we have a clear understanding of ourselves based on a foundation of true love and are able to exercise self-control.

I taught them the value of hard work. Hard work is not suffering but creation. The reason a person can work all his life and be happy is that labor is connected to God's world. The labor that people perform is nothing more than taking things that God created and shaping them in different ways. If you think that you are making something to give to

God as a memento, then labor is not something to think of in a negative way. Many American young people were so steeped in the affluent life provided to them by their materialistic culture that they didn't know the joy of working. So I taught them to work with joy.

I also awoke in them the joy of loving nature. The young people were caught up in the immoral culture of the cities and enslaved in selfish lives, so I talked to them about the preciousness of nature. Nature is given to us by God. God speaks to us through nature. It is a sin to destroy nature for the sake of a moment of enjoyment or an insignificant amount of money. The nature that we destroy eventually will make its way back to us in the form of pollutants and make life difficult for our descendants. We need to go back to nature and listen to what nature tells us. I told the young people of America that when we open our hearts and listen to what nature is saying, we can hear the word of God.

In September 1975, we founded the Unification Theological Seminary in Barrytown, New York, which is located north of New York City. The faculty was hired on an interreligious basis, and we had professors representing Judaism, Protestantism, Catholicism, Eastern Orthodoxy, and Oriental philosophy. When they lectured about their own religions, our students asked them very difficult questions. The classes always became forums for intense debate.

When all the religions were put together and debated, they began to break through the incorrect concepts they had about each other and to better understand each other. Gifted young people finished their master's-level education at our seminary and entered the doctoral programs at Harvard, Yale, and other leading U.S. universities. Today they have become people capable of leading the religious world on a global scale.

Washington Monument, 1976

In 1974 and 1975, I was invited to speak on Capitol Hill. I spoke in front of members of the House of Representatives on the topic "One Nation Under God."

I addressed the congressmen in the same manner as I had the young people on the street, saying, "America was born through God's blessing. This blessing, however, was not for Americans alone. This was God's blessing for the world, given through America. America must understand the principle of this blessing and sacrifice itself in order to save the world. To do this, there needs to be a reawakening that lets America return to its founding spirit. Christianity, which has been divided into dozens of denominations, must be united, embrace all religions, and open a new future for world civilization."

I was the first foreign religious leader to be invited to speak by members of the U.S. Congress. After I was invited for a second time, many more people became interested in finding out about this Reverend Moon from Korea.

The next year, on June 1, 1976, we held a celebration at Yankee Stadium in New York City to commemorate the bicentennial of the nation's independence. At the time, the United States could not celebrate its anniversary peacefully. It was feeling the threat of communism, and its young people were living lives far distant from the desire of God, engaging in such things as drugs and free sex. I felt that America was seriously ill. I went to the celebration feeling as though I were like a surgeon cutting open the heart of a New York that lay sick.

On the day of the celebration, torrential rains came down, and a strong wind blew the decorations all around the field, but no one tried to get out of the rain. The band started playing "You Are My Sunshine," and everyone in the stadium began to sing together. They were singing a song about sunshine, even as they were being soaked by the rain. Their mouths were singing about sunshine, but their eyes were crying. It was a moment when rain and tears were mixed together. Then, incredibly, as I went to the stage to speak, the sunshine broke through the rain clouds. It was as if God had heard their singing.

I did some boxing when I was in school. You can hit a good boxer with many jabs and still find that he is not affected. If you can land a solid upper-cut, however, even the strongest boxer will be shaken up. I was counting on landing a solid upper-cut on America. I felt that there needed to be a much larger rally than what had been held up to that point so that the name "Sun Myung Moon" would be indelibly carved into America's mind.

Washington Monument stands on the National Mall in the very center of the capital of the United States. The monument, which looks like a tall sharp pencil, stands over a hundred sixty-nine meters high. A large grassy field extends from the monument to the Reflecting Pool in front of the Lincoln Memorial. I set a plan to hold a large rally in this place, the symbolic heart of America.

Even to hold a rally there, however, we needed permission from both the U.S. government and the U.S. National Park Police. By this time, many U.S. officials did not like me very much. I had previously put ads in newspapers calling on the American people to forgive former President Richard Nixon, who was in a crisis because of the Watergate incident. My position was very unpopular. So now the U.S. government kept turning us down, and it was not until forty days prior to the event that we were finally able to receive permission.

Our members suggested to me that this was too ambitious a plan and that we should not go forward. The National Mall surrounding the Washington Monument was an open park in the middle of an urban area. There were not many trees—just a wide expanse of grass. If the crowd were small, it would be obvious for everyone to see. To fill such a large area, there would have to be hundreds of thousands of people. Our members wanted to know how this could be possible. Prior to this, only two people had held large events on the National Mall. Dr. Martin Luther King, Jr., had held a rally for civil rights on the steps of the Lincoln Memorial, and Rev. Billy Graham had held a large gathering there. So it was a place with a lot of symbolism. This was the place I was challenging.

I prayed without ceasing for this rally. Four times I wrote the speech that I was to deliver. A week before the event, I still had mixed feelings about what I should say in my speech. Finally, three days before the event, I completed the text. Generally, I don't speak from prepared texts. I made an exception in this case, because of my concern that the event go well. I knew this was going to be a particularly important occasion, though I wasn't quite certain why.

I will never forget what happened on that day, September 18, 1976. People started coming to the Washington Monument from early in the morning. Some three hundred thousand people gathered. It was impossible to tell where all these people had come from. They had all different colors of hair and skin. All the races that God sent to earth gathered on that day. It was a rally on a global scale that does not require any additional description.

I stood in front of the gathering and declared, "God prepared America for two hundred years. This is the time for awakening. America must accept her global responsibility. Armed with Godism, she must free the communist world and at last build the Kingdom of God here on earth." The speech was interrupted many times by shouts and applause.

Newsweek, in a year-end pictorial review of the major events of 1976, carried my photograph and referred to me as part of the revivalism of the 1970s. On the other hand, an increasing number of people were beginning to look at me with caution and fear. To them, I was nothing more than a strange magician who had come from the East. I was not a white man they could place their faith in and follow. The fact that I was saying things that were somewhat different from what they had heard in their churches made them feel very insecure. In particular, they could not allow a situation in which young white people were showing respect to and following an Asian with slender eyes shaped like a fish.

They began spreading rumors that I had been brainwashing innocent, young, white people. This group that opposed me gathered in the background, behind those who were shouting their support. I knew that another crisis was about to befall me. I was not afraid, however, because I was clearly doing what was right.

The United States is widely known as a country of freedom and equality, where people of all races come to realize the American dream.

In fact, however, there is a great deal of struggle stemming from racial and religious discrimination. These are chronic illnesses that are embedded deep within America's history, and they are therefore much more difficult to cure than the social diseases such as immorality and materialism that arose out of the affluence of the 1970s.

About this time, I was visiting African-American churches in an effort to foster ecumenical harmony. Among black leaders there were some who, in the footsteps of Dr. Martin Luther King, Jr., were working to do away with racial discrimination and bring about God's world of peace.

Some of these ministers had images hanging in their basements of the slave markets that had existed for hundreds of years prior to being outlawed. One frequent image was of a black man being burned alive while hanging from a tree. Another was of black men and women stripped of their clothes being looked over like merchandise by potential slave buyers. And yet another was of a black baby crying as it was being taken away from its mother. One could hardly believe that human beings were capable of the barbaric acts depicted so clearly in those images.

"Wait and see," I told a gathering in Chicago on October 24, 1975. "Within the next thirty years, there will be a president of the United States who was born into an interracial black-and-white family."

The prophecy I made that day has now come true in America with the inauguration of President Barack Obama, who spent much of his adult life in Chicago. This prophecy did not come true on its own. Many people shed their blood and sweat to do away with the struggles between the races, and those efforts have now finally blossomed.

Surprisingly, a number of ministers of established churches in America came and brought their congregations to the Washington

Monument rally. They decided that my message transcended denominations and that I was inspiring young people. I called on people to
transcend differences of denomination and religion, and those words
were realized at this rally. The Washington Monument Rally was a
miracle. The hundreds of thousands of people who attended made this
among the largest gatherings ever held on the National Mall.

"Shed Tears for the World, Not for Me"

Good is often followed by the bad. Some people drew mustaches on posters and advertisements carrying my picture, trying to make me look like Hitler. They called me "anti-Semitic" and claimed that I taught against Jews. Trouble also brewed with established Christians. As the number of young people following me grew, and the number of ministers wanting to learn my teaching, Divine Principle, increased, America's established churches began to persecute me. Finally, leftists in America reacted against my position that it was America's responsibility to stop the spread of communism in the world. They, too, began to look for ways to stop my activities.

As our popularity grew, all kinds of misgivings and doubts began to be raised about me. Young people, inspired to spread my teachings, had left college or quit their jobs to teach and raise funds for our work around the country. Their parents understandably became concerned about their well-being.

My "Forgive, Love, and Unite" campaign to protect the United States, embroiled in the Watergate crisis, sparked opposition from left-leaning media. Things that had not been an issue before suddenly came pressing down upon me. At the same time, conservatives called me too liberal, saying my teachings would break down family traditions, even though family love is my central message.

Furthermore, many Christians were unhappy about the new understanding of the cross that I was teaching: I teach that Jesus came as the Messiah, and it was not God's predestined will that he be crucified. With the crucifixion of Jesus, God's plan for the kingdom of peace went awry. If Israel had received Jesus as the Messiah, he could have brought about a world of peace, uniting cultures and religions of East and West. Instead Jesus died on the cross, and God's work of complete salvation was delayed until the Second Coming.

This teaching about the cross brought a great deal of opposition. As a result, established churches and the Jewish community both came to regard me as their enemy. They tried any number of ways to have me removed from America, each for their own different reasons.

Ultimately, I was imprisoned again. I worked with all my heart for just one purpose: to reestablish the morality of America and restore it to be a country in line with God's will. Instead I was accused of not paying my taxes. I was well past my sixtieth birthday by this time.

During the first three years I was in America, donations received from around the world were placed in a bank account in New York in my name and held in trust for the church, a practice common in some denominations. The money in this account produced interest income, and I was indicted for failing to report that interest as income on my personal tax returns for the years 1973 to 1975. The estimated tax on that income was about $7,500. Normally a fine would have been charged, but in my case, I was put on trial and convicted in 1982. In the end, on July 20, 1984, I was finally imprisoned in the federal correctional institution in Danbury, Connecticut.

On the day before reporting to Danbury prison, I met with members at the Belvedere training center in Tarrytown, New York. It was an emotional meeting. Thousands of people who had followed me were there that day, and shed tears as they prayed for me. I raised my voice and told them not to lose heart.

"I am innocent," I said. "I have done nothing wrong. I can see the bright light of hope rising from beyond Danbury." I told them, "Don't cry for me, but cry for America. Love America, and pray for America." I stood before these young people immersed in sadness and held up my hands as a sign of hope.

The moving statement I made prior to entering the prison caused a great stir among religious people. The Common Suffering Fellowship was initiated, and there was a wave of prayers to support me. The Common Suffering Fellowship was a groundswell of support from clergy of all denominations and from other religions concerned about the attack on religious freedom in America.

On the day I went to prison, I knew I had nothing to fear. I know life in jail. This was not the case with the people around me, however. They were concerned that my life could be in danger from people in prison who strongly opposed me. But I went to prison with my head held high.

"Why Does My Father Have to Go to Jail?"

Even in Danbury prison, I followed my principle of living for the sake of others. I would wake up early in the morning and clean places that were dirty. In the cafeteria, others would lean over their food and either take a nap or chat among themselves, but I kept my back straight and sat with dignity. When I was given work to do, I worked harder at it than others did, and I kept an eye out to see how others were doing.

In my spare time, I read the Bible. One prisoner, seeing how I read the Bible day and night, said to me, "Is that your Bible? Here's my Bible. Take a look!" He threw a magazine to me. It was the pornographic magazine *Hustler*.

In prison, I was known as a person who worked without talking. I read books and meditated. After going three months this way, I became friends with the prisoners and the guards. I became friends with a person who was on drugs and with the prisoner who had said the pornographic magazine was his Bible. After a month or two, the prisoners began to share with me the items they received from outside. Once we could share our hearts, it was as if spring had come to the inside of the prison.

Actually, the United States government did not really want to send me to prison. They chose to indict me while I was out of the country on a trip to Germany, and they probably would have been satisfied if I had chosen not to return. They weren't trying to put me in jail. They were trying to remove me from the country. I was becoming well known in America, and the number of people following me was increasing. So they wanted to put a roadblock in my way. Just as in Korea, I was a thorn in the side of the established churches. Because I knew this was their purpose, I chose to return to America and go to jail. I still had things that needed to be done in America.

I think that going to jail is not a completely bad thing. If I am to get people who are in the valley of tears to repent, then I must first shed tears. Unless I first experience such a wretched heart, I cannot get others to submit themselves to God. Heaven really works in mysterious ways. After I was imprisoned, seven thousand ministers and other religious leaders accused the U.S. government of violating religious freedom and began an effort to save me.

Among them were the conservative Rev. Jerry Falwell of the Southern Baptist Convention and the liberal Dr. Joseph E. Lowery, who years later would give the benediction during the inauguration of President Obama. They stood at the forefront of the effort to save me. Also, my daughter, In Jin, still in her teens, marched with them. She stood before several thousand religious leaders and read in tears a letter she had written in appeal to the judge who had handed down my sentence:

"My father's life has been dotted with tears and suffering, as he sought to carry out God's will. He is now 64 years old. His only crime was that he loved America. Yet, at this moment, he is either washing dishes in the prison cafeteria or mopping its floors.

"Last week, I visited my father and saw him for the first time in his prison uniform. I cried and cried. My father told me not to cry for him but to pray for America. He told me to take my anger and sorrow and transform these into a powerful force that will make this a truly free country.

"He said that while he was in prison he would endure any hardship, bear any injustice, and carry any cross. Freedom of religion is the basis of all freedoms. I am truly grateful to everyone who has stood up to support religious freedom."

My sentence was reduced by six months for good behavior, and I was released after serving thirteen months. The day I left prison, a banquet to celebrate my release was held in Washington, D.C. Seventeen hundred Christian ministers and Jewish rabbis were gathered and waiting for me. In my remarks to the gathering, I repeated my position in favor of transcending religions and denominations. I spoke in a loud voice to the world at large, feeling no need for concern for the reaction from those opposed to me.

"God is not a denominationalist. He is not bound by secondary arguments over doctrine. There are no distinctions over nationality or race in God's great parental heart. Neither are there any walls between nations or cultures there. Even today, God continues to do everything He can to embrace all the world's people as His children. America today suffers from racial issues, issues resulting from the confusion of values and moral degradation, issues of spiritual drought and the decline of Christian faith, and the issue of atheistic communism. These are the reasons I answered the call of God and came to this country. Christianity today must have a great awakening and come together as one. Clergy, too, must reexamine the roles that you have been playing until now and repent. The situation that played out two thousand years ago, when Jesus came and called on people to repent, is being repeated today. We must fulfill the important mission that God has given to America. The situation cannot continue as it is now. There needs to be a new Reformation."

Once I had been released from prison, there was nothing to hold me back. I spoke with an even louder voice than before to give a message of warning to a fallen America. I repeatedly spoke in strong words that returning to God's love and morality is the only way to revitalize America.

I was imprisoned without my having done anything wrong, but God's will was there as well. After my release, the people who worked for my release took turns coming to Korea to learn more about my work. They came to find out what it was about Reverend Moon's spirit that had attracted so many young people in America. On their return to the United States, one hundred twenty of these ministers organized the American Clergy Leadership Conference.

CHAPTER FIVE

LOVING FAMILIES CAN CHANGE THE WORLD

My Wife, Hak Ja Han Moon

The first time I saw my wife, she was a young woman of fourteen who had just graduated from elementary school (sixth grade). She was a quiet girl who never raised her voice and never sought to bring attention to herself. She always took the same route to and from the church. When she was first introduced to me, I was told she was the daughter of one of our early church members, Mrs. Soon Ae Hong.

"What is your name?" I asked her.

"My name is Hak Ja Han," she answered with a clear voice.

In that moment, before I knew what was happening, I said, "So Hak Ja Han has been born in Korea!" I said this three times in repetition, and then prayed, saying, "God! Thank you for sending to Korea such a wonderful woman as Hak Ja Han." I then looked at her, and said: "Hak Ja Han, I'm afraid you are going to have to do a lot of sacrificing."

All of these words came out of my mouth spontaneously. Later, Mrs. Hong told me that she thought it strange that I would say the same thing three times after meeting her daughter for the first time. My wife has told me that she also remembers that first, short meeting. She told me she remembers everything I said then as if I had delivered a sermon just for her, and she kept it in her heart. She said she felt like she had received an important revelation about her future that she could not forget.

Her mother was from a faithful Presbyterian family, so she was raised in a Christian home. Her hometown was Jeongju, which is my hometown as well, but she had lived in Anju until coming to South Korea during the Korean War. When Mrs. Hong first began attending our church, she lived a very faithful life in Chuncheon and raised her daughter strictly. My wife attended a nursing school that was operated by the Catholic Church. I am told that the rules of this school were so strict that it was as if she were living in a convent. She had a gentle character, and during the time she was raised by her mother, she never went anywhere except to school and to our church.

Years passed, and I was approaching forty. I sensed that the time was coming for me to marry again. All I needed to do was wait for God to tell me, "The time has come, so get married," and I would do as I was told. Seung Do Ji, an elderly woman in our church, began an effort in October 1959 to prepare for my engagement, even though there was still no bride-to-be. Another church member who had been praying for seven years about a wife for me told me one day that she had had a dream in which she saw that Hak Ja Han was my wife.

Mrs. Ji told me about a strange dream she had. "What kind of dream is this?" she exclaimed. "I saw hundreds of cranes come flying. I tried to wave them away with my arms, but they kept coming and they finally covered you with their white feathers. Is this some kind of omen for the future?" The "Hak" in Hak Ja Han is the Chinese character for crane.

Then, Hak Ja Han herself had a dream in which I appeared and told her, "The day is near, so make preparations." My wife later told me that in her dream she said to me in a humble tone, "I have been living until now in accordance with the will of God. In the future, as well, I will follow God's will as His servant, no matter what that will may be."

A few days after my bride-to-be had this dream, I asked Mrs. Hong to bring her daughter to me. This was our first meeting since she had been introduced to me at age fourteen. That day, I asked this young lady many questions. In every case, she responded with composure and spoke clearly. In this meeting, I asked my future wife to draw a picture. Without hesitation, she picked up a pencil and started drawing on a sheet of paper. When she had finished and placed her picture before me, I was very impressed by what I saw. I then looked at her face, and her shy expression was very beautiful. Her heart was as wonderful as the picture she had drawn.

We were engaged on March 27, 1960, and had our marriage ceremony barely two weeks later, on April 11. I did not set a date at the time, but when I called Miss Han several days later, I told her, "Tomorrow morning, we will have a marriage ceremony." She responded simply, "Is that so?" and did not ask any questions or try to speak in opposition. She seemed entirely obedient to Heaven. That was how pure and gentle she was. Then as now, when it comes to the will of God, she has a strong determination.

At the marriage ceremony I wore a *samokwandae*, the formal dress of government officers that now is commonly used in traditional wedding ceremonies, and she wore traditional Korean attire that included a *jokdori* bridal tiara. My bride, who was then seventeen and more than twenty years younger than I, looked confident and radiant with her tightly closed lips and pretty face. During the ceremony, I told my bride that she was about to embark on a difficult course.

"I think you are already aware that marrying me will not be like any other marriage. We are becoming husband and wife to complete the mission given to us by God to become True Parents, and not to pursue the happiness of two individuals, as is the case with other people in this world. God wants to bring about the Kingdom of Heaven on the earth through a true family. You and I will travel a difficult path to become True Parents who will open the gates to the Kingdom of Heaven for others. It is a path that no one else in history has traveled, so even I don't know all that it will involve. During the next seven years, you will experience many things that will be difficult to endure. Don't forget, even for a moment, that the life we live is different from others. Don't do anything, no matter how trivial, without first discussing it with me, and obey everything I tell you."

She responded, "My heart is already set. Please do not worry."

I could see in her expression that day that she had made a strong determination. Her difficult challenges began the day after our marriage. The first difficulty she faced was that she could not see her mother as freely as before. My wife, her mother, and her maternal grandmother were all only daughters. As a result, the relationship between mother and daughter was particularly strong. In order to take on her public mission and develop the proper focus, I asked her to live what amounted to an ascetic life for three years. That meant she could not see her mother or any of her relatives for three years. She lived in a room rented from a church member. She came to the church no more than once a day, usually in the evening. So as not to create disruption, she left through the back door.

I myself was often involved in worship services or praying through the night and was rarely at home, but the separation was not for practical reasons. The separation was to establish a spiritual condition of unconditional devotion to her mission. As the outrageous rumors about me continued to circulate, this separation from her relatives and me made it even more difficult for my young wife to endure.

At the time of our marriage, the Unification Church already had been established in over one hundred twenty communities around Korea. Even in our church, however, there were those who were critical of our marriage. Some envied her, some hated her, and many stories circulated. As if that were not enough, she lived in someone else's home, while older women of our church followed me everywhere I went.

Eventually, my seemingly cold treatment of my wife brought an end to all the criticism and envy against her. In fact, people began to sympathize with her. For example, many members criticized me when I couldn't go to see my wife even though she was suffering postpartum illness and was shivering in a poorly heated room after the birth of our first daughter. Some of them said, "How can he even call himself her husband?"

"You're going too far, sir," I was told. "If you married her, you should live with her. What are you doing, making it difficult for her even to see your face?" The people who had been criticizing my wife one by one began to take her side instead.

In spite of her young age, it was necessary that my wife receive harsh training. During the time we lived together, the pressures on her were relentless. She never had even a single free moment for herself. She constantly was on edge, as if she were walking on a thin layer of ice, wondering, "Will today be peaceful? Will tomorrow be peaceful?" Because she had to attain God's standard of motherly love, I corrected her for even a single wrong word. Sometimes even her affection for me had to be curtailed for the sake of her eternal mission. It was all necessary for her to become True Mother, but I am sure it caused much grief in her heart.

I might say a word in passing and not think much of it. She, however, had to harmonize herself with my every word, so I am sure her suffering was great. It took us seven years to conform ourselves to each other. I relate these things because the most important thing in a marriage relationship is trust. It is what makes it possible for two people to become as one.

An Incomparable Inner Beauty

My wife and I made a promise to each other after we were married. We agreed that no matter how upset or angry one of us might become, we would not allow anyone to think, "It looks like Reverend and Mrs. Moon had a fight." We agreed that no matter how many children we might have, we would not let them see any sign that we might have had a fight. Children are God. Children are God with very small hearts. So when a child says, "Mom!" and calls, you must always answer, "What is it?" with a smile.

After going through such a harsh course for seven years, my wife became a wonderful mother. All the gossip about her disappeared, and a peaceful happiness came to our family. My wife gave birth to fourteen children, and she has embraced each one with so much love. When she is away from home on our speaking tours and mission life, she sends letters and postcards to our children every day.

While it was difficult for her to raise fourteen children over the course of over forty years, she never complained. Several times I had to be overseas when my wife was about to give birth. She had to bear such times alone. There were days when I could not do anything for her. Once a member wrote me about my wife's difficult financial situation.

There was concern over whether she was getting sufficient nutrition. Even then, my wife never complained about her difficulty. Because I sleep only two or three hours a night, she has dutifully done the same throughout our life together. These sorts of matters pain me to this day.

My wife has such a tremendous heart of love and care that she even gave a special ring I bought her to someone in need. When she sees someone in need of clothes, she buys that person clothes, or gives them some of ours. When she comes across someone hungry, she buys the person a meal. There have been many times when we have received presents from others that she would give away to someone else she felt needed them more.

Once we were touring the Netherlands and had a chance to visit a factory that processed diamonds. Wanting to express my heart of regret toward my wife for all her sacrifices, I bought her a diamond ring. I didn't have much money, so I couldn't buy her a large one. I picked out one I liked and presented it to her. Later, she even gave away that ring. When I saw the ring wasn't on her finger, I asked her, "Where did the ring go?"

She answered, "You know by now I can't keep something like that when someone has a greater need."

On another occasion I saw her pulling out a large wrapping cloth, and she was working quietly to pack some clothes. "What are you going to do with those clothes?" I asked her.

"I have a use for them," she said.

She filled several wrapping cloths with clothes without telling me what she planned to do with them. When she was finished, she told me she was getting ready to send the clothes to our missionaries working in foreign countries.

"This one's for Mongolia, this one's for Africa, and this one's for Paraguay," she said. She had a slightly self-conscious smile that made her look so sweet when she told me. Still today, she takes it upon herself to look after our overseas missionaries.

My wife is the patron of the International Relief and Friendship Foundation established in 1979. It has done service projects in numerous countries, such as Congo, Senegal, and the Ivory Coast. The foundation gives food to impoverished children, medicine to those who are sick, and clothing to those in need. In Korea, she created the Aewon charity organization in 1994. Its activities include managing a canteen serving free food to the poor and supporting low-wage earners, the handicapped, children taking care of families in place of parents, and others. It also provides aid to the North Korean people.

My wife has also been active in women's organizations for some time. The Women's Federation for World Peace, which she established in 1992, has branches in some eighty countries and is in general consultative status with the Economic and Social Council of the United Nations as a nongovernmental organization.

Throughout history, women have been persecuted, but I predict this will change. The coming world will be one of reconciliation and peace based on women's maternal character, love, and sociability. The time is coming when the power of women will save the world.

Unfortunately today, many women's organizations apparently believe that standing in opposition to men is the way to demonstrate the power of women. The result is an environment of competition and conflict. The women's organizations my wife leads, on the other hand, seek to bring about peace on the principle that women should work together, take initiative, and empower one another across traditional lines of race, culture, and religion to create healthy families as the cornerstone of the culture of peace. The organizations she works with do not call for a liberation of women from men and families. Instead, they call for women to develop and maintain families filled with love.

My wife's dream is to see all women raised as true daughters with filial hearts who can create peace at home, in our communities, in our nations, and in the world. The women's movement being carried out by my wife serves the goal of true families, which are the root of peace in all areas of life.

During one of the most intense periods of my public work, our children had to live close to half the year without their parents. In our absence, they lived in our home, cared for by church members. Our home was always filled with church members. Every meal in our home had guests at the table, guests who always received priority over our children. Because of this environment, our children grew up with a sense of loneliness that is not experienced by children in other families. Even worse was the suffering they had to endure because of their father. Wherever they went, they were singled out as sons and daughters of "the cult leader Sun Myung Moon." This suffering sent them through periods of wandering and rebellion, but they have always returned home. We were not able to support them properly as parents, but five have graduated from Harvard University. I could not be more grateful for their courageous accomplishments. Now they are old enough to help me in my work, but even to this day, I am the strict father. I still teach them to become people who do more than I do to serve Heaven and live for the sake of humanity.

My wife is a woman of incredible strength, but the death of our second son, Heung Jin, was difficult for her. It happened in December

1983. She was with me in Kwangju, Korea, participating in a Victory over Communism rally, when we received an international phone call that Heung Jin had been in a traffic accident and had been transported to a hospital. We boarded a flight the next day and went directly to New York, but Heung Jin was lying unconscious on the hospital bed.

A truck traveling over the speed limit as it came down a hill tried to brake and swerved into the opposite lane, where Heung Jin was driving. Two of his best friends were in the car with him at the time. Heung Jin cut the wheel to the right so the driver's side took most of the impact from the truck. By doing so, he saved the lives of his two friends. I went to the place near our home where the accident had occurred, and the black tire marks veering off to the right were still visible.

Heung Jin finally went to the heavenly world in the early morning of January 2. He had turned seventeen just a month before.

Words cannot describe my wife's sorrow when she had to send a child she had raised with love to the heavenly world before her. She could not cry, however. In fact, it was important that she not shed any tears. We are people who know the world of the eternal spirit. A person's spirit does not disappear like so much dust, just because the physical life is lost. The soul ascends to the world of spirit. As parents, the pain of knowing that we would never be able to see or touch our beloved child in this world was almost unbearable. My wife could not cry; she could only lovingly put her hands on the hearse that carried Heung Jin's body.

This tragic accident occurred as we planned for the betrothal of Heung Jin to Hoon Sook Pak, who was studying ballet. I had to speak to Hoon Sook about his departure from this world and find out from her what she wanted to do. I told her I knew it wouldn't be easy or fair to her parents if she chose to go ahead with such a marriage. I told her it was best to forget the betrothal. Hoon Sook was adamant, however. "I am aware of the existence of the spirit world," she said. "Please let me spend my life with Heung Jin." In the end, Hoon Sook became our daughter-in-law fifty days after Heung Jin's departure. My wife and I will never forget her bright smile as she was accompanied by a framed photograph of Heung Jin throughout the spiritual marriage ceremony.

It would seem that my wife would be devastated each time she faced such difficult situations, but she always remained unshaken. Even in the most difficult and unbearable circumstances, my wife never lost her serene smile. She always crossed over life's most difficult peaks success-fully. When church members ask my wife's advice on raising their own children, she tells them: "Be patient and wait. The period when children wander is only temporary. No matter what they do, embrace them, love them, and wait for them. Children will always return to the love of their parents."

I have never raised my voice toward my wife. This is not because of my character, but because my wife has never given me cause to do so. Throughout our life together, she has labored to care for me with com-plete, loving devotion. She is even the one to care for my hair. So this great saint of world affairs is also the best barber in the world. Now that I am old I make many new demands on her, and she always responds. If I ask her to cut my toenails, she will do it cheerfully. My toenails are mine, but I can't see them very well. She sees them perfectly well, though. It's a strange thing. The older I become, the more precious my wife is to me.

Promises That Must Never Be Broken

During our matching and marriage ceremonies, I ask the brides and grooms to make promises to each other that must never be broken. First, a husband and wife must always trust and love each other. Second, they must not cause any pain to the heart of their partner. Third, they must educate their children and grandchildren to maintain sexual purity. Fourth, all members of their family must help and encourage each other so they become a true ideal family. Chastity before marriage and fidelity in marriage are of utmost importance. This is what I teach so people can live to their highest potential as human beings, creating and maintaining healthy families.

Marriage is more than a simple coming together of a man and woman. It is a precious ceremony of commitment to carry on God's work of creation. Marriage is the path by which a man and woman become as one, create new life, and establish true love. Through marriage, a new future is created: Societies are formed; nations are built. God's world of peace is realized with married families at the center. It is in the family that God's Kingdom of Heaven is brought about. So husbands and wives must be centers of peace. Not only must there be love between the husband and wife, but the couple must also be able to bring harmony to their extended families. It is not enough that the husband and wife live well together in love. All the relatives must love each other as well. I tell brides and grooms to have many children. To bear many children and raise them is God's blessing. It is unthinkable that human beings apply their own standard of judgment and arbitrarily abort precious lives given to them by God. All life born into this world embodies God's will. All life is noble and precious, so it must be cared for and protected.

Naturally, a husband and wife must maintain mutual trust and nurture their love. The promise I emphasize the most to people preparing to marry is "teach your children to maintain sexual purity."

This is an obvious promise, but it has become difficult to keep in today's society. The worse the world becomes, however, the more important it is to strictly keep the promise of sexual purity.

The perfection of human beings and peace in the world come about through the family. The purpose of religion is for everyone to become people of goodness who can then bring about an ideal world of peace. No matter how much politicians may put their heads together, they will not bring about peace. Formidable military power will not bring peace. The starting point for bringing about peace is the family.

When I arrived in America in 1971, the wind of promiscuous free sex was blowing across the country, and the entire society was in the midst of confusion. Young people who had received wonderful educations were being destroyed one by one. Sexual immorality was so bad that it was becoming the norm. Sexually transmitted diseases were beginning to skyrocket.

The seriousness of the problem was compounded by politicians, academics, and clergy. They knew about this problem, but most of them ignored it. They tried to look away from the ugly reality because they themselves had not maintained sexual purity. People who are not sexually pure themselves cannot urge their children to be so.

The degradation of sexual morality among adults destroys families and leads to the ruin of children. Immorality and licentiousness in the personal lives of adults ultimately destroy the lives of their children. The reason today's society does not have a level of happiness to match its level of material affluence is that families are being destroyed. To save families, adults must first live proper lives. Then, it is possible to raise children in sexual purity.

The mother is the fortress that protects the family. No matter how much society may change, the family is healthy and peaceful only if the mother has the heart to sacrifice and serve. It is in such a family that beautiful children can grow. In educating our children, what the children see and learn in the family is most important. A crab that walks sideways cannot tell its offspring to walk straight ahead. The parents must show a good example. True children come from true families. Truth is always very simple.

The most difficult aspect of family life is raising children properly. We give birth to them in love and raise them in love, but they don't necessarily grow up the way their parents desire. What's worse, today's materialistic culture is destroying the innocent minds of young people. Young people who should be growing up to become responsible adults capable of extraordinary achievements are being lost to drugs. Drug-induced states make people lose touch with their own spirit. Young people who have lost touch with their spirit eventually can only fall into crime and sexual immorality.

During adolescence, children think everything should be centered only on themselves, and so there is the tendency to rebel against things the parents may say. If the parent does not respond with understanding, there is the possibility that the child may go to self-centered extremes. On the other hand, a child in adolescence can be deeply moved by anything that seems to connect with his heart. Perhaps on an autumn day, the child will see a persimmon fall from a tree that has lost all its leaves. The child cannot explain it, but somehow it connects with his heart and he will smile and experience happiness. This is a sign that God's original character is dwelling in his heart.

But if adolescents involve themselves in sexual relationships, their perceptions become clouded and their power of judgment diminished. When an adolescent boy and girl meet and start talking with each other, they can feel flushed and there may be a change in their heart rate. If their minds are not brought into harmony with God's standard in that moment, they will surely be moved in the direction of self-centeredness. They lose the means with which to control their bodies.

During adolescence, our cells open wide all the doors of love in both the physical body and the spirit. The desires of our mind and the desires of our body are meant to become one and function together. When we acquire the nose of love, we start to love smells that we used to hate. When we acquire the mouth of love, we start to love tastes that we used to hate. We want to listen all night to the stories of love. We want to keep touching the person we love. Adolescents start to think they can be happy simply by entering into a love relationship.

However, the doors of love are designed by God and are to open only when the time is right. Children must understand that they need to wait for the right time. Parents must teach these things to their adolescent children very carefully. Love is a process by which we grow to resemble God. Despite what the world may tell us, it is not something to be enjoyed anytime we please.

During adolescence, a child may want to try really hard to copy the activity in a thrilling movie. People ask, "What's wrong with that?" It is wrong because irresponsible actions lead to destruction. When children mature and acquire wisdom and knowledge, they can control their social and environmental experiences and are truly free to do so, but not during adolescence.

Why do we say, "Do not give a knife to a child"? It is because the child would wave it around. The child might understand how to cut with a knife, but he cuts without control. The child might even cut his mother's fingers. Because children do not yet fully understand the consequences, we do not give them knives.

The combination of parents not teaching their children the value of purity and children rebelling against their parents leads to broken families. Because of this, societies are being broken. Because of this, nations are being destroyed. Because of this, humanity is being destroyed.

To Love Is to Give and Forget

The family is the only institution created by God. It is the school of love where people can learn how to love each other and live together in peace, and it is the training center where we practice how to build a palace of peace in the world. It is where we learn how to become a husband or wife who will live for the sake of our spouse and how to become a husband and wife who will travel on the eternal path of love. The family is the base camp for world peace, and it must be such that the children will say, "We have never seen our mother and father fight."

We come up against all sorts of things in life. Even the most loving couple can have times when they may bicker with each other, become angry, and raise their voices. When the children come into the room, however, it all must stop immediately. No matter how angry a husband may be, he must relate to his spouse in peace when the children are present. The children must grow up thinking their family is filled with joy and their parents always love each other.

Parents are like a second God to their children. If you ask your young children, "Whom do you like better—God or Mommy and Daddy?"—and they say they like their mom and dad better, then that means they also like God. The most precious education takes place in the family. You won't find happiness and peace in some other place. The family is intended to be the Kingdom of Heaven. It would not matter if a person possesses incredible wealth and fame or even possesses the whole world. If all is not right with that person's family, then he cannot be happy. The Kingdom of Heaven begins in the family. If a husband and wife are bound together in true love and they build an ideal family, this will connect directly with the world.

I saw something interesting when I was in Danbury prison. We were using a bulldozer to level a slope and make a tennis court. When it rained, we would wait for it to stop, and start up again when the sun came out. This process of starting and stopping went on for months. We had a long stretch of rain for one period, and we couldn't work for twenty consecutive days. When the rain cleared and we went out to start the work again, we found that some kind of waterfowl had created a nest where there were some water weeds. It was a place not more than a few meters from where the prisoners would walk for exercise.

At first, we didn't even realize the bird was there. Its camouflage was so perfect that the bird's feathers could easily be mistaken for the water weeds. Once the bird laid its eggs, though, we could see there was a bird in among the weeds. The bird was sitting on some eggs that looked like pieces of black gravel. Once the chicks hatched, the mother would go find some food, bring it back to the nest, and put it in the beaks of the chicks. When the mother was returning to the nest with food, however, she never flew directly to the nest. She would land a little distance from the nest and then walk the rest of the way. Each time, she approached the nest from a different direction. This was her wisdom to make it more difficult for others to discover the location of the nest where the chicks were. The chicks ate the food their mother brought them and grew larger. Sometimes, when a prisoner would walk near the nest, the mother would fly out and chase him away with her sharp beak. She was afraid the prisoner might harm her chicks.

The water bird understood the true love of parents. True love is willing to give up its own life, and there is no calculation there. The heart of the bird that was willing to sacrifice its life, if necessary, to protect its offspring was true love. Parents go the path of love, no matter how difficult it becomes. A parent is prepared, if needed, to bury his life for the sake of love, and this is true love.

The essence of love is to cast aside any thought of having others live for oneself; it is to live for the sake of others and give for the whole. Love gives, but then forgets even the fact that it has given and continues to give without ceasing. This is a love that gives in joy. It is the heart that a mother feels when she takes her infant in her arms and lets it feed from her breast.

Parents will suffer for their children until it seems their bones are going to melt away, yet they never feel that the work is difficult. That is how much they love their children. True love begins with God and comes to us from God. So when the parents say to their married children, "When you like each other, it is because of the grace of your parents," the children must be able to respond, "If you had not found such a spouse for me, I don't know what I would have done."

The family is a bundle of love. When we go to the Kingdom of Heaven and unpack that bundle, a wonderful father and mother will jump out. Beautiful children will jump out. A benevolent grandfather and grandmother will jump out. This is the bundle of love. The family is the place where God's ideal is realized and the place where we can see the completion of God's work. God's will is to bring about a world in which love is made real, and the family is the place where God's love overflows.

We only need to hear the word *family* for us to begin smiling. This is because the family is overflowing with true love that truly lives for the sake of all members. True love gives love, then forgets even the fact that it gave, and then gives again. The love that has parents living for their children and grandparents for the grandchildren is true love. The love that lets a person give up his or her life for the country is true love.

The Peaceful Family Is the Building Block of Heaven

Many Western people live truly lonely lives. Their children leave home once they turn eighteen, and the parents may only get to see their faces at Thanksgiving or Christmas. Many children never visit their parents just to find out how they are doing. Once people marry, they live with their spouse, independent from their family, until their parents become so old they can no longer take care of themselves. At that point, they move their parents into a nursing home.

So it is understandable that some Westerners envy the culture of the East. Many elderly people in the West think, "In the East, the grandparents live in the family as the senior members of the family, and it is really wonderful. The children respect their old parents. This is how people are supposed to live. What good is it to be lying in a nursing home, not able to see my children, not even knowing what day it is, just staying alive?"

Unfortunately, though, the Eastern family structure is also gradually deteriorating. We too are abandoning traditions that have been handed down to us for thousands of years. We have thrown away our traditional clothing, our food, and our family structure. The number of senior citizens living alone in Korea is on the rise. Each time I see stories in the news of senior citizens alone, it makes me sad. The family is where generations live together. If family members are scattered and the parents are left alone, then that is no longer a family. The extended family system is a beautiful Korean tradition.

I recommend that three generations live together as one family. This is not simply because it is a way of maintaining our country's tradition. When a husband and wife have a child, they pass on all they can to that child. There is a limit, however, to how much the parents can pass on. The parents represent the present and the children the future. The grandparents represent the past. So it is only when the grandparents, parents, and children live together that the children can inherit all the fortune of the past and present. To love and respect your grandfather is to inherit the history of the past and to learn from the world of the past. The children learn precious wisdom from their parents on how to live in the present, while the parents prepare for the future by loving their children.

The grandparents are in a position to represent God. No matter how intelligent a young man may be, he cannot know all the secrets of this big world. Young people cannot know all the different secrets of life that come to us as we grow older. This is the reason the grandfather represents the history of the family. The grandfather is a precious teacher who passes on to the grandchildren all the wisdom he has acquired through the experiences he has accumulated during the course of his life.

The world's oldest grandfather is God. So a life of receiving the grandfather's love and of living for the sake of the grandfather is a life of coming to understand God's love and of living for His sake. We need to maintain such a tradition in order to open the secret storehouse of God's Kingdom and receive His treasure of love. Any country that ignores its old people abandons its national character and ignores its roots. When autumn comes, the chestnut tree gradually loses its moisture, and its leaves begin to fall. The outer shell of the chestnut falls off, and even the inner shell that surrounds the actual nut dries up. This is the cycle of life. Human beings are the same way. We are born as infants, grow up in the love of our parents, meet a wonderful partner, and get married. All this occurs in the chain of life made up of love. In the end, we become like chestnuts drying up in the autumn. Old people are not a separate category of people. We all become old. We must not treat old people disrespectfully, no matter how senile they may become.

There is a saying, "Anything can be accomplished when there is harmony in the home." When there is peace in the family, everything goes well. The peaceful family is the building block of the Kingdom of Heaven. The family operates on the power of love. If we love the universe as we love our families, then there is nothing to stop us from going anywhere we want. God exists in the center of love, as the Parent of the entire universe. That is why the love in the family needs to link directly to God. When the family is completed in love, the universe will be completed.

Ten Years of Tears Melt a
Father-in-Law's Heart

Not long ago the Korean media carried a story about a Japanese woman living in Milyang, Korea, who received an award for her filial service to her family. The article said that the woman had come to Korea as the wife of a Korean man who had met her through an introduction by a certain religious group and married her despite opposition from his family. The Japanese wife had cared for her Korean mother-in-law, who had difficulty moving around, and her aged father-in-law with great devotion. The people in the community then recommended her to be recognized for her filial actions, the article said.

The mother-in-law was paralyzed from the waist down and classified by the Korean public health authorities as being in the second-highest level of physical handicap. From the first day of her marriage, the daughter-in-law carried her mother-in-law on her back to different hospitals so she could be treated. Because she spent so much time devoting herself to her parents-in-law, she rarely had time to visit her own family in Japan. When she heard that she was going to be awarded for her actions, she protested, saying she was merely doing what was right.

This Japanese daughter-in-law in the news is Kazuko Yashima. She came to Korea through the international and intercultural marriages of our church. These are marriages where men and women are matched across religious, national, or racial differences. There are many young men in Korea's rural areas who cannot find brides. The brides who come to Korea in these international and intercultural marriages do so unconditionally.

They care for their aged parents-in-law, inspire their husbands to have strength and hope, and bear and raise children. They go to live in the rural communities that Koreans have left behind because it is so difficult to live there. What a wonderful and precious thing they are doing! This program has been going on for more than thirty years.

Thousands of women from other countries have settled in Korea through such international and intercultural marriages. In rural Korean communities where the young people have left for the cities and the sound of a baby's cry has not been heard for a long time, the old people are overjoyed to see the birth of babies to these couples, and they treat the babies as if they were their own grandchildren. In one elementary school in Choongcheong Province, more than half the eighty students are children of the international and intercultural marriages arranged by our church. The school's principal has said the school will have to close if its student body declines any further, and so he prays daily that our church members will not move away from the community. In Korea today, some twenty thousand children of international and intercultural marriages are enrolled in elementary schools around the country.

Every year around the anniversary of Korea's independence from Japan, television news programs carry stories about some very special Japanese who stand before the camera and apologize for the actions of their country in Korea during the period of occupation. They themselves did not commit those crimes, but they apologize for the actions of their ancestors. Most of these people are members of our church who have torn down the walls separating nations by means of international and intercultural marriages. Because of their actions, the walls in the hearts of Koreans who think of the Japanese as our enemies are increasingly crumbling.

In 1988, a young and well-educated man who had joined our church wanted to get married and sought to be matched. He was matched with a Japanese woman. The father of this young man reacted very negatively to the match. "Of all the women in the world, you have to marry a Japanese?" he asked.

During the Japanese occupation, the father had been one of the Koreans conscripted into forced labor and taken to a coal mine in Iwate Prefecture in northeastern Japan. He risked his life to escape the mine and walked for well over a month to Shimonoseki, where he was able to board a ship back to Korea. He harbored a tremendous hatred for Japan. On hearing the news of his son's match to a Japanese woman, he threatened to disown him.

"You betray the family," he said. "I will have your name taken out of the family register. No woman from that enemy country will ever set foot in this house, so take her and go away. She is not right for you, so I don't care whether you go or whether you die."

The father was adamant. The young man, however, went ahead and did what he felt was right. He married the Japanese woman and took his bride to his hometown in Nagan, Korea. The father would not even open the front gate for them. Sometime later, he reluctantly accepted their marriage, but his persecution of his daughter-in-law continued. Every time she seemed to have difficulty with something, he would say, "That's nothing, compared with what your people did to me. You should have expected this much when you decided to marry into our family."

Every time the relatives would gather for a major holiday, the father-in-law would have her sit near him, and he would tell her all the things that were done to him in the Iwate coal mine. Each time, the daughter-in-law would respond by saying, "Father, I apologize to you on behalf of Japan. I am sorry." She would shed tears and ask for his forgiveness. For as long as he would vent his anger at her, she would listen to him tell the same stories over and over until he was finished, and she would continue to apologize.

This went on for about ten years, and then it stopped. Relatives noticed that his cold attitude toward the daughter-in-law had become much warmer and that he even seemed to like her. So they asked him, "Why are you behaving so kindly toward your daughter-in-law? She's a Japanese woman. Don't you still hate her?"

"I don't hate her anymore," he said. "All the hatred that had accumulated in my heart has gone away.

"I never really hated her," he added. "I was just venting on her all the hatred that was in me for having been conscripted to work in the mine. Because of her, the hatred has all disappeared. From now on, I'm going to be kind to her, because she's my real daughter-in-law."

The daughter-in-law paid for the sins of the Japanese. This is an example of the path of redemption that will lead humankind into a world of peace.

The True Meaning of Marriage

International and intercultural marriages are the quickest way to bring about an ideal world of peace. Things that would take seemingly forever can be accomplished like miracles through these types of marriages in just two or three generations. People should marry across national and cultural boundaries with people from countries they consider to be their enemies so that the world of peace can come that much more quickly. A person may hate people from a certain country or culture and think he never wants to set eyes on them. But if someone from that country becomes his spouse, then the person is halfway to becoming a person of the new country. All the hatred melts away. If this is repeated for two or three generations, the roots of hatred can be eliminated.

White and black people will marry each other; Japanese will marry Koreans and people from Africa. Many millions are entering into such international and intercultural marriages. A completely new lineage is being created as a result. A new kind of human being who transcends white, black, and yellow is being born. I am not just referring to marriages across international boundaries. The same is true for marrying people from other religions or denominations. In fact, marriages between people of different religions are even more difficult than international marriages. Even if two religious groups have been fighting each other for centuries, it is possible to bring harmony between them by having their followers marry each other. In such a marriage, one spouse will not close himself off from the other just because he or she was raised in a different tradition.

It is most important to teach young people about the sanctity and value of marriage. Korea today has one of the lowest birthrates in the world. Not to have children is dangerous. There is no future for a country that has no descendants. I teach young people that they should remain sexually pure during their youth, receive the marriage Blessing, and then have at least three children. Children are blessings given to us by God. When we bear children and raise them, we are raising citizens of the Kingdom of Heaven. That is why it is a great sin to live immorally and to abort babies conceived in this lifestyle.

We marry not for ourselves but for the sake of our partners. When looking for a spouse, it is wrong to look only for a beautiful person or for a person living well. Human beings must live for the sake of each other. We should apply this principle to marriage, too. No matter how uneducated or homely your prospective spouse may be, you should marry with a heart that you will love him or her even more than if the spouse were educated and beautiful. God's love is the most precious of all blessings. In marriage, we receive that blessing of love and put it into practice in our own lives. We must understand this precious meaning of marriage, conduct our lives in marriage in the context of true love, and bring about true families.

From this perspective, world peace is not such a huge undertaking. It starts with peaceful families that create peaceful societies and eliminate conflict among countries. This will lead to world peace.

This example shows the importance of families that are intact and the immense responsibility such families must bear. The thinking that says "It's enough that I live well and that my family lives well" is completely alien to me.

Marriage is not something that involves just the bride and groom. Marriage creates a relationship between two families, and it brings reconciliation between clans and countries. Each accepts the other's different culture and overcomes the resentment and hatred built up through history. When a Korean and Japanese marry, it contributes to reconciliation between the two countries; when a white person and a black person marry, it contributes to reconciliation between the two races. The children of such marriages represent harmony because they inherit the lineage of two races. They represent a new beginning for humanity that transcends the races. When this continues for a few generations, division and hostility among nations, races, and religions will disappear, and humankind will become one family living in a world of peace.

In recent years, more and more Koreans are marrying foreigners, and we see more families with people from different nationalities and religions. Koreans have even coined a phrase for it that means multicultural families. It is not easy for a man and woman who have been raised in different cultures to create a family and live with love for each other. Particularly in Korea, which traditionally has had a homogeneous culture, the partners in such marriages need to make extra effort to understand and care for each other. The reason our members who enter into international and intercultural marriages succeed is because they live together centering on God. Various social welfare groups in Korea try to encourage the success of multicultural families by offering programs that teach Korean language and culture. Such efforts will be useless, however, unless our concept of marriage changes. Whoever thinks, "Why did I marry this man? If I hadn't married this man, I would have had a better life," is setting the tone for a marriage that will be hell. Coming to a correct understanding of marriage is more important than learning Korean language and culture.

Marriage is not a simple matter of a man and woman of marriageable age coming together and combining their two lives. Marriage is something built on the basis of sacrifice. The man must live for the sake of the woman, and the woman for the sake of the man. As you continue to live for the sake of your spouse, your selfish mind disappears completely. The heart that seeks to sacrifice this way is the heart of love. Love is not a man and woman meeting each other and having a good time. Love is offering up your life. If you marry, you must do so on the basis of your determination that your life is for your spouse.

True Love Is Found in True Families

No matter how much a man and woman may love each other, a complete and happy family must have parents who act as a protective shield around the home, and there must be at least one child for the parents to love. When a family is protected, it becomes a nesting place for happiness. Even a person with great success in society will have an unhappy family if this protection collapses.

The basis of love is the heart that sacrifices everything for the sake of the other. The reason parental love is true love is that parents are willing to give everything to their children, and when they have given everything, they want to give even more. Parents who love their children do not even remember what they have given. No parent would keep track of all the shoes and clothes he bought for his child and say, "This is how much I spent on you." Instead, a parent gives everything he has and says, "I wish I could do more for you than I have, and I'm sorry that I cannot."

As a child, I would follow my father around as he tended his bee colonies, and I saw how the bees behaved. When a bee flying around in a garden caught the fragrance of a flower, it would fly there, and place its legs firmly on the flower. It would then stick its nose deep into the flower, so that its rear end was pointing upward while it sucked up the nectar. If you grabbed the bee by its abdomen, it would not let go of the flower. It risks its life to keep its hold on the flower.

The love of parents cultivating a family is like the honeybee attached to the flower. Even if a parent should lose his own life, he will never let go of the bond of love that ties him to his child. Parents will lay down their lives for the sake of the child and then later forget they had done so. This is the true love of parents. No matter how far or dangerous the path may be, the parents will gladly travel it. Parental love is the greatest love in the world.

A person can live in a wonderful house and eat exotic foods from the mountains and the oceans, but if he has no parents, there will be a large void in his heart. A person who has grown up without receiving parental love has a loneliness and emptiness in his heart that cannot be filled with anything else. The family is the place where we receive true love and learn true love. Children who do not receive true love when they are young live their entire lives hungering for love and suffer emotional pain. Not only that, they don't have the opportunity to learn the lofty moral duties they must fulfill for the family and society. True love is a value that cannot be learned any place other than in the family.

A true family is a place where a husband and wife each love the other and live for the sake of the other, as if the spouse were his or her mother, father, or sibling. It is a place where the husband loves his wife as he loves God, and the wife respects her husband as she respects God. We cannot forsake our siblings, no matter the difficulties we may face. Neither can we forsake our mothers. So the term *divorce* cannot even exist. The husband is in the place of the father and older brother to the wife. Just as a wife could never forsake her father or older brother, she can never forsake her husband. In the same way, a husband could never forsake his wife. A true family is a place where each spouse lives with the acknowledgment of the absolute value of the partner.

It doesn't matter if a husband and wife come from different races or cultures. If they have formed a family after having received God's love, then there can be no conflicts of culture among the children born into this family. These children will love and value the culture and tradition of their mother's country and father's country with the same love they have for each parent. Resolving conflicts in multicultural families is not a matter of providing them with particular knowledge. Instead, it is a matter of the parents of these families raising their children in true love. The parents' love soaks its way into the flesh and bone of the children and becomes the fertilizer that enables the children to accept their mother's and father's countries as one and become wonderful citizens of the world.

The family is the school where love for humanity is taught and learned. When children who are raised in the warm love of their parents go out into the world, they will care for people in difficulty in the manner they learned in their home. People raised in loving relationships with their own brothers and sisters will go into society and share their caring hearts with their neighbors. People raised in love will look upon each person they meet in the world as a member of their own family. The starting point toward a true family is the heart of love that treats strangers as family and shares with them.

Another reason the family is important is that it expands to become the world. A true family is the basis for forming a true society, true nation, and true world. It is the starting point of world of peace that is God's Kingdom. Parents will work for their children until their bones melt away. They are not working just to feed their own children, how-ever. A person whose heart overflows with love is capable of working for the sake of others and God.

The family is where we receive so much love that it overflows from our hearts. The family protects its members in its embrace, but its func-tion is not to prevent love from getting out. In fact, the love in the fam-ily should overflow into the surrounding community. No matter how much love may overflow, the love in the family will never run dry. This is because it is received from God. The love we receive from God is such that we can continue to dig it out but never see the bottom. In fact, the more we dig, the more love wells up like pure spring water. Anyone who has been raised in this love can lead a true life.

Leaving Behind a Legacy of Love

A true life is a life in which we abandon our private desires and live for the public good. This is a truth taught by all major religious leaders past and present, Eastern and Western, whether it be Jesus, Buddha, or the Prophet Mohammad. It is a truth that is so widely known that, sadly, it seems to have become devalued. Yet the passage of time and changes in the world cannot diminish the value of this truth. This is because the essence of human life never changes, even in times of rapid change all around the world.

The teacher with whom we have the closest relationship is our heart. Our heart is more precious to us than our closest friends and even more precious than our parents. So, as we live our lives, we need periodically to ask our hearts, "Am I living a good life now?" Anyone can hear his heart speaking to him. If he comes to the realization that his heart is his master, he "polishes" his heart and maintains a close relationship with his heart throughout his life. If a person hears the sound of his heart tearfully sobbing, then he needs to stop immediately whatever he is doing. Anything that makes the heart suffer will ruin him. Anything that makes the heart sad will eventually make the person fall into sadness.

For a person to polish his heart to the point that it becomes as clear as crystal, he absolutely must spend time in direct conversation with his heart in an environment where he is away from the world and alone with his heart. It will be a time of intense loneliness. The moment we become close to our hearts is the time of prayer and meditation. It is a time when we can take ownership over our hearts. When we isolate ourselves from the noise around us and allow our thoughts to settle, we can see into the deepest parts of our hearts. It will take a lot of time and effort to go all the way down to where the heart has settled. It will not happen in a day.

Just as love is not for our own sake, so happiness and peace are not for ourselves. Just as love can never exist without a partner, happiness and peace cannot exist without a partner. All these can exist only in the context of a relationship with a partner. Nothing can be accomplished if we live alone. We cannot be happy alone or speak of peace alone. Since a partner is what enables us to have happiness and peace, the partner is more important than we are.

Think about a mother carrying a baby on her back, sitting at an entrance to the subway in Seoul, selling homemade snacks to the people passing by. To be at that spot in time for the morning rush hour, she will have spent the whole night preparing the snacks, and then put her fussing child on her back to come to the station. People passing by might say, "Oh, you could get along well if only you didn't have that child to care for," but it is for the sake of the child that the mother lives her life.

Today people can expect to live about eighty years. Eighty years of joy, anger, sorrow, happiness, and all the other emotions mixed together may seem like a long time. But if we take away the private time a person spends sleeping, working, and eating, and then the time we spend talking, laughing, and having fun with family members and friends, attending weddings and funerals, and lying sick in bed, only about seven years will remain. A person may live eighty years but spend only about seven years living for the public good.

Life is like a rubber band. The same seven years, given to two different people, can be spent either as seven years or as seventy. Time, by itself, is empty. We need to put things in it. The same is true about a person's life. Everyone wants to live his life with a comfortable place to sleep and good things to eat. Eating and sleeping, however, are simply ways of letting time slip by. In the moment that a person has lived out his life and his body is laid to rest in the ground, all wealth and glory become nothing more than a bubble and disappear at once. Only the seven years that he lived for the public good will remain and be remembered by posterity. Those seven years are all that is left in the world of a life that lasted eighty years.

We do not come into this world, or depart from it, of our own accord. We have no ability to make choices with regard to our fate. We are born, though we did not choose to be born. We live, though we did not choose to live. We die, though we do not choose to die. We have no authority over these aspects of our lives, so how can we boast that we are somehow better than others? We cannot be born by our own wish, possess things that will forever be our own, or avoid death. So any boasting on our part would only be pathetic.

Even if we rise to a position higher than others, the honor is only temporary. Even if we gather more possessions than others, we must leave them all behind at the gates of death. Money, honor, and knowledge all flow away from us in time, and all disappear with the passing years. No matter how noble and great a person might be, his is nothing more than a pitiable life that will end the moment he loses hold of his lifeline.

Human beings have always struggled to understand who we are and why we live. We must realize that just as we were not born of our own accord, we are not meant to live our lives for our own sake. So the answer to the question of how we should live our lives is simple. We were born of love, so we must live by traveling the path of love. Our lives were created by receiving the boundless love of our parents, so we must live our entire lives repaying that love. In the course of our lives, this is the only value we can choose on our own. The success or failure of our lives depends on how much love we pack into those eighty years that are given to us.

At some point, everyone will shed his physical body like old clothing and die. In Korean, "to return" is a common expression for dying. To return means to go back to where we came from, that is, to go back to our fundamental roots. Everything in the universe moves in cycles. The white snow that collects on the mountains will melt and flow down the slopes, first forming streams and then a river, and eventually go into the ocean. The water that flows into the ocean will absorb the heat of the sun's rays, become water vapor, go back up into the sky, and prepare to become either snowflakes or drops of rain. To return to our original place in this way is what we call death. Then, where do we human beings return to when we die? Body and heart come together to bring about human life, and death is the act of shedding the body. So we go to the place from which the heart came.

We cannot talk about life without also talking about death. We must accurately understand what death is, even if we do so only to understand the purpose of life. The type of life that has true value can be understood only by the person who finds himself in a difficult situation when death appears imminent and he cries out to Heaven in desperation, pleading to be allowed to live even just one more day. If our days are as precious as this, how should we live them? What are the things we must accomplish before we cross over the boundary line of death?

The most important is not to commit sin — to lead a life that is without shadows. There is much religious and philosophical debate over what constitutes sin, but what is clear is that we should not engage in acts that prick our conscience. When we do things that give us a guilty conscience, it always leaves a shadow in our heart.

The next most important thing is to resolve to do significantly more work than others have done. All of our lives are limited, whether that limit is sixty years, seventy years, or some other time period. Depending on how we use that time, we can lead a life that is two or three times more abundant than others. If you cut your time into segments and then live each segment in a meaningful way, your life will be truly precious. Live with an attitude of devotion and diligence, telling yourself, for example, that you will plant two or three trees in the time it takes others to plant one.

Do not live for yourself. You must live not for yourself but for others; for your neighbors more than for your family; for the world more than for your own country. All sin in the world comes about when the individual is put first. Individual desires and ambitions harm a person's neighbors and ruin the society at large.

Everything in the world will eventually pass. The parents we love, the husband or wife we love, and the children we love will all pass away. All that we face at the end of our lives is death. When a person dies, only his legacy remains.

Please consider for a moment what you can do to show that you lived a life of value. The possessions and social position you have accumulated during your life will pass away from you. Once you cross the river of death, such things will have no meaning. Because we were born in love and lived our lives in love, love is also the only thing that remains with us when we are in our graves. We receive our lives in love, live by sharing love, and return into the midst of love. It is important that we live in a way that we can leave a legacy of love behind us.

CHAPTER SIX

LOVE WILL BRING UNIFICATION

The Power of Religion to
Turn People to Goodness

On August 2, 1990, Iraqi President Saddam Hussein invaded Kuwait, igniting the possibility of war in the Persian Gulf. This area has long been a tinderbox, and I could see the world was about to be swept up into war. I concluded that Christian and Muslim leaders must meet to prevent the conflict. I acted quickly to do all I could to stop a war in which innocent people were sure to die.

On October 2, I convened on short notice an emergency conference of the Council for the World's Religions in Cairo, Egypt, to deliver my urgent message of peace to the highest spiritual authorities of the Middle East and the Muslim world. Many wondered why I, a person with no apparent ties to the Middle East, would convene such a meeting, but to me it was simple. I believe every religion should contribute to world peace. A conflict between Christianity and Islam would be far worse than the conflict between democracy and communism. There is nothing more fearful than a religious war.

I sent a message imploring President George H.W. Bush, who already was trying to limit the conflict, to avoid war in the Arab world and instead work to bring about Saddam Hussein's retreat through diplomatic means. President Bush may have thought he was going to war against Iraq only, but that is not how Muslims would think. For Muslims, religion is in a higher position than the nation-state. I was very concerned that, if Iraq were attacked, the Arab world would join in opposition to the United States and the Christian world.

Our emergency conference in Cairo involved top Muslim leaders and grand muftis from nine countries, including the grand muftis of Syria and Yemen. At the core of the meeting was my desperate appeal to the Arab and Muslim world not to support Saddam Hussein's claim that this was a holy war. Whether the United States won or Iraq won, what good would it do? What value would it have if it meant that bombs rained down, destroying houses, schools, and precious innocent lives?

The Cairo conference was just one of our many peace activities. Every time a crisis arose in the Middle East, our members worked fearlessly, risking their lives at the scenes of danger. For years, during the violence and terror in Israel and Palestine, our members, traveling at a moment's notice, collaborated with major organizations to work for peace.

I am always uneasy sending our members to places where their lives are at risk, but it is unavoidable when working for the cause of peace. I may be in Brazil tilling the soil under the blazing sun, or speaking far away in Africa, but my heart is constantly drawn to those members who insist on working in the dangerous environment of the Middle East. I pray that peace will come to the world quickly, so I no longer need to ask our members to go to such places of death.

On September 11, 2001, we all felt utter horror when the World Trade Center twin towers in New York City were destroyed by terrorists. Some people said this was the inevitable clash of civilizations between Islam and Christianity. But my view is different. In their purest form,

Islam and Christianity are not religions of conflict and confrontation. They both place importance on peace. In my view, it is bigoted to brand all Islam as radical, just as it is bigoted to say that Islam and Christianity are fundamentally different. The essence of all religions is the same.

Immediately following the collapse of the towers, I organized religious leaders from New York and around the country to pray and minister to the victims and first responders at Ground Zero. Then, in October I convened a major interfaith conference for peace in New York City. Ours was the first international gathering in New York after the tragedy.

These dramatic contributions to peace in times of war did not spring up from nothing. For decades prior, I had invested in promoting inter-religious harmony. It is on the foundation of this investment that we have the trust of major faith leaders who would travel to Israel during the Intifada or to New York in the wake of the 9/11 attacks.

In 1984, I brought together forty religious scholars, instructing them to compare the teachings that appear in the sacred texts of Christianity, Islam, Buddhism, and other major world religions. The book that resulted from their efforts was *World Scripture: A Comparative Anthology of Sacred Texts,* published in 1991. What they found was that the sacred texts of religions convey the same or similar teachings more than seventy percent of the time. The remaining thirty percent are teachings that represent unique points of each religion. This means that most of the teachings of the major world religions are the same at their core. The same is true of religious practice. On the surface, some believers wear turbans, some wear prayer beads around their necks, others wear a cross, but they all seek the fundamental truths of the universe, and try to understand the will of the Divine One.

People often become friends even if all they have in common is the same particular hobby. When two strangers meet and discover they have the same hometown, they can immediately communicate as if they had known each other for decades. So it is truly tragic that religions, which share the same teachings more than seventy percent of the time, still struggle to understand each other and communicate happily. They could talk about the things they have in common and take each other by the hand. Instead, they emphasize their differences and criticize one another.

All religions in the world talk about peace and love. Yet they fight each other over peace and love. Israel and Palestine talk of peace and justice, yet both practice violence until children are bleeding and dying. Judaism, the religion of Israel, is a religion of peace, and the same is true of Islam.

Our experience when compiling *World Scripture* leads us to believe that it is not the religions of the world that are in error but the ways the faiths are taught. Bad teaching of faith cultivates prejudice, and prejudice leads to conflict. Muslims were branded terrorists after the 9/11 attack. But the vast majority of these simple, believing families are peace-loving people, just like us.

The late Yasser Arafat led the Palestinians for a long time. Like all political leaders, he had hoped for peace, but he was also associated with strife in the region. As chairman of the Palestine Liberation Organization, Arafat embodied the determination for the Gaza Strip and the West Bank to become an independent Palestinian state. Many argue he shifted from his past associations and began to deter the activities of extremist organizations after he was elected president of the Palestinian National Authority in 1996.

In the interest of seeking peace in the Middle East, I communicated with Arafat on twelve separate occasions. Of course, my words to him never wavered. God's way is always the way of harmony, seeking for peace.

The road to Arafat's office was literally a difficult one. Anyone approaching his office had to pass between heavily armed guards and submit to at least three body searches along the way. But when our members arrived, Arafat, wearing his *keffiyeh* (traditional head gear), would warmly welcome them.

These sorts of relationships cannot be built in a day or two. They come from years of pouring out our sincerity and devotion for the sake of Middle East peace. It was our arduous efforts and constant willingness to risk our lives in terror-ridden conflict areas that prepared the way for us to be welcomed into relationships with the religious and political leaders at these levels. It took large amounts of resources. Finally, we could gain the trust of both Arafat and top Israeli leaders, which allowed us to play a mediating role during outbreaks of conflict in the Middle East.

I first set foot in Jerusalem in 1965. This was before the Six-Day War, and Jerusalem was still under Jordan's territorial control. I went to the Mount of Olives, where Jesus shed tears of blood in prayer just prior to being taken to the court of Pontius Pilate. I put my hand on a two-thousand-year-old olive tree that could have witnessed Jesus' prayer that night. I drove three nails in that tree, one for Judaism, one for Christianity, and one for Islam. I prayed for the day when these three families of faith would become one. World peace cannot come unless Judaism, Christianity, and Islam embrace as one. Those three nails are still there.

Judaism, Islam, and Christianity are sharply divided against each other in today's world, but they share a common root. The issue that keeps them divided is their understanding of Jesus. To address this problem, on May 19, 2003, I asked that Christians de-emphasize the cross in relations among the Abrahamic faiths. Thus, we enacted a ceremony of taking down the cross. We brought a cross from America, a predominantly Christian culture, and buried it in the Field of Blood in Israel. This is the field that was bought with the thirty pieces of silver that Judas Iscariot received for the betrayal of Jesus that ended in Jesus' crucifixion.

Later that year, on December 23, some three thousand Ambassadors for Peace from all religions, and from around the world, joined with seventeen thousand Israelis and Palestinians in Jerusalem's Independence Park to symbolically remove the crown of thorns from the head of Jesus and replace it with a crown of peace. They then marched for peace through Jerusalem. Local authorities granted permissions and protected our efforts, and Palestinian and Israeli families supported our march for peace by placing a light in front of their homes.

Through that march, which was broadcast live via the Internet to the entire world, I proclaimed that Jesus had his authority as King of Peace restored to him. After centuries of misunderstanding and division, an opportunity was created for Christianity, Judaism, and Islam to reconcile with one another.

Al-Aqsa Mosque, the third-holiest mosque in Islam after those in Mecca and Medina, is located in Jerusalem. It is the spot from which the Prophet Mohammad is said to have ascended to heaven. Ours was the only mixed religious group welcomed to all parts of this house of worship. The mosque leaders guided the Christian and Jewish leaders who had participated in the peace march to the sacred spaces of the mosque. We were able to open a door that had been closed tightly, and prepared the way for many Muslim leaders to communicate at a new level with their Christian and Jewish brothers and sisters.

Human beings like peace, but they also enjoy conflict. People will take the most gentle of animals and make them fight. They will have roosters fight and peck each other with their sharp beaks until pieces of soft flesh begin to fall away. Then, these same people will turn around and tell their own children, "Don't fight with your friends. Play nice."

The fundamental reason that wars occur is not religion or race. It is connected to what lies deep inside human beings. People like to attribute the causes of armed conflicts to such things as science or the economy, but the actual fundamental problem lies within human beings ourselves.

Religion's role is to turn human beings toward goodness and eliminate their evil nature that finds enjoyment in fighting. Examine the major religions of the world. They all hold a peaceful world as their ideal. They all want to see a kingdom of heaven, utopia, or paradise. Religions have different names for this ideal, but they all seek such a world. There are numerous religions in the world, and virtually everyone is divided into countless factions and denominations. But the essential hope for all is the same: They want the Kingdom of Heaven and a world of peace. The human heart has been torn to shreds by the violence and enmity at our core. The kingdom of love will heal it.

The River Does Not Reject the Waters That Flow into It

Selfishness is rampant in the world. Ironically, however, the individual is destroyed by this, and not just the individual, but those around him and the nation as a whole. The greatest obstacle to the world of peace is greed in people's hearts. It starts in individuals and expands to the nation, and hearts stained with avarice cause division and conflict at every level. Countless people throughout history have shed their blood and died in conflicts caused by greed.

To eliminate such conflicts, we need a great revolution to change the erroneous values and thinking that are widespread in the world today. The complex problems our societies face today can be resolved quickly if there is a revolution in people's thinking. If each individual and nation begins to look out for the other first, working together with the other, the problems of modern society will be resolved.

Throughout my life, I have dedicated myself to efforts for peace. Whenever peace is discussed, I become emotional. Tears begin to well up in my eyes, my voice chokes, and I can hardly swallow. It moves me deeply just to imagine the day when the world becomes one and begins to enjoy peace. That is the nature of peace. It links people who think differently, are of different races, and speak different languages. Our hearts yearn for this world and harbor a hope that it will be realized.

However, peace comes through concrete action, not just having a vague dream. But building a movement for peace has not always been easy. There have been many difficulties, and it has required large sums of money. I have not done this for my own honor, or to make money. All I did was invest my full effort so that we can have a world where a strong and true peace takes root. For as long as I have been doing this work, I have never been lonely. This is because, ultimately, peace is the desire of every person in the world. It is strange though. Everyone wants peace, but still it has not come.

It is easy to talk about peace. But to bring peace is not easy. This is because people push aside the most elemental truth needed to bring about a world of peace. They pretend not to know this truth is there. Before we talk about peace among individuals or nations, we must talk about peace between ourselves and God.

Each religion today thinks of itself as the highest, rejecting and looking down on other religions. It is not right to build fences against other religions and denominations.

Religion is like a wide river flowing toward an ideal, peaceful world. The river flows for long distances before it comes to the wide expanse of peace. On its way, many streams flow into it. The streams cease to be streams from the point they meet the river. From that point, they, too, become part of the river. In this way, they become one.

The river does not reject any of the streams that flow into it. It accepts them all. It embraces all the streams and forms a single flow as it continues toward the ocean. People in the world today do not understand this simple truth. The streams that seek out the river and flow into it are the numerous religions and denominations of today. Each stream traces its origin to a different spring, but they are all going to the same destination. They are seeking the ideal world overflowing with peace.

Peace will never come to this earth unless we first tear down the walls between religions. For thousands of years, religions have grown in alliance with particular ethnic groups, and so they are surrounded by high cultural walls. Tearing these down is an extremely difficult task. For thousands of years, each religion has surrounded itself with such high walls, insisting that it is the only correct religion. In some cases, religions have expanded their influence and entered into conflicts and fights with other religions, using God's name in activities that had nothing to do with His will.

The will of God lies in peace. A world fragmented by differences in nationality, race, and religion, where people attack and fight one another and shed one another's blood, is not what God wants. When we shed blood and fight each other in His name, we only cause Him pain. A world torn to shreds has been created out of the desires of people to promote their own wealth and glory. It does not represent the will of God. God clearly told me so. I am only His errand boy, receiving His words and carrying them out on earth.

The path to bring about a world of peace in which religions and races become united has been exhausting. Many times I was rejected by people, or my own abilities fell short, but I could not put aside this mission. When members and colleagues who worked with me would cry out in anguish because of the difficulty of the task, I would even feel envious of them.

"If you decide this path isn't for you, you have the option to stop and turn back," I told them. "Or if you try and try and still can't accomplish it, you have the option to die trying. But you should pity me," I said. "I am a person with no such options."

There are close to two hundred countries in the world. For all these countries to enjoy peace, the power of religion is absolutely necessary. The power of religion is in the love that overflows from it. I am a religious person whose role is to convey love, so it is natural that I would work for world peace. There is no difference between Islam and Christianity in their commitment to bring about a world of peace.

In America, I lead a movement for peace, bringing together thousands of clergy who transcend denomination. Through this movement, we discuss ways that people of all faiths — Christians, Muslims, Jews, Buddhists, etc. — can come together. We devote our full efforts to change the hardened hearts of people.

My purpose is the same today as it was yesterday. It is to create one world with God at the center, a world brought together like a single nation without boundaries. All humanity will be citizens of this world, sharing a culture of love. In such a world, there will be no possibility for division and conflict. This will mark the beginning of a truly peaceful world.

"Allow Freedom of Religion
in the Soviet Union"

There are a number of materialism-based theories that are popularly held but not verified. One is Charles Darwin's theory of evolution. Another such theory comes from the writings of Karl Marx. The idea that spirit originates from matter is wrong down to its root. Human beings are created by God, and all beings are unified bodies having both material and spiritual aspects. In short, the core theory and philosophy underlying communism is wrong.

While studying in Japan, I worked together with communists for the independence of Korea. They were my good friends who were prepared to give their lives, if necessary, for the liberation of our homeland; but our way of thinking was fundamentally different. So, once independence was achieved, we had to go our separate ways.

I am opposed to the historical materialism of communism. I have carried out a movement for victory over communism throughout the world. I have advised successive U.S. presidents to protect the free world, standing up to the communist strategy of turning the world red. Communist countries that were unhappy with my actions attempted to remove me through acts of violence, but I do not hate them. Nor do

I consider them my enemy. I oppose the philosophy and ideology of communism, but I have never hated its people. God wants all people, including communists, to be brought into His oneness.

In that sense, my visit to Moscow in April 1990 for a meeting with President Mikhail Gorbachev and my visit to Pyongyang the next year for a meeting with President Kim Il Sung were not simple journeys; they were taken at the risk of my life. It was my destiny to go on these journeys to convey Heaven's will to these men. I said only half-jokingly at the time that Moscow, pronounced in English, sounds similar to "must go," and so I had to go.

I had a long-held conviction regarding communism. I could foresee that signs pointing to the fall of communism would begin to appear after about sixty years from the Bolshevik Revolution, and that the Soviet edifice would fall in 1987, the seventieth anniversary of the revolution. So I was excited in 1984 when I heard that Dr. Morton Kaplan, a noted political scientist at the University of Chicago, was proposing to hold an international conference titled "The Fall of the Soviet Empire." I asked him to pay me a visit in Danbury prison so that we could discuss the details. The first thing I said to him when we met was that I wanted him to declare "the end of Soviet communism" before August 15 of that year.

Dr. Kaplan responded, "Declare the end of Soviet communism so soon? How can I do such a risky thing?" and said he was not inclined to do this. In 1985, when the conference was to take place, the Soviet Union was increasing its worldwide influence, and there were no outward signs of its decline. But, it's the final flame that burns the brightest.

So it was natural that Dr. Kaplan would be reluctant. If he made a declaration predicting such a specific event and it turned out to be false, his reputation as a scholar could be destroyed overnight.

"Reverend Moon," he said, "I believe you when you say that Soviet communism will fall. But I don't think it will happen just yet. So instead of declaring 'the end of Soviet communism,' how about if we say 'the decline of Soviet communism'?"

I burned with anger when I saw that he was proposing to soften his original title to something other than "The Fall of the Soviet Empire." It was a compromise I could not accept. I felt strongly that if a person has conviction, he should be brave and put all his energy into the fight, even if he feels afraid.

"Dr. Kaplan," I said, "what do you mean? When I ask you to declare the end of communism, I have a reason. The day you declare the end of communism, that declaration itself will take energy away from it and help bring about its peaceful collapse. Why are you hesitating?"

In the end, Dr. Kaplan did indeed declare "the end of Soviet communism" at a conference of the Professors World Peace Academy (PWPA) held in Geneva under the title, "The Fall of the Soviet Empire: Prospects for Transition to a Post-Soviet World." It was something that no one had dared consider up until that time.

Because Switzerland was a neutral country, Geneva was a major staging area for the Soviet Committee for State Security (KGB), and many KGB agents worked from there to carry out espionage and terror activities around the world. The Intercontinental Hotel, where the PWPA conference was held, faced the Soviet Embassy across the street, so I can well imagine how nervous Dr. Kaplan must have felt. A few years later, however, he became well known as the scholar who first predicted the end of Soviet communism.

In April 1990, I convened the World Media Conference in Moscow. Unexpectedly, the Soviet government gave me head-of-state-level protocol, beginning at the airport. We were transported to the center of Moscow in a police-escorted motorcade. The car that carried me traveled on the yellow section of the road, which was used only by the president and state guests. This happened before the collapse of the Soviet Union. The Soviet government afforded this exceptional treatment to me, an anticommunist.

At the conference, I gave an address praising the move toward *perestroika*. I said this revolution must be bloodless and that it must be a revolution of the mind and spirit. The purpose of my visit was to attend the World Media Conference, but my mind was focused on meeting President Gorbachev.

At the time, President Gorbachev was popular within the Soviet Union, following the successes of his *perestroika* policies. Over the years, I have been able to meet with many U.S. presidents, but meeting President Gorbachev was much more difficult. I was concerned that even one meeting might be difficult to achieve. I had a message to give him, and it was important that I do this in person. He was reforming the Soviet Union, giving rise to the winds of freedom there, but as time passed, the swords of reform were being increasingly pointed at his back. If the situation were left unchecked, he would fall into great danger.

I explained, "If he does not meet me, he has no way to catch the wave of heavenly fortune, and if he cannot do that, he will not last long."

Perhaps President Gorbachev heard this expression of my concern. The next day, he invited me to the Kremlin. I rode in a limousine provided by the Soviet government and entered deep into the Kremlin. On entering the presidential office, my wife and I took our seats, and

Cabinet ministers of the Soviet Union took seats next to us. President Gorbachev smiled a big smile and gave us an energetic explanation of the successes of his *perestroika* policies. Then he showed me into an anteroom, where we met one on one. I used this opportunity to give him the following message:

"Mr. President, you have already achieved much success through *perestroika*, but that alone will not be sufficient for reform. You need immediately to allow freedom of religion in the Soviet Union. If you try to reform only the material world, without the involvement of God, *perestroika* will be doomed to fail. Communism is about to end. The only way to save this nation is to allow the freedom of religion. The time is now for you to act with the courage that you have shown in reforming the Soviet Union and become a president who works to bring about world peace."

President Gorbachev's face hardened at the mention of religious freedom, as though he had not been expecting this. As one would expect from the man who had allowed the reunification of Germany a few months earlier, however, he quickly relaxed his expression and soberly accepted my words to him. I continued, saying, "South Korea and the Soviet Union should now open diplomatic relations. In that context, please invite South Korean President Roh Tae Woo to visit." I also explained a list of reasons why it would be good for the two countries to have diplomatic relations.

After I had finished all I wanted to say, President Gorbachev made a promise to me with a tone of certitude that I had not heard him express prior to that point.

"I am confident," he said, "that relations between South Korea and the Soviet Union will develop smoothly. I, too, believe that political

stability and the relaxation of tensions on the Korean peninsula are necessary. Opening diplomatic relations with South Korea is only a matter of
time; there are no obstacles. As you suggested, I will meet President Roh
Tae Woo."

As I was about to leave President Gorbachev that day, I took off my
watch and put it on his wrist. He seemed a little bewildered that I would
treat him as I might an old friend. So I told him firmly, "Each time your
reforms face difficulty, please look at this watch and remember your
promise to me. If you do that, Heaven will surely open a path for you."

As he promised me, President Gorbachev met President Roh in San
Francisco in June that year for a bilateral summit. Then, on September
30, 1990, South Korea and the Soviet Union signed a historic agreement
to open diplomatic relations for the first time in eighty-six years.

Of course, politics is the job of politicians, and diplomacy is the job
of diplomats. Sometimes, though, when a door has been closed for a
long time, a religious person who has no self-serving interests at stake
can be more effective.

Four years later, President and Mrs. Gorbachev visited Seoul, and
my wife and I hosted them at our residence in Hannam-Dong. He had
already been removed from power by a coup d'état. Following the coup
by anti-reformist forces opposed to *perestroika*, he had resigned his position as general secretary of the Soviet Communist Party and dissolved
the party. As a communist, he had eliminated the Communist Party.

The former president and first lady used chopsticks to eat the *bulgogi*
(a deliciously seasoned grilled beef) and *jabchae* (made from noodles
and vegetables) we had carefully prepared. When he was served *sujeong-
gwa* (a sweet, refreshing, cold persimmon drink) as dessert, Mr. Gorbachev repeated several times, "Korea has excellent traditional foods."

He and the first lady appeared relaxed and quite different from the tense days when he was in office. Mrs. Gorbachev, who had previously been a thoroughgoing Marxist-Leninist lecturing at Moscow State University, wore a necklace with a crucifix.

"Mr. President, you did a great thing," I told him. "You gave up your post as general secretary of the Soviet Communist Party, but now you have become the president of peace. Because of your wisdom and courage, we now have the possibility to bring world peace. You did the most important, eternal, and beautiful thing for the world. You are a hero of peace who did God's work. The name that will be remembered and honored forever in the history of Russia will not be 'Marx,' 'Lenin,' or 'Stalin.' It will be 'Mikhail Gorbachev.' "

I gave such high praise to Mr. Gorbachev for his decision to bring about the breakup of the Soviet Union, the mother country of communism, without shedding blood.

In response, Mr. Gorbachev said, "Reverend Moon, I have been greatly comforted by your words. Hearing your words gives me energy. I will devote the remainder of my life to projects that are for the sake of world peace." And he firmly took my hand in his.

Korea's Unification Will
Bring World Unification

As I was leaving the Kremlin after meeting President Gorbachev, I turned to Bo Hi Pak, who had accompanied me, and gave him a special instruction.

"I need to meet President Kim Il Sung before the end of 1991," I told him. "There's no time. The Soviet Union is going to end in the next year or two. Our country is now the problem. Somehow, I need to meet President Kim and prevent war from occurring on the Korean peninsula."

I knew that when the Soviet Union collapsed, most other communist regimes in the world would also fall. North Korea would find itself forced into a corner, and there was no telling what provocation it might commit. North Korea's obsession with nuclear weapons made the situation even more worrisome. To prevent a war with North Korea, we needed a channel to talk to its leadership, but we had no such channel at that point. Somehow, I needed to meet President Kim and receive his commitment not to strike first against South Korea.

The Korean peninsula is a microcosm of the world. If blood were shed on the Korean peninsula, it would be shed worldwide. If reconciliation occurred on the peninsula, there would be reconciliation worldwide. If the peninsula were unified, this would bring about unification in the world. Beginning in the late 1980s, however, North Korea had been working hard to become a country possessing nuclear weapons. Western countries were saying they would stage a first strike against North Korea, if necessary. If the situation continued to the extreme, there was no telling what desperate move North Korea might attempt. I knew I needed to open a channel of communication with North Korea somehow.

It was no easy task. Bo Hi Pak communicated with North Korean Vice Premier Kim Dal Hyun, but Pyongyang's response was firmly negative.

"The people of North Korea know President Moon only as the ringleader of the international movement for victory over communism," the vice premier said. "Why would we welcome the leader of a conservative, anticommunist group? A visit to North Korea by Chairman Moon absolutely cannot be permitted."

Bo Hi Pak did not give up. "President Nixon of the United States was a strong anticommunist," he reminded the North Korean official. "But he visited China, met Chairman Mao Zedong, and opened diplomatic relations between the United States and China. It was China that profited from this. Until then, China had been branded an aggressor nation, but it is now rising as the central country on the world stage. For North Korea to have international credibility, it should establish a friendship with a worldwide anticommunist such as Chairman Moon."

Finally, President Kim Il Sung invited my wife and me on November 30, 1991. We were in Hawaii at the time, so we quickly flew to Beijing. While we were waiting in the VIP lounge of Beijing Capital International Airport, which the government of China had arranged for us to use, a representative of the North Korean government came and handed us the official invitation. The official stamp of the Pyongyang government was clearly visible on the document.

"The Democratic People's Republic of Korea extends an invitation to Chairman Moon Sun Myung of the Federation for World Peace, his wife, and entourage to enter the Republic. Their safety is guaranteed during the period of their stay in the North." It was signed "Kim Dal Hyun, Vice Premier, Cabinet of the Democratic People's Republic of Korea. November 30, 1991."

Our group boarded a special flight, Air Koryo 215, arranged for us by President Kim. A special flight from President Kim had never been arranged for any foreign head of state, so this was very exceptional and special treatment.

The aircraft flew over the Yellow Sea, up to Sineuiju, over my hometown of Jeongju, and on to Pyongyang. I was informed that the special route had been charted to let me see my hometown. My heart began to pound as I looked down at my hometown, dyed red by the light of the setting sun, and I felt numb deep in my being. I wondered, "Can this really be my hometown?" I wanted to jump out right away and start running around the hills and valleys.

At Pyongyang's Sunan International Airport, family members whom I had not seen for forty-eight years were there to greet me. My younger sisters, who used to be as beautiful as flowers, had become grandmothers entering their senior years. They grasped my hands, creased their eyebrows, and began to cry wildly. My older sister, now more than seventy, grabbed me by the shoulder and cried. I, however, did not cry.

"Please," I said, "don't do this. It's important for me to meet my family, but I came to do God's work. Please don't do this. Get hold of yourselves."

Inside my heart I was shedding tears like a waterfall. I was seeing my sisters for the first time in more than forty years, but I could not embrace them and cry with them. I maintained control of my heart, and made my way to our place of lodging.

The next morning, as has been my custom throughout my life, I awoke early in the morning and began to pray. If there were any surveillance apparatus in the guesthouse, my tearful prayer for the unification of the Korean peninsula would have been recorded in its entirety. That day, we toured the city of Pyongyang. The city was well fortified with the red slogans of Kim Il Sung's *Juche* ideology.

On the third day of our visit, we boarded an aircraft to tour Mount Kumgang. Though it was the winter season, the Kuryong Falls had not frozen and still spouted a strong flow of water. After touring all the different areas of Mount Kumgang, we boarded a helicopter on our sixth day, to be transported to my hometown.

In my dreams, I had felt such a strong yearning for my childhood home that I felt as though I could run to it in one bound. And now, there it was, appearing before me. I could hardly believe my eyes. Was this real, or was I dreaming? For what seemed like the longest time, I could only stand there, like a statue, in front of my home. After several minutes, I stepped inside.

It used to be in the shape of a hollow square, with the main wing, guest wing, storehouse, and barn built around a central courtyard. Now, only the main wing remained. I went into the main room, where I had been born, and sat on the floor with my legs crossed. Memories of what it had been like in my childhood came back to me as clearly as if it were only yesterday.

I opened the small door that led from the main room to the kitchen and looked out at the backyard. The chestnut tree I used to climb had been cut down and was gone. It seemed as though I could hear my mother calling to me sweetly. "Is my little tiny-eyes hungry?" The cotton cloth of her traditional dress passed quickly before my eyes.

I visited my parents' gravesite and offered a bouquet of flowers. The last time I saw my mother was when she came to visit me in prison in Heungnam and cried out loud. Her grave was thinly covered by the snow that had fallen the night before. I brushed it away with the palm of my hand and gently caressed the grass that had grown over her grave. The rough touch of the grass reminded me of the roughness of my mother's skin on the back of her hand.

My Meeting with President Kim Il Sung

I had not gone to North Korea because I wanted to see my home-town nor because I wanted to tour Mount Kumgang. I wanted to meet President Kim Il Sung and have a serious discussion on the future of our homeland. Yet, six days into my visit, there was no word on whether a meeting with President Kim could be arranged. When we arrived back at Pyongyang's Sunan Airport by helicopter after visiting my hometown, however, I found that Vice Premier Kim Dal Hyun had unexpectedly come to meet me.

"The Great Leader Kim Il Sung will receive you tomorrow," he told me. "The place will be the Majeon Presidential Residence in Heungnam, so you will need to board a special flight immediately and go to Heungnam."

I thought to myself, "They say he has many presidential residences. Why, of all places, Heungnam?"

On my way, I noticed a large sign for the Heungnam Nitrogen Fertilizer Factory, where I had been forced to labor. It reminded me of my time in prison and gave me an odd feeling. I spent the night in a guesthouse and went the next day to meet the president.

As I approached the official residence, I found President Kim at the entrance, waiting to greet me. The two of us simultaneously embraced each other. I was an anticommunist and he was the leader of a communist party, but ideology and philosophies were not important in the context of our meeting. We were like brothers who were meeting for the first time after a long separation. This was the power of belonging to the same people and sharing the same blood.

Right at the outset, I said to him: "Mr. President, because of your warm consideration, I have been able to meet my family. There are, however, ten million Koreans who are members of families separated between North and South, and they are unable even to know whether their relatives on the other side are alive or dead. I would like to ask you to grant them the opportunity to meet each other."

I spent a little more time telling him about my visit to my hometown and appealed to his love for the Korean people. He and I spoke the same dialect, so we were at ease with one another.

President Kim responded, "I feel the same way. From next year, let's begin a movement that allows separated compatriots of North and South to meet one another." His acceptance of my proposal was as natural as the snow melting in spring.

After speaking of my visit to Jeongju, I moved on to my views on nuclear weapons. I respectfully proposed that North Korea agree to a declaration on the de-nuclearization of the Korean peninsula and sign a safeguards agreement with the International Atomic Energy Agency.

He responded with candor, "Think for a moment. Who am I going to kill by making nuclear weapons? Kill my own people? Do I look like that kind of person? I agree that nuclear energy should be used only for peaceful purposes. I have listened attentively to what you have to say, and I expect it will be all right."

At the time, North-South relations were at a difficult point over the issue of nuclear inspections in North Korea, and so I had made my proposal with some reluctance. Everyone present, however, was surprised that President Kim responded in such a pleasant tone. At this point, we adjourned our meeting to a dining room, where we took an early lunch.

"Are you familiar with frozen potato noodles?" he asked. "It's a dish I ate quite often when I was active as a partisan on Mount Baekdu. Please try some."

"Well, of course I know it," I said, responding to his words with delight. "We used to enjoy this dish in my hometown."

"Well, I'm sure in your hometown you ate it as a delicacy," he continued. "But we ate it to survive. The Japanese police used to search for us all the way to the top of Mount Baekdu. We didn't have a chance to sit down to a decent meal. What else is there to eat at the top of Mount Baekdu other than potatoes?

"We would start to boil some potatoes, and if the Japanese police came after us, we would bury the potatoes in the ground and run away. It would be so cold that by the time we got back, the potatoes would be frozen solid in the ground. The only thing we could do was dig up the potatoes, thaw them, and then turn them into powder, so we could make noodles out of them."

"Mr. President," I said, "you are an expert on frozen potato noodles."

"That's right. They taste good mixed in bean soup, and they also taste very good if you eat them in sesame soup. It's a dish that is easy on the digestion, and because potatoes have a tendency to stick together, it is very filling.

"Also, Chairman Moon," he continued, "it tastes really good if you do like they do in Hamgyung Province and take some mustard leaf *kimchi*, like this, and put it over the noodles. You should try it."

I did as he suggested and ate my frozen potato noodles with some mustard leaf *kimchi* over them. The tasty flavor of the noodles matched well the spicy *kimchi* and left my stomach feeling light.

"There are many delicacies in the world," President Kim said. "I'm not interested in any of those. There's nothing better than the potato cakes, corn, and sweet potatoes that I used to eat in my hometown."

"You and I even share similar tastes in food," I said. "It's good that people who share the same homeland can meet like this."

"How was it when you visited your hometown?" he asked me.

"I was filled with many emotions," I said. "The home where I lived was still there, and I sat in the main room to think about the past. I almost expected to hear the voice of my late mother, calling me. It was an emotional feeling."

"I see," he said. "It shows that our country needs to be unified imme-diately. I hear that when you were young, you were quite mischievous. Did you have a chance to run around while you were there this time?"

Everyone at the table laughed at the president's comment.

"I wanted to climb a tree and go fishing," I said, "but I heard that you were waiting for me, so I quickly came here. I hope you will invite me to come again sometime."

"Well, of course. Of course I will. Chairman Moon, do you like to hunt? I like hunting very much. I think if you go bear hunting on Mount Baekdu, you will enjoy it very much. Bears have big bodies and look uncoordinated, but they are actually very nimble.

"I once came face to face with a bear," he continued. "The bear looked at me and didn't move a muscle. If I had started to run, you know what would have happened, don't you? So what was I going to do? I stared right back at him and just stood there. One hour passed, then two hours, three hours. But the bear just kept staring at me. You know how Mount Baekdu is famous for being cold. I was afraid I might freeze to death before the bear ate me."

"So what happened?" I asked.

"Well, Chairman Moon, do you see the bear sitting here, or do you see me?"

I laughed out loud, and President Kim immediately followed with a suggestion.

"Chairman Moon," he said, "the next time you come, let's go hunting together on Mount Baekdu."

I responded quickly with my own invitation.

"You like to fish, don't you? On Kodiak Island in Alaska, you can catch halibut that are as big as bears. Let's go fishing for those sometime."

"Halibut as big as bears? Well, I will definitely have to go."

The two of us were able to communicate well about our shared hobbies of hunting and fishing. At one point, we each felt we had so much to say to the other that we just started talking like old friends meeting after a long separation. Our laughter echoed around the dining room.

I also talked about Mount Kumgang.

"I went to Mount Kumgang, and it really is a beautiful mountain," I said. "It needs to be developed as a tourism destination for our people."

"Mount Kumgang will be an asset to our unified homeland," he said. "So I have made sure that only certain people can touch it. If it's developed in the wrong way, it could be ruined. You have an international eye, and I could trust someone like you to take it over and develop it for us." President Kim went so far as to ask that we consider developing Mount Kumgang together.

"Mr. President," I said, "you are older than I, so you are like my older brother." He responded, "Chairman Moon, from now, let's refer to each other as older brother and younger brother," and he grasped my hand tightly.

He and I held each other's hand as we walked down the hallway and took commemorative photographs. Then I left the residence.

After I had gone, I was told that President Kim told his son, Kim Jong Il, "Chairman Moon is a great man. I have met many people in my life, but none were like him. He has a broad scale of thinking, and he overflows with heart. I felt close to him. It made me feel good to be with him, and I wanted him to stay for a long time. I want to meet him again. After I die, if there are things to discuss pertaining to North-South relations, you must always seek the advice of Chairman Moon."

So it seemed that we had communicated very well.

Soon after I ended my week-long stay and left Pyongyang, Prime Minister Hyung Muk Yeon led a North Korean delegation to Seoul. Prime Minister Yeon signed an agreement to de-nuclearize the Korean peninsula. On January 30 of the following year, North Korea signed a nuclear safeguards agreement with the International Atomic Energy Agency, thus fulfilling the commitments that President Kim had made to me. There is more work to do, but these were the results I accomplished by going to Pyongyang at the risk of my life.

The Land May Be Divided, but Not Its People

T he Korean peninsula is one of the last remaining divided countries on earth. We have the responsibility to unify the peninsula. We cannot pass a divided homeland on to our descendants. It is impermissible that a single people should be divided and for peace-loving people to be unable to see their parents or siblings. The line that divides North and South Korea was drawn by human beings. Land can be divided that way, but not people. That we do not forget each other and continue to yearn for each other even after some sixty years of separation shows that we are one people.

The Korean people were traditionally known as "people of white clothing," because of the color of our traditional clothes. White is the symbol of peace, and our people are people of peace. During the time of the Japanese occupation, Koreans, Chinese, and Japanese lived in Manchuria and Siberia, sometimes helping each other and at other times killing each other. Throughout that time, Koreans never carried swords or knives as did the Japanese and Chinese. Instead, we carried flint rocks. Lighting fires in the frozen land of Manchuria and Siberia was a way of protecting life.

This is the kind of people we are. We respect Heaven, uphold moral principles, and love peace. Our people shed much blood during the time of the Japanese occupation and the Korean War. This, however, did not bring about the unification of our country or the establishment of a sovereignty of peace. Our country was broken at the waist into two pieces, and half became a dark world of communism.

We need unification to restore the sovereignty of our people. We must end the division between North and South so we can have peace. Only after we first accomplish peaceful unification and restore our sovereignty can we bring peace to the world.

The Korean people were created to bring peace to the world. Everything has a name, and names have meaning. Our traditional white garments are easy to see, both by day and night. White is good to use for signs during the night because it is easy to see in the dark. In the same way, our people are destined to convey messages of peace around the world, both day and night.

North and South are divided by a ceasefire line, but this is not the problem. Once we remove that line, we will find an even larger barrier between us and Russia and China. For our people to enjoy true peace, we will need to overcome those ceasefire lines as well. It will be difficult, but it is not impossible. The important thing is our own attitude.

I believe that when a person sweats, he should sweat every last drop that he has in him. He should sweat even the last little bit that is in his heart. That way, he will have no regrets, and everything will become clean and set in order. The same is true when we attempt anything difficult. The difficulty will end only when you have gained victory at every stage, and everything has been made clear. Whatever you are dealing with needs to be completely put in order. Then it can bear fruit. We cannot restore our people's full sovereignty without going through such tearful difficulties.

Today, many people talk about peaceful unification. I, however, spoke about this at a time when people did not dare even use the phrase "peaceful unification," for fear of being charged with violating the Anti-Communist Law and the National Security Law. Today, when people ask me what must be done to bring about unification, I tell them what I have always said on this matter: "If South Koreans love North Korea more than they love the South, and North Koreans love South Korea more than they love the North, we could unify the peninsula today."

I was able to risk my life to go to North Korea in 1991 and meet President Kim because I had a foundation of such love within me. I made agreements then with him regarding meetings of separated families, North-South economic cooperation, development of Mount Kumgang, de-nuclearization of the Korean peninsula, and working toward a North-South summit conference. No one thought an anticommunist could go to a communist country and open the floodgate of unification, but I surprised the world.

Before my meeting with President Kim, I delivered a two-hour address titled "Blood Is Thicker Than Water," at the Mansudae Assembly Hall, seat of the Supreme People's Assembly, North Korea's legislature. I spoke that day to the leadership of North Korea about a way to unify North and South through love. I stood before the leadership of North Korea, who were armed with Kim Il Sung's philosophy, and told them exactly what I believed.

"North and South must be unified," I said, "but guns and swords will not make us one. North-South unification will not happen with military force. Even the Korean War failed in this respect, and it is foolish for anyone to think they can make another attempt through military force. Neither will unification happen with the *Juche* ideology that you espouse. What will do it, then? The world does not operate only by the power of human beings. Because God exists, nothing can be done by human effort alone. Even in situations of evil, such as war, God carries out His providence. That is why North and South cannot be unified through the *Juche* ideology that puts man at the center.

"Bringing about a unified homeland can be done only with Godism," I continued. "God is protecting us, and our time of unification is coming. Unification is the destiny; it is the task that must be accomplished in our era. If we cannot accomplish the sacred task of unifying the homeland in our time, we will not be able to hold our heads high in the presence of our ancestors or descendants for the rest of eternity.

"What is Godism? It is the practice of God's perfect love. Neither the right wing nor the left wing can unify North and South. It will be possible only when there is a 'headwing thought' that is able to harmonize these two.

"To travel the path of love, you must apologize before the world for your invasion of the South. I understand that North Korea has planted twenty thousand resident espionage agents in the South. Send an order immediately to all of them, instructing them to turn themselves in to the South Korean authorities. If you do that, I will give them an education that will rectify their ideology and turn them into patriots who will contribute to the peaceful unification of North and South."

I pounded on the table in front of me as I spoke. The expressions of Mr. Yun Ki Bok and Vice Premier Kim Dal Hyun grew tense. I was aware of what dangers I might be exposed to for making such statements, but I needed to say what I had come to say. I was not simply trying to shock the audience. I knew that my speech would be reported immediately, word for word, to President Kim and his son, Chairman Kim Jong Il. So I wanted to state my purpose clearly.

When I finished, some of the North Koreans present even protested, demanding to know how I could dare to speak in such a manner. I looked at my entourage and saw that their faces were white. Our members who were with me told me: "The speech had a very strong tone, and the atmosphere of the audience was not good."

I was adamant, however. "Why did I come here?" I asked them. "I didn't come to see the land of North Korea. If I were to leave here without saying what needed to be said, Heaven would punish me. Even if today's speech is used by them as an excuse to deny me a meeting with President Kim and to expel us from the country, I still needed to say what I came to say."

On July 8, 1994, President Kim suddenly died. His death came when North-South relations were at an all-time low. Patriot missiles had been deployed on South Korean soil, and hawks in the United States advocated the destruction of nuclear facilities in Yeongbyon. It appeared that war might break out at any time. North Korea announced it would not receive any mourners from outside the country, but I felt it was important we send someone. I wanted to fulfill my obligation, as I had formed a brotherly relationship with President Kim.

I called Bo Hi Pak. "Go immediately to North Korea as my representative to mourn President Kim's death." I said.

"No one can get into North Korea now," he said.

"I know it's difficult, but somehow you have to go. I don't care if you have to swim across the Yalu River. Get in there and convey my condolences."

Bo Hi Pak first traveled to Beijing and risked his life to communicate with North Korea. Then, Chairman Kim Jong Il gave the instruction, "An exception will be made for a mourning representative from Chairman Moon. Escort him to Pyongyang."

After condolences had been expressed, Chairman Kim Jong Il met with Bo Hi Pak and politely greeted him, saying, "My father always said that Chairman Moon was working hard for the unification of our homeland. I am glad you came."

In 1994, the Korean peninsula was in such a crisis that it could have exploded at any time. In that moment, we were able to resolve the nuclear crisis on the Korean peninsula because of the relationship I had formed with President Kim Il Sung. Sending a representative to express my condolences was not a simple matter of mourning.

I described my meeting with President Kim in considerable detail to illustrate my point about the importance of faith and loyalty between two people. I met him for the sake of the peaceful unification of our homeland. I was able to convey my concerns for the destiny of our people with faith and loyalty. As a result, after his death, his son, Chairman Kim Jong Il, accepted our mourning representative. There is no wall that cannot be scaled and no dream that cannot be realized when we share our love with a sincere heart.

When I went to North Korea, I thought of it as my homeland and the home of my brother. I didn't go there with a desire to get something from them. I went with the purpose to share with them my heart of love. The power of love touched not only President Kim Il Sung but also his son, Chairman Kim Jong Il. Since then, and continuing to this day, we have maintained a special relationship with North Korea. Each time North-South relations become difficult, we have played a role in opening the gateway. It is all based on the fact that I met with President Kim Il Sung, conveyed to him my sincere heart, and built a relationship of trust with him. That is the importance of trust.

Following my meeting with President Kim, we now operate the Pyeonghwa Motors plant, the Potonggang Hotel, and the World Peace Center in North Korea. There are billboards for Pyeonghwa Motors around Pyongyang. When the South Korean president visited North Korea, North Korean officials took him to the Pyeonghwa Motors plant. South Korean business leaders who accompanied the president stayed at the Potonggang Hotel. Non-North Korean members of our church who work in North Korea gather at the World Peace Center each Sunday for worship service.

All of these projects are efforts for the sake of peaceful exchanges and unification of North and South. They are not being done to make a profit. They are efforts to contribute to the unification of North and South as an expression of love for the Korean people.

Not by Guns or Swords, but by True Love

It is not just the ceasefire line that divides our people. The Young-nam and Honam regions are also divided by an invisible line. Also, Koreans who live in Japan are divided between the Korean Residents Union in Japan, or Mindan, who are pro-South Korea, and the General Association of Korean Residents in Japan, or Chongryon, who are pro-North Korea. The conflict between the two organizations in Japan is based on the hometowns of their respective members. Second and third-generation Korean residents in Japan, who have never been to their parents' hometowns, still live in conflict with each other, as they live within the lines drawn by their parents. The members of the two organizations use slightly different language, send their children to different schools, and do not intermarry.

In 2005, I put into effect my long-cherished plan to create oneness among Koreans in Japan, as well as among Koreans in the Young-nam (southeastern) and Honam (southwestern) regions. I invited one thousand members of Mindan and one thousand members of Chongryon to Seoul, and matched them in sisterhood and brother-hood relationships to one thousand people from Youngnam region and one thousand from Honam.

It is next to impossible for Chongryon and Mindan to sit down together in Japan and talk about the peaceful unification of North and South. The task of gathering these people in one place was difficult, but it was deeply moving for me to see them sitting together and embracing each other.

One Chongryon official at the event was visiting Seoul for the first time. He spoke in tears as he commented that he deeply regretted the many years he had spent fighting a war that was not his own, particularly as he was not even certain which part of the peninsula his father actually came from. He said he felt immeasurably ashamed for having lived his life with a meaningless line of division drawn in his heart.

To fully understand the division of the Korean peninsula and the conflict between the two sides, we must look comprehensively at the past, present, and future. Every incident has a root cause. The division of the Korean peninsula was created by the history of struggle between good and evil. When the Korean War broke out, the Soviet Union, China, and other communist countries came to the aid of North Korea.

In a similar way, sixteen countries, led by the United States, sent armed forces to the aid of South Korea. Also, five countries sent medical teams, and twenty nations provided war supplies. What other war in history involved so many countries in the fighting? The reason that the entire world became involved in a war that took place in the tiny country of Korea is that this was a proxy war between the forces of communism and the forces of freedom. It could be said that Korea came to represent the world, and that good and evil fought fiercely on its soil.

Retired general and former U.S. Secretary of State the late Alexander Haig made an unexpected statement in his congratulatory remarks at the tenth anniversary celebration of *The Washington Times*, which I founded in 1992.

"I am a veteran of the Korean War," he said. "As a commander, I was in charge of the attack against Heungnam, and we staged the strongest attack we could. I am deeply moved to hear that Reverend Moon, who was being held by the communists, was set free by that day's attack. It seems I was sent there to free Reverend Moon. Now, Reverend Moon is here to save America. *The Washington Times* is a newspaper that will save the American people by providing a balanced view of history that is neither right nor left, and show us the way forward. As we see, there is no such thing as coincidence in history."

A few years ago in Korea, there were people making the argument that the statue of the famous Gen. Douglas MacArthur in an Incheon park should be removed. They believed that if United Nations forces had not joined the war effort, the country would not be divided be-tween North and South, as it is today. I was shocked to hear this, and spoke strongly against it. Such an argument can only be made from the position of the Communist party of North Korea.

Great sacrifices were made on a global level, and yet the peninsula remains divided. We do not know the exact date when unification will come, but it is clear that we are making strong strides in that direction. There are many obstacles to be overcome on the road to unification. As we come face to face with each obstacle, we need to work to tear it down and then move on. Though it may take a long time and prove difficult, unification will absolutely come if we work with the same desperation we would have if we were swimming across the Yalu River.

Following the breakup of the Soviet Union, Romania resisted change the longest among the communist countries of Central and Eastern Eu-rope. Then, at the end of 1989, Romania experienced a bloody uprising

LOVE WILL BRING UNIFICATION

by its people. As soon as the regime was toppled, Nicolae Ceaucescu, who had ruled the country for twenty-four years, was executed, along with his wife. He was a brutal dictator who mercilessly massacred those who opposed his policies. In any country, one reason a dictator will tend to tighten his grip is that he fears for his life in the event he may lose power. I think that if a dictator can be certain that his own life will not be placed in danger, he will not go headlong down a dead-end street in the manner of Ceausescu.

Our country, too, will be unified before long, by one means or another. So politicians and economists need to make the necessary preparations in their own fields of expertise. As a religious person, I will work hard to prepare to greet the unified Korea in which we can embrace North Korean people with love and share in a common peace.

I have studied the unification of Germany for a long time. I have listened to the experiences of those who were involved with regard to how it was that unification could come without a single bullet being fired or a single drop of blood being spilled. In so doing, my hope has been to find a way that is appropriate for Korea. I have learned that the main reason Germany could be unified peacefully was that East German leaders were made to understand that their lives would not be in danger following unification. If East German leaders had not believed this would be so, they would not have allowed unification to occur so easily.

I came to believe we need to have a similar understanding toward rulers of North Korea. A novel based on North Korea was published in Japan not long ago. In this book of fiction, the rulers of North Korea repeatedly watch a video of Ceausescu's execution and cry out, "That is what will happen to us if we lose power. Under no circumstances can we lose our hold on power!"

Of course, that is only a novel published in Japan. We should, however, devote our attention to this real problem and find a solution for North Korean leaders, to bring about Korea's speedy unification.

Building a world of peace on the Korean peninsula is not as difficult as we may think. When South Korea lives fully for the sake of North Korea, North Korea will not try to fight the South, and peace will come naturally to the peninsula.

The power that can move a rebellious child is not the fist or brute power. It is the power of love that wells up naturally from within the heart. More than rice or fertilizer, it is important for us to give love to North Korea. We must never forget that it is only when we consider North Korea's situation and live for its sake with a loving and sincere heart that the North will open its heart to us and the world.

CHAPTER SEVEN

FUTURE OF KOREA, FUTURE OF THE WORLD

Global Harmony Starts on the Korean Peninsula

Imiss my hometown so much that I visit it often in my dreams. My hometown is far beyond Seoul, in Jeongju, North Korea. It is an area that has both mountains and the sea. Wherever I am and whatever time it may be, my heart is always reaching out to that place where there is love and life.

All of us are born into our parents' lineage, and as we grow up we are nourished by our parents' love. We cannot forget our hometowns because that is where the ground is soaked with our parents' love. That is why the older we get, the more we miss our hometowns. It is where our roots are and where we must return. It is difficult for people to cut themselves off from things that are fundamentally important to them. In 2004, I ended my activities in the United States after thirty-four years and returned to the Korean peninsula, where heavenly fortune resides.

We are not aware of the exact time when morning becomes noon. Neither are we aware of the exact time that evening becomes night. In the same way, human beings have no way of knowing the moment when Heaven does its work. That is how it is with our lives as well. Our moments of success and failure all pass us by without our being fully

aware of exactly when they began to unfold. The same is true with nations. We cannot know the moment when good or ill fortune comes to a
nation. Heavenly fortune is a force that moves the world; it is a principle
that makes the universe go round. Though we may not know it, there is
clearly something called heavenly fortune, which the One who created
this world uses to conduct His providence.

The universe moves in perfect accordance with its own order. All beings in the world bear within them a certain principle that is put there
even before they exist. When a baby is born, no one has to teach it
how to breathe or to open its eyes. The baby does these things without
being compelled. Things that happen on their own hold within them
important keys to the secrets of the universe.

Many natural phenomena seem to just happen on their own. In
reality, though, they don't happen in this way. Hidden within natural
phenomena in the universe is a directional force that we are not aware
of and do not understand. This is the same with the forces of fortune in
the universe, or heavenly fortune.

As the universe turns, it is certain that there will be a period of powerful fortune. If we understand the principle of the universe whereby
spring follows winter and is then followed by summer, then we can
foresee a bright future for Korea after a long winter of misfortune.

Those who are wise will align themselves with the laws and rhythms
of the universe. When I was in America I would often fish in the Hudson
River near my home. I have been a very skilled fisherman since I was a
young boy, but there were days on the Hudson when I could not catch
so much as a minnow and had to return home disheartened. Fish have
paths they travel at certain times. If we don't know where these paths
are and what times they are on these paths, we won't catch any fish. Just

because there is water, it does not mean there will always be fish passing by. A person who doesn't understand this could keep his line in the water all day and all night, and it won't do him any good. The same is true with heavenly fortune. If we don't have an eye to see the future, we will not see heavenly fortune, even if it is staring us in the face. That is why it is important to have a keen understanding of heavenly fortune and an ability to sense its movements.

Human civilization developed throughout history in a westerly direction. Egypt's continental civilization gave way to the peninsular civilizations of Greece and Rome and then developed to the island civilization of Britain before moving on to another continental civilization, this time in America. Civilization continued its westerly move, crossing the Pacific Ocean to Japan. The movement of civilization didn't stop there. The force that raised up Japan to such a great position is now moving to the Korean peninsula. Civilization is about to come to its fruition in Korea.

For Japan's island civilization to link up with the continent, it must pass through a peninsula. Asia, of course, has other peninsulas, but only Korea possesses sufficient foundation to inherit contemporary civilization. The Korean peninsula is in a most exquisite geopolitical position. It faces Japan and the United States across the Pacific Ocean. It also is connected to the continents of Asia and Europe and shares common borders with China and Russia. This is the reason Korea has been a focal point in the power struggles among the world's great powers and has suffered a great deal as a result.

During the Cold War, we fought for our very existence in a war against communism. Even now, the concerns and interests of the world's great powers continue to involve the Korean peninsula, so Korea remains a divided country unable to be completely at peace. The time has come when the Korean peninsula, where the interests of the great powers collide, will take on an important role in preventing conflict between these countries. As a result it will be in a position to lead the rest of the world into prosperity and peace.

Heavenly fortune comes with tremendous responsibility. Now that the Korean peninsula has come into its heavenly fortune, it must play a role similar to a ball bearing, making sure these countries not only do not collide with each other but instead cooperate closely for the sake of the prosperity and peace of the world. The functions of a ball bearing are to hold the axle of a machine in place while also allowing the axle to rotate freely. Korea needs to maintain smooth relationships with the great powers and thus become a ball bearing that allows peace to rotate freely throughout the world.

For a long time I have been making intensive preparations for Korea to play this role. I supported the *glasnost* policies of President Gorbachev and pushed the goal of improving relations with the Soviet Union. I also supported the reform and openness policies of Deng Xiaoping in China, starting in the late 1980s. I began my work in China by supporting Yanbian University to establish a college of engineering. Even after the Tiananmen Square incident, when foreign capital was leaving China, we remained in China and invested hundreds of millions of dollars in Huizhou, in Kwangtung Province.

I did not do this just for economic reasons. I am a religious person, not a businessman. A religious person is someone who sees into the future and prepares for it. Russia, China, Japan, and the United States must learn to cooperate with each other while using the spiritual bearings of the Korean peninsula. The Korean peninsula is destined to become the axis for world peace.

When I began working to improve relations between Korea and the Soviet Union and China, I discovered that Korea did not even have something as basic as a Russian or Chinese dictionary. Very little was going to get done as long as we could not understand each other's languages. When I heard that there were groups of academics who had the foresight to begin work on a Chinese-Korean dictionary and a Russian-Korean dictionary, I supported these two projects.

The Chinese-Korean Dictionary Project was led by Professor Il Shik Hong of the Korea University's Institute of Korean Culture, and several professors in the university's Russian Studies Department were behind the effort to publish a Russian-Korean dictionary. These dictionaries are playing crucial roles in the exchanges between the two Koreas and China and Russia.

When a rock sits atop the highest mountain peak, once it begins to fall it will fall all the way to the deepest part of the valley. This describes the changing fortunes of Western civilization. It is common knowledge that the West achieved incredible development through the use of science, but now moral decay is sending it down to the depths of the valley floor. That valley floor is the East, which has been developing a spiritual culture for thousands of years.

In particular, the Korean peninsula is the place where Eastern and Western cultures meet, as well as the place where continental and oceanic civilizations meet. The historian and philosopher Oswald Spengler put forth a cyclical theory of the rise and decline of civilizations that took a dim view of democracy and described it as the type of government that is leading Western civilization into decline. He argued that democracy is driven by money and that democracy's corrupting power and its signs of moral decline include the rise of materialism and cults of science.

Looking at today's Western culture, it appears that some of his thoughts were prophetic. The Atlantic civilization that has prospered until now is clearly facing a new era, the era of a pan-Pacific civilization that is on the rise. Asia, with Korea poised to take a central role, is becoming the lead actor in a new world history. Two-thirds of the world's population lives in Asia. All the world's major religions began in Asia. It has long served as humanity's spiritual root.

It is inevitable that the Western and Eastern civilizations come together in harmony on the Korean peninsula. As the world rapidly changes, heavenly fortune is moving in Korea's direction at an ever-increasing speed. However, if the Korean peninsula is to properly perform its important role in leading the world to harmony and peace during an era of chaos, then it must prepare itself well. It must do away with a past marked with prejudice and selfishness and greet the new age with clear eyes and a new heart.

From Suffering and
Tears to Peace and Love

There is deep meaning in the tragic history the Korean people have experienced up to this point. Korea has suffered a great deal because it is destined to become the foundation from which world peace will emerge. Because it has endured suffering and difficulty for such a long time, Korea can now become the central nation from which God brings peace to the world. Even though Koreans have experienced countless hardships, we have never made anyone our enemy or hated anyone. Several of our neighbors have caused difficulty for us, but we have never made them our irreconcilable enemies.

The Korean people have developed a culture of heart that enables us to forgive our enemies. It takes mastery over oneself to love and accept an enemy. The ability to love one's enemy comes only after an individual is victorious over his own internal conflicts.

People who are persecuted are the closest to God. To understand God's heart, one must experience His tearful heart. Even a person who normally would not shed tears will do so if he loses his family and his country. He would desperately plead with God in tears. Suffering difficulties causes one to have a heart that sheds tears, but it is through this type of heart that one can receive God's blessing. God comes to a heart that is soaked with tears. Korea has become a land of heavenly fortune because so many tears have been shed within the hearts of its people.

Korean people honor their ancestors. No matter how hungry we may be, we will never sell the land where our ancestors are buried in order to buy food. Historically we have maintained a way of thinking that respects Heaven. We are a modern, civilized nation that still honors the world of the spirit. When we accepted Buddhism and Confucianism, they gave rise to a beautiful religious culture. More recently Christian and Muslim traditions have begun to thrive here as well. All these religions live without conflict within Korea. They blend together and coexist peacefully. What is it that has made us such a unique people?

From ancient times we have always had religious minds, and our hearts have always been open to receive the word of God. In addition, Koreans have always placed a high priority on education and excellence. As a result the Korean language and the *Hangeul* alphabet are considered treasures handed down by Heaven. Our language is rich with adjectives and adverbs that can be used to express the human heart.

I love the alphabet that we use. I am very fond of the term *Hunminjeongeum*, which means "correct sounds for the instruction of the people." This is the original idea of *Hangeul* (Korean letters). It has such a beautiful meaning. The excellence of *Hangeul* has survived for centuries and continues to contribute beauty to human communication, even in this digital age. To me it is truly amazing that through a simple combination of consonants and vowels humans can communicate and even imitate all the sounds of the creation. For the past thirty years, I have been telling the members of our church in other countries to prepare for the future by learning Korean.

Recently, the term *hallyu*, or "Korean wave," was coined in China by journalists to describe the rapid spread of Korean popular culture throughout Asia. The popularity of Korean pop music, TV dramas, and movies has generated a large increase in the number of people learning the Korean language. There are now people in Japan, Mongolia, Vietnam, and even Africa who can speak Korean.

This is certainly not a coincidence. The soul dwells within language. The reason the Japanese tried so hard to eliminate the Korean language during their occupation was to destroy the soul of the Korean people. The fact that people around the world now speak Korean means that the heart and soul of the Korean people are thriving in today's world. It is because of heavenly fortune that Korea's cultural influence continues to grow.

The Korean people never want to burden others. When I was in America, I saw the stubborn character of Korean people. The United States is a country that has many types of social safety nets, but Koreans almost never want to take advantage of these. Rather than relying on the support of the government, they find ways to earn money in order to raise their children and take care of their older parents. This is how Koreans show self-reliance. I also see this in the missionaries we have sent across the world. They don't fear going to a country they know little about. This is true not only for missionaries but also for businessmen. Once they are given a mission, no matter where that mission may take them in the world, they drop everything and go. They are not indecisive or reluctant.

Koreans have such an enterprising spirit that they can go anywhere in the world and live a productive life. Our suffering history has taught us that no obstacle is too great. We have learned to face the worst kinds of situations and overcome them.

When there is a neighborhood celebration, people compete for the best spot to view the celebration. This is a very self-centered kind of behavior. The person who quietly sits down in the worst seat will be the leader of the coming age. Anyone who worries first about putting food in his own mouth will be a failure in the coming age. Even if we are going to eat only one spoonful, we must think of others first. If we are to receive the heavenly fortune that is coming to the Korean peninsula, then we must be aware in the deepest part of our hearts that "others" are more valuable than "myself."

In the past, everything we loved was taken from us. During Japan's occupation, our country was taken away. Our country was split in two, and we were forcibly separated from our loving parents and siblings. So Korea became a land of tears. Now, however, we must cry for the world. From now on, rather than shedding tears for ourselves, we must shed tears more sincerely and more desperately for the sake of the world. This is what we must do on the Korean peninsula if we want to continue to receive heavenly fortune. When we do this, the heavenly fortune on the Korean peninsula will then spread out to the world. Korean people have a great opportunity to be at the center of an era of world peace.

The Goal of Twenty-first Century Religion

The twentieth century was a time of tremendous change. More happened in that hundred-year period than during the past two thousand years. It was the century when there were two world wars and when communism rose to great strength and then virtually disappeared. It was also the century when humanity turned its back on God and buried itself in material things. What about the twenty-first century, then? Some say that advances in science have proven that many religious beliefs are mere superstition and irrelevant to the modern world. I contend, however, that the role of religion will always be relevant as long as the spiritual aspect of human beings remains a reality and a world of peace has not been established.

What is the purpose of religion? It is to bring about God's ideal world. The reason religions evangelize is because they desire to increase the number of citizens under God's sovereignty. If everyone were to live under God's sovereignty, we would have a world of peace where there would be no war or division. The ultimate destination of the path followed by religions should be peace.

God created this world out of a desire for love and peace. If we create division by insisting that our own religion is the only path to salvation, we go against God's desire. God wants everyone in the world to work hard for peace, reconciliation, and coexistence. If people say that coming to church creates division in their family, then I do not hesitate to tell them that they should put their family first. Religion is only a means to bring about God's perfect world; it is not an end in itself.

Humankind's destiny is to bring together all the points of view that are now divided against each other. The philosophy that will lead humanity in the future must be able to bring together all religions and philosophies. The days have ended when one country stands at the forefront and leads humanity. The era of nationalism has also ended.

If we continue the era of people congregating together only by religion or race, then humanity cannot avoid a repetition of war. The age of peace absolutely cannot come unless we transcend cultural customs and traditions. No ideology, philosophy, or religion that has influenced humanity in the past is capable of bringing about the peace and unification that is needed for the future. We need a new ideology and philosophy that goes beyond Buddhism, Christianity, and Islam. For my entire life, I have called on people until my voice is hoarse to transcend their religious factions and even their religions.

There are close to two hundred countries in the world, and each has its own national borders. A border separates one country from another, but countries separated by borders cannot endure eternally. Only religion can overcome national borders. However, religions that should be bringing people together have instead divided themselves into many factions that are busy fighting each other. They have fallen into a selfish thought process that puts their religion or faction first. They are oblivious to the fact that the world has changed and a new era of selflessness has dawned.

It will not be easy to tear down the religious walls that have stood for thousands of years, but these walls must come down if we are to advance into a world of peace. Religions and their factions must stop their meaningless fighting, find a middle ground for their differing opinions, and develop concrete ways to advance the world of peace. For humanity to be happy in the future, material affluence alone will not be sufficient. It is urgent that the struggles of modern ideologies, cultures, and races be overcome through interreligious understanding and spiritual harmony.

All my life I have made the following appeals to the wide variety of religious people I have met around the world: First, respect the traditions of other religions and do everything you can to prevent conflict and discord among religions. Second, all religious communities should cooperate with each other to serve the world. Third, the leaders of all religions should work together to develop a structure that will let us accomplish our mutual mission of establishing world peace.

The right eye is there for the left eye, and the left for the sake of the right. The two eyes together exist for the sake of the whole body. The same can be said for every other part of the body. Nothing exists only for its own sake. Religion, too, does not exist for its own sake but for the sake of love and peace. Once world peace is accomplished, there will be no further need for religion. The ultimate purpose of religion is to bring about the reality of a human community filled with love and peace. This is God's will.

It is not easy to create an environment where people's hearts are filled with a craving for peace. Continuous education is the only solution.

This is the reason why I devote myself to projects in the field of education. We founded the Sunhwa Arts School even before our church had developed enough to stand on its own.

A school is a holy place where truth is taught. What are the most important truths that should be taught in school? The first is to know God and recognize His existence in the world around us. The second is to know the fundamental origin of human beings, our responsibilities, and how to fulfill our responsibilities for the sake of the world. The third is to realize the purpose for the existence of human beings and to then create an ideal world for that existence. These things can be understood only after they have been taught with sincerity and dedication over a long period.

Education today is focused on creating a winner-take-all society where those who finish first are rewarded with a monopoly on happiness. This is not the right way to educate children. Education must be a means for creating a world where all humanity can live well together.

The philosophies and methods of education that have dominated us until now must be changed to ones that let us advance toward humanity's common goals. If the United States were to educate only for the sake of the United States, and Britain only for sake of Britain, then humanity's future would be dark. Educators must not teach how to live selfishly but instead impart the wisdom needed to resolve the myriad social problems we face today.

The role of religious scholars is even more important. Religious scholars do not need to be teaching complex theories and the superiority of their own religions. Instead, they need to give their students the wisdom to love humanity and build a world of peace. They need to teach the principle of selflessness. We cannot expect a future of happiness for humanity if scholars do not take the lead in teaching our descendants the principles of peace. Humanity is one brotherhood and sisterhood, and the world is one family.

The most important wisdom needed by humankind comes from knowing God's heart and His ideal. For this reason, the role of religion continues to be important, especially in the twenty-first century, when science and technology seem to be replacing the role of religion in understanding how the universe operates.

Religions around the world must understand the destination of the human journey and immediately cease all major and minor struggles. They should not be fighting for the purpose of protecting their own honor. Religions must pool their wisdom and combine their energies and work diligently to build the ideal world. They must forget the past struggles filled with hatred and work out peaceful solutions.

No matter how much we have done for world peace, there is always more to be done. Religious people, whose mission is to lead humanity into the ideal world, must not forget for a moment that truly their only mission is to be apostles of peace.

Cultural Projects Express
God's Creativity

In 1988, Seoul hosted the Summer Olympics. I saw this as a potential festival of peace in my own backyard and had many of our
members from around the world come to Seoul for the event. The
members helped guide the international athletes and officials, cheered
the athletes, served them food, and presented them with mementos of
their visit to Korea.

Since China and the Soviet Union were both participants in the
Games, I saw it as an event that could critically alter the Cold War era.
Seeing the Olympic Games as a festival of peace gave it the potential to
create harmony between the communist bloc and the free world. On
the day of the opening ceremony I sat in the general seating area of
Jamsil Main Stadium and watched with great joy.

After the Olympics, I carried on the energy of the Games by
founding the Ilhwa Chunma professional soccer team in Korea. The
Ilhwa team has won several championships and built up a strong
fan base. We have since founded the soccer teams Clube Atlético
Sorocaba and Centro Esportivo Nova Esperança (CENE) in Brazil,
the home of samba football, and continue to operate them today.

The reason I chose to create soccer teams is that I enjoy the sport. I have enjoyed sports since I was young, and for a time I did some boxing and some traditional martial arts. Soccer, however, is the one sport that I continue to enjoy into my old age. In my school days I used to run around the schoolyard diligently kicking the ball, but now I enjoy watching it. When the World Cup was held in Seoul, I had three television sets set up side by side so that I could watch all the games. I never missed a game that Korea played.

Soccer is a microcosm of life. No matter how well I might dribble the ball down the field, if someone from the opposing team who is faster and more skilled comes along and steals the ball away from me, then in an instant everything I did until then is for nothing. Also, even if I dribble all the way down the field and take a shot at the goal, if the ball hits the goalpost and bounces back, that's the end. It's up to me to dribble the ball, but it takes more than one person to get the ball into the goal. I need a teammate like Ji Sung Park, who will assist me at the critical moment, or someone like Young Pyo Lee, who will adroitly draw the other team away from me.

The most important person on the team is the coach, who watches over the entire team from the sidelines. The coach doesn't run or score goals, but his power is greater than that of all the players put together. Similar to a coach who sees things that the players cannot see and gives signals, God sees things that we cannot see and gives us signs. If the players follow the coach's signs well, they will almost always win. But if the coach sends signs and foolish players either don't understand them or ignore them and play according to their own thinking, the team can only lose.

Soccer is a sport where competition takes place and someone wins or loses, but it also has the potential for significantly influencing countries and increasing their cooperation toward peace. I was told that twice as many people watched the World Cup as watched the Olympics. This provides an idea of how many people around the world love soccer. Therefore, just like the Olympics, it has the power to become a force for harmony between countries, races, religions, and cultures. I see soccer and peace among countries as potentially powerful partners.

Pelé, who was appointed as Brazil's Extraordinary Minister for Sport in 1995, once visited Korea and spent time in the Hannam-Dong neighborhood of Seoul. People remember him as the greatest soccer player in the world, but the Pelé I met was a peace activist. He wanted to bring world peace through soccer.

When I met him, he laughed as he told me the story of a game in Africa. He said, "I once played in Nigeria, but the country was at war then. How do you think we were able to play in a place where bombs were exploding all around? Thankfully, there was a short ceasefire called so that the game could be played. That's when I realized deeply that football (meaning soccer) was more than just a sport. Football is a means shared by all people in the world for creating world peace. After that, I decided that I had to carry out a movement for world peace through football."

I was so impressed with Pelé in that moment that I firmly grasped his hand.

We live in a competitive society where there is a great deal of stress. Stress creates tension in our lives and takes away our peace of mind. When stress accumulates, people can become irritated and sometimes fight each other. Sports and the arts are examples of things that help us to lower our levels of stress. These things help us to vent our pent-up urges and bring humanity together. The reason for my devotion to soccer teams, symphony orchestras, and ballet companies is that these activities are means to bring world peace.

Pelé understands this kind of thinking. Finding ourselves in agreement, Pelé and I created a new competition of international dimensions called the Peace Cup, and tournaments have been held every two years since 2003. We brought famous soccer teams from around the world to Korea. A corresponding women's tournament called the Peace Queen Cup is held in alternate years.

In the summer of 2009 we held the first men's tournament outside Korea. The 2009 competition was held in Spain's Andalusia region. All profits from the tournaments are used to support soccer events for children and youth in developing countries. In particular, we use soccer to help children with physical disabilities keep their dreams alive.

Working with the Office of the U.N. High Commissioner for Refugees, the U.N. refugee agency, we held a soccer tournament for young people in Liberia. This is a country where fifteen years of tribal warfare have left its people exhausted. It receives special protection from the United Nations because of its precipitous drop in population. The children of this war-torn country gathered together to play soccer and sing songs of peace. In the process of kicking the ball around, they were learning skills of teamwork and fair play that are necessary for bringing harmony between tribes.

The Peace Cup organization also has a goal of building a peace stadium in the Israel-Palestine-Jordan region, as close as possible to the Israel-Palestine border. The stadium would be freely available to all as a peace-building venture. We want to bring famous coaches from Europe and start a soccer academy for the children in the region. The adults may want to point guns at each other, but the children will want to come to the soccer stadium and kick the ball around. People say it is unrealistic and shake their heads, but we will do this.

Already a member of the Israeli cabinet has said the stadium should be built in the Israeli area, and a member of the Palestinian cabinet says it should be in the Palestinian area. I am determined, however, to build it in a way that connects the two sides. I am not one to be pressured into giving up my dreams. I have a bull-headed strength of will that I use to pursue dreams that will lead to a world of peace.

The creation of our ballet company is another example of the same strength of will. People said it couldn't be done. We established the Universal Ballet in 1984. Today more people in Korea are enjoying ballet than ever before. When we first created our ballet company, Korea was like a barren wasteland as far as ballet was concerned. Korea now even has its own world-renowned ballerinas.

Every time I watch ballet, I feel that this must be what art in the Heavenly Kingdom is like. When a ballerina stands on her toes and holds her head toward the heavens, this stance strikes me as a perfect pose for the way we should hold God in awe. It has the look of ardent desire. In ballet, human beings can use the beautiful body given to them by God to express their love for Him. It is the highest form of art.

The Universal Ballet began by performing *Swan Lake* and the *Nutcracker Suite*. It has added *Don Quixote, Giselle*, and its own original creations *Shim Chung* and *The Love of Choonhyang*. It has developed to the point of being internationally acclaimed. The Universal Ballet receives invitations from the world's most famous venues. Its dancers are credited with adding a uniquely Korean beauty to the energetic moves of Western ballet. They are praised for the way they harmonize

Eastern and Western styles in their performances. The Universal Ballet has an academy in Washington, D.C. I also created the New York City Symphony Orchestra and the New Hope Singers.

The arts enable humankind to reflect the high ideals embodied in God's own creative work. God poured His entire heart into human beings and the world He created, just as artists invest their entire being into their works. The Book of Genesis makes it seem as though things came into being simply by God speaking a word, but that is absolutely not how it was. God invested all His energy into creating the waters and the land.

In the same way, the movements of the ballerinas onstage are fruits of a creative process that requires total investment. The same thing can be said about soccer. A successful soccer team will invest its full energies into a ninety-minute game. In making a single run for the goal, a player will invest every bit of energy he can summon, as if his life depended on it. This is similar to what God went through as He created the world.

To pour out everything we have, to offer ourselves up completely for the sake of one moment in time—this is how greatness is achieved and how humankind comes to resemble God.

Master of the Seas and
the Future of the World

Histstory has shown that the country that controls the seas will become a world leader. Consider Britain. It was once invaded by the Vikings from Norway and Sweden. In the sixteenth century, soon after she was crowned, Queen Elizabeth I realized that if Britain didn't have control of the sea it could lose everything. She strengthened her country's maritime policy, and through her dedicated effort Britain became a powerful maritime nation. She mobilized capital and technology to have strong ships built, manned the ships with brave sailors, and sent them out to sea. They did not know what was waiting for them beyond the seas, but they risked their lives to go. As a result, Britain, a small island nation in the Atlantic, came to possess colonies on all the continents and oceans and built an empire.

Western civilization centering on Britain saw tremendous development in science and technology. With the aid of the compass, British ships journeyed to many different places in the world. The country's highly developed material knowledge and technology gave it abilities with which it sought to dominate the entire world. Korea, and most of the rest of the East, has taken a different approach. The

Eastern world does not discard the spirit in the pursuit of the material. If there is a conflict between the material and the spiritual, the East would rather discard the material. So generally speaking, life in the East has been more difficult than in the West because it is less materially developed. In the West, however, spirit will not be dominated by the material forever. As a totally materialistic culture brings degradation, the opportunity presents itself to learn from the more spiritually oriented East.

Civilization developed from Egypt, to Greece and Rome, to Britain and the United States, and is now moving toward the Pacific region surrounding the Korean peninsula. The era of a Pacific civilization is opening, bringing together Western science and Eastern spirituality. The leaders in this new era will be nations like Korea and its Asian neighbors. It is not by mere coincidence that Korea and Japan have been able to rise to international prominence in a short time. This development was a historical inevitability pointing to the Asian era.

The United States and Russia, however, will not stand by and watch as our country rises to a leadership role in the world. It is possible that there could be a major conflict involving the United States, Japan, Russia, and China in the vicinity of Korea. We must prepare for this contingency in two ways.

First, we must create a strong bond between Japan and the United States and link this to Russia and China so as to protect Korea. How can we do this? With a philosophy and a heart that create oneness. The only philosophy that can prevent wars between religions and open a path to a peaceful world is one that proclaims that humanity is one, transcendent of race, nationality, and religion. To protect itself from the dangers of war, Korea must plant a philosophy of oneness in the world.

Second, we must prepare ourselves for the new oceanic era. The Pacific era is at hand. Anyone who cannot rule the ocean cannot become a leader in the Pacific age. If heavenly fortune comes and we are not prepared, we cannot take advantage of the opportunity. If we know that an oceanic era is about to begin and Korea wants to be the leader of that era, then Korea must make the necessary preparations.

Fish are not the only resources in the ocean. A greater treasure is its ability to provide energy. As crude oil reserves decrease, a sense of crisis over sources of energy is growing day by day. If the world runs out of oil, humanity will immediately find itself in the dark. There is an effort to develop alternative energy from corn, but this does not seem realistic when there is not enough food being distributed to feed the world's population as it is.

The true alternative energy source is the ocean. Energy from hydrogen in the seawater represents the future of humanity. Two-thirds of the earth's surface is water. This means that two-thirds of the raw materials humanity needs for the future are contained in the ocean. A new future for humanity cannot be accomplished without the ocean's resources. Developed countries are already extracting oil and natural gas from the seabed and selling it at high prices. The world has only begun to discover the resources in the ocean. The day is at hand when humanity will find itself dependent on the ocean.

The oceanic era will not begin without human effort. We must first go out onto the oceans. We must go out on boats and fight the waves. Without such courage we cannot prepare ourselves for the oceanic age. The country that conquers the oceans will become a dominant power in the world and find the world eager to study its culture and language. Korea must become the champion steward of the Pacific Ocean. It must understand the will of the Creator and manage His resources well.

Great Opportunity in the Oceanic Era

The oceans can become a central point for bringing the world together. To take ownership over the ocean we must be trained to live on it with the same ease as we live on land. When I train people to fish, I send ten small boats out with one large boat. When the boats leave port, the small boats are towed by the large boat. Once they are out on the open sea, however, the small boats are responsible for themselves. They must know the direction of the wind, what is on the ocean floor, and what route the fish are taking. They must learn all this on their own.

I like to use the phrase "Alaska spirit." By this I mean the habit of getting up at five o'clock in the morning, going out to sea, and not returning until well after midnight, when in the summer it is still light. The person with "Alaska spirit" stays out on the ocean until he catches the daily allowance. One cannot become a true fisherman unless he learns how to endure this way.

Catching fish is not a pleasure cruise. No matter how many fish may be in the ocean, they are not going to just jump into the boat. It takes specialized knowledge and much experience. A person must know how to mend a net and how to tie an anchor rope. Once a person receives intense training to become a fisherman, he can go anywhere in the world and become a leader of people. Learning to be a fisherman is good leadership training.

Dominance at sea will require ships, including submarines, that can go anywhere in the world. Korea is already the largest shipbuilding country in the world. It has the ability to become a great sea power. What Korea needs now is more people willing to go out to sea.

Koreans are the descendants of Chang Bo Go, that wealthy man of the ninth century who ran an international maritime trading business and was called "Ocean King." We have a long tradition of going out to sea on ships, fighting the waves, and winning battles.

People naturally fear the waves. When waves catch the wind, they become swells. Waves and swells are needed for oxygen to be mixed into the ocean. If the ocean is calm for an extended period, without wind or waves, it begins to die. When we realize the value of waves, they are no longer something to be feared. Even if a strong wind blows and the waves become fearsome, we understand that this is the way to help the fish live. Then the waves become part of the attraction of the sea.

Thirty meters below the surface of the ocean there are no waves. If we were to take a submarine to the bottom of the ocean it would be so cool that there would be no need for air conditioners. The fish choose the depth that has the temperature that is right for them and then perform wonderful dances as they swim in schools in their favorite waters. Similar to our Little Angels dance troupe with their fans, the fish have their colorful outfits and gently wave their fins. It is a beautiful and peaceful environment they live in. The world, too, will soon be as peaceful as this.

The fact that an oceanic era is coming means that Korea will soon have the opportunity to change the world. People who live in peninsular countries have had to contend with invasions from both land and sea throughout history. To survive they had to be brave and develop a steely national character. It is not by coincidence that civilizations developed in peninsular countries such as Greece and Italy. Civilizations could blossom in these countries because they had the enterprising and tough, adventurous spirit needed to spread their influence across both continents and seas.

Have you heard about the Black Stream, a boundary current in the western part of the North Pacific Ocean? It travels sixty-four hundred kilometers a year, based on the gravitational pull of the moon. It is an oceanic gyre that revolves all the way around the Pacific Ocean. To describe it simply as "tremendous" is not sufficient.

All the oceans of the world move by the same power that moves the Black Stream and other ocean currents. If these currents did not exist, the waters would not move, and would die. Just as even the largest and mightiest rivers eventually must flow into the sea, even the largest oceans must move in accordance with currents like the Black Stream.

The Korean people must become like the Black Stream and cause the flow of their peace-loving culture to influence the whole world. We must become a source of strength in the world, the place where all of life's forces come together in a peaceful concentration.

I have visited Korea's southern coast many times in an effort to find the place that could become the center of a Pacific civilization, and I believe that Yeosu and Sooncheon are suited to the task. The sea off the coast of Yeosu is as tranquil and clear as a mirror. It is where Admiral Yi Soon Shin dealt the Japanese a heavy defeat in 1592, and it is also where he died in battle. Yeosu has a great history of sea battles, and it is also the point where the Youngnam and Honam regions meet. It is at the end of the foothills of Mount Jiri, where leftists and rightists fought each other following the Korean War. In this sense, it is a land imbued with the pain of our people.

Sooncheon Bay, famous for its reed beds, has a beautiful and world-famous coastline. Out on the sea, with its clear waters that shimmer in the sunlight, we can catch many different types of fish. Abalone and brown seaweed grow in the tranquil waters of the bay. The large tidal flats are filled with cockles and other types of shellfish and small octopus. I have been out on the seas in that area and also climbed the mountains, and it is clear that this is a beautiful land that has everything necessary for the coming Pacific age.

I am now developing Korea's southern coast, with the focus on Yeosu. As a part of the preparations for this, I have been to Geomun Island and other islands in the area and lived there for several months. I consider people who live there, farming and fishing for the past several decades, to be my teachers.

I ate and slept in humble inns as I studied everything in detail. I didn't just study books. I went everywhere, using my eyes and feet to check everything. As a result, I now know what kinds of fish can be found in what areas of the ocean, what kinds of nets need to be used to catch them, what kinds of trees grow in the mountains, and which home on the island has an old man living alone after having suffered a stroke.

The day I finished my studies of the southern coast I took the village mayor, who had been helping me, on an airplane to Alaska. He had taught me everything he knew, so I wanted to return the favor by teaching him what I knew about Alaska. I went fishing with him in Alaska and told him about the different kinds of fish and how they can be caught. Even if I know only a little about something, I don't feel comfortable unless I share it with others.

Very soon after I began developing Yeosu, it was chosen as the venue for an international maritime exposition to be held in 2012. Together with the Olympic Games and the World Cup, international expositions are among the three largest festivals on a global scale. During the six months that Expo 2012 will be held in Yeosu, the one hundred fifty-four member countries of the International Exhibitions Bureau will operate various exhibits. This will focus the world's attention on Yeosu, and the technology and culture of developed countries will flow into Yeosu.

Have you ever looked up at a summer sky and seen clouds blowing by at an amazing speed? Once clouds catch the wind, they move quickly over mountains and oceans. Now is not the time to be hesitating. In a way similar to those clouds, heavenly fortune will be blowing the world toward Yeosu and the Korean peninsula.

I plan to connect all the islands along the southern coast with bridges and build condominiums where boat-loving people from around the world can come and stay. These will not be resorts just for play. Americans, Germans, Japanese, Brazilians, and Africans will all come. They may go out on different boats to catch fish, but I will encourage them to stay under the same roof to show that humanity is one family.

The coming era will also be an era of aeronautics and even space travel. The time is coming when possessing a well-developed aeronautic technology will be an absolute necessity. It will be too late for Korea to prepare its space industry if it doesn't start now. For this reason, I am preparing an aeronautic industrial park in Gimpo, in Kyeonggi Province.

I plan to produce world-famous helicopters as fine as Sikorsky. Soon the day will come when helicopters bearing the *Taeguk* symbol of Korea will fly through the skies all over the world. (The *Taeguk* is the Yin and Yang symbol on the Korean flag.)

A Single Dandelion Is
More Precious Than Gold

Three of the greatest challenges of modern society are solving pollution problems, creating a consciousness for protecting the environment, and increasing food production. The earth has already been extensively damaged. Our endless greed for material possessions has brought about serious air and water pollution that is destroying nature, including the ozone layer that protects us. If present trends continue, humanity will find itself unable to escape the consequences and traps of the reckless pursuit of material goods.

For the past twenty years, I have been working to sustain and preserve Brazil's Pantanal region. The Pantanal — a region that overlaps areas of Brazil, Bolivia, and Paraguay — is the world's largest wetlands area. It is listed with UNESCO as a World Heritage Site. I am carrying on a worldwide environmental movement to preserve the living creatures of the Pantanal in a pristine state of natural purity, as God intended at the time of Creation.

The Pantanal, where the water, land, animals, and plants exist in harmony, is truly a magnificent place. Simple words such as *beautiful* and *fantastic* cannot begin to describe its value. Photos of the area taken from the sky are so beautiful that a collection of these is one of the best-selling nature photo collections in the world. The Pantanal is one of humanity's treasure troves, where rare species such as the white throated capuchin, red howler monkey, macaw, jaguar, anaconda, the ostrich-like rhea, and the caiman live.

The flora and fauna of the Pantanal and the Amazon basin seem to exist as they might have on the first morning of Creation. The Pantanal is like a modern-day Eden. Human beings have destroyed a great many life forms that God created. Too many species of plants and animals have become extinct because of human greed. In the Pantanal, though, the original forms that God created still remain. I am planning to establish an aviary and an insect preserve in the Pantanal to save some of these unique species from extinction.

In addition to being a habitat for many plants and animals, the Pantanal is also an important source of oxygen for the earth, and a storehouse to absorb greenhouse gases. The Pantanal is changing rapidly, however, due to industrial development. If the Pantanal, which along with the Amazon provides such a large amount of oxygen for the earth, is destroyed, the future of humanity will be dismal.

Hundreds of species of fish live in the Pantanal. One is a gold-colored fish called the dorado, which often reaches a weight of more than twenty-six kilos. When a dorado first took my hook, it felt like my body was about to be pulled into the river. As I was reeling in the line with all my strength, it jumped out of the water several times. After several jumps it still had plenty of strength left to fight. It was so strong it seemed more like a bear or a tiger than a fish.

The lakes in the Pantanal are almost always clean. No matter what is put into the water, it quickly becomes clean again. The water is cleansed quickly because the wetland environment filters sediments and pollutants, and this is why there are so many different species of fish living there. Each species feeds on something different. Living together in a complex system, they also devour organic wastes that dirty the water. Even their act of feeding has the function of keeping the water pure. In this respect, fish are very different from human beings because they never live for their own sakes, but as part of a larger balanced system. They help clean their environment and make it better.

The back of a water hyacinth's leaf in the Pantanal wetlands is black with bugs. If all the bugs were to remain there, the hyacinth would not be able to live, but there are fish that eat those bugs off the leaves. So the bugs live, the hyacinth lives, and the fish live. This is what nature is like. No creature lives for itself. Instead, they live for each other. Nature teaches us this tremendous lesson.

No matter how many fish there are in the Pantanal, if people are given the freedom to fish there, the population is bound to decrease. To protect the fish we need to develop fish farms. Because the fish in the Pantanal are so precious, we need to develop many fish farms. Similar facilities to protect insects, birds, and mammals are also needed. Raising insects will help increase the bird population. The Pantanal provides a perfect environment for all these creatures, and by focusing on how to increase their population humankind can continue to enjoy them for centuries to come.

It is not just fish that are plentiful in the Pantanal. The riverbanks have pineapples, banana trees, and mango trees. Rice grows so well there that it is possible to have three harvests a year, even without irrigated fields. That's how rich the soil is. Crops such as beans and corn can be grown just by spreading the seeds over the ground. Very little human labor is needed.

Once while traveling down the Paraguay River on a boat, we stopped at a house near the bank. The farmer who lived there realized we were hungry, so he went into his field and dug up a sweet potato. It was the size of a watermelon! He told us that as long as he leaves the root in the ground it will continue to produce potatoes for several years. The thought that potatoes can be harvested without annual planting left me with a strong desire to take them to countries where food is lacking.

People who advocate developing wetlands stress the economic benefits of such development. The Pantanal, however, provides plenty of economic benefit just as a wetland. The area has vast tracts of virgin hardwood forest, and natives claim that a person could drive a spike into one of these trees and it would still live more than a hundred years. These massive trees produce woods such as brown ebony, which does not rot and is said to last longer than iron.

Imagine what it looks like to have forests filled with such precious trees. I had some seedlings of these trees planted on four hundred hectares (nine hundred eighty-eight acres) of land in the Pantanal. The trees our members planted have made the Pantanal even more beautiful.

Human selfishness is destroying nature. Competition for the shortest route to economic success is the main reason that the earth's environment has been damaged. We cannot allow the earth to be damaged any further. Religious people must lead the way in the effort to save nature. Nature is God's creation and His gift to humankind. We must work quickly to awaken people to the preciousness of nature and the urgent need to restore it to the rich and free state it enjoyed at the time of Creation.

Because it has become widely known that the Pantanal is a treasure trove, a struggle over its future has begun. The place that we should be protecting is about to become a battlefield for greedy human beings.

For the past ten years, I have been taking leaders from countries around the world to the Pantanal and sponsoring discussions on how to protect this region and the rest of the world's environment. I am gathering the world's environmental experts and scholars and encouraging them to take an interest in preserving the Pantanal. I am working to stop the Pantanal from being destroyed by the merciless material desires of human beings.

As the environmental issues grow more serious, many environmental groups have sprung up. The best environmental movement, however, is the one that spreads love. People generally take care of things that belong to them or to people they love. They do not, however, take care of or love the natural environment that God created. God gave this environment to humanity. It is His will that we use the environment to obtain food, to have it in abundance, and to experience the joy of living in the beauty of nature. Nature is not something to be used once and thrown away. Our descendants for many generations to come must be able to rely on it just as we have.

The shortcut to protecting nature is to develop a heart that loves nature. We must be able to shed a tear at the sight of even a blade of grass that we see as we walk along the road. We must be able to grab hold of a tree and weep. We must understand that God's spirit is hidden inside a boulder or a gust of wind. To care for and love the environment is to love God. We must be able to see each creature made by God as an object of our love. If our spiritual eyes were open we could see that a single dandelion by the roadside is more valuable than the gold crowns of kings.

Solution to Poverty and Hunger

I f you are never hungry, you cannot know God. The times when you are hungry are opportunities to be nearest to God. When you are hungry if you are able to look humbly at each approaching person as if he were a close family member whom you want to help, you are more likely to be fed. In such situations, it is important to maintain a sympathetic heart of goodness.

Hunger is not an issue relegated to less-developed areas of the world. Even in the United States, which enjoys one of the highest standards of living in the world, there are millions of people who are undernourished and hungry. When I went to the United States, one of my first projects was to purchase trucks to be used for the distribution of food to the poor.

The situation in impoverished countries is far worse than in the United States. When I look at the world situation, I feel that securing sufficient food supplies is the most pressing problem. Solving the food crisis cannot be put off for even a moment. Even now, some twenty thousand people around the world die of hunger-related causes every day. We cannot afford to be apathetic just because we and our immediate families are not facing hunger.

Simply distributing food supplies by itself will not resolve hunger. A more fundamental approach to the problem is needed. I am considering two fundamental and concrete methods. The first is to provide ample supplies of food at low cost, and the second is to share technology that people can use to overcome hunger on their own.

The issue of food will present humankind with a very serious crisis in the future. We cannot build a world of peace without first resolving the food issue. Sufficient food supplies for all the world's population cannot be produced on the limited amount of land area that is currently available. We must look to the oceans for a solution. The oceans hold the key to solving the food crisis of the future. This is the reason I have been pioneering the oceans for the past several decades.

In Alaska, pollock smaller than thirty-eight centimeters long are used for fertilizer. They would make wonderful food, but people don't know how to prepare them, so they use them just for fertilizer. As recently as twenty or thirty years ago, Koreans could ask Westerners to give us the tail of an ox (a delicacy) and they would let us have it for free. Koreans are fond of food prepared with the bones or the intestines of cows, but some Westerners do not know these are edible.

The same is true with fish. About twenty percent of the world's fish catch is routinely thrown out. Whenever I see this, I think of the people who are dying of hunger, and I feel pain. Fish is a much more reliable source of protein than beef. How wonderful it would be if we made fish cakes or fish sausages to give to people in impoverished lands!

Once this thought came to me, I started projects to process and store large volumes of fish. It does not do any good to catch large amounts of fish if you cannot handle them properly after the catch. Even the best fish cannot be kept well for more than eight months. Even if they are frozen and placed in refrigeration, air gets in through cracks in the ice, and water escapes. You could pour water on the fish and freeze them again, but by then the best flavor is already gone and the fish might as well be thrown out.

We gathered fish that were being thrown out and researched how to turn them into fish powder. We sought to do something that even advanced countries like France and Germany have not done. Fish turned into powder could be transported and stored easily, even in hot and humid climates. Fish powder is ninety-eight percent protein, among the very highest protein content of all food products. For this reason it can be used to save people from dying of hunger. Fish powder could also be used to make bread. We are still searching for ways to make it available to impoverished countries around the world.

The oceans contain limitless food supplies, but the best method for saving humanity from the food crisis is fish farming. I foresee that there will be buildings, similar to the skyscrapers we see in our cities today, devoted to fish farming. By using water pipe systems, we can farm fish in tall buildings or even on the tops of mountains. With fish farming we can produce more than enough food to feed all the world's people.

The ocean is a blessing bequeathed to us by God. When I go out on the ocean, I am completely absorbed in fishing. I have caught all kinds of fish in different countries. One reason I fish is so I can teach people who don't know how to fish. In South America I spent several months showing local people my fishing methods. I took in tangled fishnets myself and spent three or four hours showing them how to untangle them.

To secure adequate supplies of food at low cost, humankind will need to develop the ocean. This and the great grasslands that are still in their prehistoric state are our final storehouses of wealth. This task, though, will not be easy. It will require us to go to places that are so hot and humid that moving around and working hard with a strong sense of dedication become very difficult. Developing the grasslands in tropical regions cannot be done without a love for humankind that is passionate and dedicated.

Jardim, in Brazil, is just such a place. It is quite difficult to live there. The weather is hot, and bugs that have not even been named yet are continually biting. I lived in that place and made friends with all its various creatures. I walked around barefoot, feeling the red soil of Jardim beneath my feet, looking just like a peasant farmer. When I was at the river catching fish, I looked like the local fishermen.

It is only when the local people look at you and say, "You really are a farmer," or "You really are a fisherman," that you are qualified to receive their knowledge and share your own knowledge with them. It is not something that can be done by someone who needs to sleep eight hours a night in a clean and comfortable bed, eat three square meals a day, and take naps under a shady tree.

When we were developing a project in Paraguay, a group of our members and I were living in a small hut in Olimpo, close to the Paraguay River. There was only one toilet, and each morning we had to take turns using it. I would get up each morning at three o'clock, do some exercises, and then go fishing. Because of this, the members who were with me went through some very difficult times. They were not used to cutting bait early in the morning before they were completely awake.

When we took the boat out, we had to cross through a number of other properties in order to reach the mooring site. Unlocking the gates to these properties in pitch darkness was difficult. One morning when the members were fumbling with a lock, unable to open it, I yelled at them, "What are you doing?!" I shouted so loudly and fiercely that I surprised even myself, so I am sure it must have been difficult for them.

But I feel that I cannot afford to waste so much as a single second. I don't have any time to be idly standing around. I can clearly see a list of all the things I must accomplish before there can be a world of peace, so my heart is always in a hurry.

When I fished there on the river before dawn, the mosquitoes would swarm like a dark cloud. Their stingers were so sharp they would pierce right through a pair of jeans. In the predawn darkness we could not see the floats on our fishing lines, so we had to attach white plastic bags to them. I could not wait for the sun to come up. I was in too much of a hurry.

I still miss Jardim. I miss everything about it. When I close my eyes, I can still feel the heat of the Jardim air pressing against my face. The minor inconveniences to my body were nothing. Bodily suffering passes quickly. What is important is that this place can one day play a significant role in serving the world. Being in Jardim brought great happiness to my heart.

Going Beyond Charity to End Hunger

To solve the problem of hunger we must have a patient heart that is willing to plant seeds. Seeds are planted and wait unseen under the soil until they are able to germinate and break through their outer cover. Similarly, it is better in the long term to teach a person how to plant and harvest wheat and then turn it into bread than it is to give a piece of bread to a person who is about to die. The former may be more difficult and not result in as much public recognition, but it is the only way to arrive at a fundamental and sustainable solution to world hunger. We need to begin now to study the climate, the soil, and the character of the people in areas that suffer from hunger.

There is a species of tree called the moringa. The people in the Congo feed the leaves of this tree, which are high in nutrition, to their children to supplement their diet. They pound these leaves on a stone mill, add some oil, and fry them in batter. They also feed them to their cattle to fatten them up before taking them to market.

It may be a good idea to plant many moringa trees and make powder out of the entire tree after throwing out the root, which is poisonous. The powder can be used to make bread. Many countries could follow this example and plant moringa trees. Also, Jerusalem artichokes, which look like sweet potatoes, grow very quickly once they are planted. The amount that can be harvested is three times greater than that of other famine relief crops. Planting a lot of Jerusalem artichokes is another way to contribute to resolving the hunger problem.

In Jardim, a large earthworm is used in farming, and this makes the soil quite fertile. This earthworm exists only in South America, but perhaps we can study its ecology and use it to help agriculture in other areas. Koreans are working in Brazil's Mato Grosso region to study silkworms. If the cultivation of silkworms is successful there, it will be possible to make silk cheaply and sell it to buy food.

There is no quick fix to the problem of world hunger. People in each country have different tastes for food and different customs, and the plants and animals are different. The important point is concern for our neighbors. We first need to develop the heart that, when we are eating enough to fill our own stomachs, we think of others who are going hungry and consider how we can help them. True peace will not come as long as humanity does not solve the problem of hunger. If the person next to me is about to die of hunger, peace is a mere luxury.

It is as important to teach the skills needed to become self-sufficient in producing food as it is to distribute food directly to those in need. To teach such skills, we need to build schools in remote areas to combat illiteracy. Technical schools will need to be established in order to give people the ability to support themselves. The Westerners who conquered Africa and South America did not do enough to provide technology to the people who were already there. They only used the people as laborers as they sought to dig up and take away the resources buried in the ground. They did not teach the people how to farm or how to operate a factory. This was not right. Our church has, from the early stage of our foreign mission work, established schools in places such as the Congo for teaching agriculture and industrial technology.

Another problem faced by people suffering from hunger is that they cannot afford proper medical treatment when they become ill. On the one side of the world, developed countries are seeing an overuse of drugs, while on the other side of the world people who are hungry often die because they cannot afford simple medicine for diarrhea. Therefore, as we work to eradicate hunger we must also provide medical support. We must establish clinics and care for those who suffer from chronic illness.

For example, centering on the New Hope Farms in Jardim, Brazil, I donated ambulances and medical equipment to over thirty surrounding small towns. I created New Hope Farms as a model to show how humanity can live together in peace. We tilled a wide expanse of land to make farmland, and there is a cattle ranch in the higher elevations.

Although New Hope Farms is in Brazil, it does not belong only to the people of Brazil. Anyone who is hungry can go to New Hope Farms, work, and be fed. Some two thousand people from all races and from all over the world can always eat and sleep there. We will establish schools all the way from elementary levels to university. People will be taught how to farm and how to raise cattle. We will also teach how to plant and grow trees and how to catch, process, and sell fish. We do not have only a farm. We use the numerous lakes in the vicinity of the river to create fish farms and fishing grounds.

Paraguay's Chaco region occupies sixty percent of that country's territory, but it has been a neglected land. The Chaco region was formed when the sea rose to cover the land, and even now you get salty water gushing up when you dig into the ground. I was in my seventies when I first went to Paraguay. The lives of the people living in this long-neglected land were impoverished beyond words. It caused me great pain in my heart to see them. I sincerely wanted to help them, but they were not prepared to easily accept me, a person of a different skin color who spoke a different language.

I did not give up, however. I traveled the Paraguay River for three months, eating and sleeping with people from the area. At more than seventy years of age, I was taking on a task that people said was impossible. I taught the people I met what I knew about fishing, and they taught me their language. We were on the boat like this together for three months and became friends.

Once they began to open their hearts, I talked to them again and again about why the world must become one. At first their reaction was indifferent. Year by year, though, the people of Paraguay began to change. After ten years, they changed so much that they held a global peace festival with great enthusiasm.

Resolving the food situation does not mean that peace will follow immediately. After the hunger issue has been resolved, it is important to carry out educational programs on peace and love. I have built schools in places such as Jardim and Chaco. At first people didn't send their children to school but instead had them help raise their cattle. We worked hard to convince them that the children and young people needed an education. As a result, we now have many students. We built a light industrial factory where they could produce items using simple technologies, and the students became more interested in attending school so they could work in the factory.

We are all responsible for the people around the world who die of hunger. We need to take action to help them. We need to feel a clear sense of responsibility and find a way that they can be fed and saved. People who live well should come down to a slightly lower position and raise up those who live poorly, to bring about a world where all people live well.

CHAPTER EIGHT

NEW VISION FOR
YOUTH

Find Your Purpose, Change Your Life

When we meet someone new, we are always curious about who he or she is. God has the same curiosity about each human being. He is especially curious about young people, and it brings Him great joy when He gets to know them intimately. Why is this? It is because our youth is the most important and beautiful period of our lives. This period should be a time of tranquility as one prepares for the future. The process of growing to maturity is a building block that opens the way to a new era.

It is difficult to find young people today who are passionate about their lives. We find so many young people who, with no goal or purpose for their life, are just wandering around. All great leaders in history had a definite sense of purpose in life from the time they were children. From childhood they nurtured that purpose held within their hearts and exerted great energy to achieve it. Whether they were sleeping or playing with their friends, these great leaders geared every youthful action toward preparing for the stage they would stand on in the future. Is that how you are living your life?

We are all created to be great men and women. God did not send us into this world without purpose. When God created us He invested

His complete love into each person. So we are all created for greatness. Because God exists, we can accomplish anything.

I became a completely different person when I began to love God. I loved humanity more than myself and was more concerned with the problems of others than with the problems of my family. I loved everything that God created. I deeply loved the trees on the hills and the fish in the waters. My spiritual senses developed so I could discern God's handiwork in all things of creation.

As I was changing my heart to conform to God's love, I also strengthened my body so that I could fulfill my mission. I wanted to be ready to go anywhere, anytime that God called on me. I played soccer and did boxing, some traditional Korean martial arts, and *wonhwado*, a form of martial arts that I developed. In *wonhwado* the athlete moves his body in a smooth, circular motion, almost as in a dance. It is based on the principle that greater power comes from circular motion than moving in a straight line.

Even now I begin each day with stretching exercises for my muscles and joints and a breathing exercise that I developed. Sometimes when I am traveling around the world on speaking tours, I may not have time for these exercises in the morning. Still I will find the time, sometimes while sitting on the toilet. I never miss a day of exercise. When I was young, thirty minutes a day was plenty, but now that I am older I have increased it to an hour a day.

In 2008 I was involved in a helicopter crash. The helicopter was suddenly surrounded by black rain clouds and in an instant crashed onto a mountainside. The helicopter rolled over, and I was left hanging upside down by my seatbelt. Instinctively I tightly grabbed the armrests on both sides of my seat. If I had not been so diligent in my exercises, I think I would have broken my hip the instant I was suspended upside-down. The body is the container to hold a healthy spirit. It is important for us to be diligent about training our bodies.

Few students go to school because they like to study. They usually go because their parents tell them to, not because they look forward to studying. As students continue to study, however, they gradually learn to enjoy it. From that point they will start to study on their own and find their own path. An interest in learning is a sign of maturity.

Parents cannot wait until their children mature enough to study on their own. They tell them, "You have to study. Please make up your mind to study," and put pressure on them. Parents do this because they know that children need to study in order to prepare for the future. They worry that if their children don't study at the proper age level, they will face the future unprepared.

There is, however, something more important than studying to prepare for the future. Before unconditionally focusing entirely on studies, young people must realize what they want to do in life. They must make a determination to use their talents to help the world rather than just serve themselves. Many young people today seem to be studying just for study's sake. Unless you have a purpose in life, your studies will lack the passion needed for happiness.

Once I came across a Korean student working hard on his English schoolwork. I asked him, "Why are you working so hard to learn English?"

He answered, "To get into a university."

What could be more short-sighted? Getting into a university is not a purpose. A university is a place to go to study particular subjects in the course of pursuing a larger objective. It cannot be the objective itself.

Also, do not define your life goal in terms of how much money you want to make. I have never received a salary, but I managed to eat and stay alive. Money is a means to do something, not the goal. Before you make money, have a plan for spending it. Money gained without a prior objective will soon be wasted.

Your choice of occupation should not be based only on your talents and interests. Whether you become a firefighter, a farmer, or a soccer player is up to you. But what I am referring to transcends your occupation. What kind of life will you lead as a soccer player? How will you live as a farmer? What is your objective in life?

To set your objective is to give meaning to the life you will lead. If you are going to be a farmer, then you should set your objective to test new agricultural methods, develop better species of crops, and help eradicate world hunger. If you are going to be a soccer player, then set a meaningful objective such as to heighten your country's image in the world or to establish soccer camps that will nurture the dreams of economically deprived children.

To become a world-class soccer player takes incredible work. If you do not have a definite purpose in your heart, you will not be able to endure the difficult training required to reach the top. Only if you have an objective will you have the power to maintain your course and live a life that is a cut above those around you.

Embrace the World

Setting a goal in life is similar to planting a tree. If you plant a jujube tree in your front yard, you will have jujubes in your home. If you plant apple trees on the hill behind your home, then they will produce apples. Think carefully about your choice of goals and where you intend to plant them. Depending on the goal you choose and where you plant it, you can become a jujube tree in Seoul or an apple tree in Africa. Or you can become a palm tree in the South Pacific. The goal you plant will bear fruit in the future. Think carefully where the best place is to plant your goal so that it will bear the best fruit.

When you are setting your goal, be sure to consider the entire world. Consider Africa, which continues to suffer from poverty and disease. Consider Israel and Palestine, where people continue to aim their weapons at each other and fight over matters of religion. Consider Afghanistan, where people barely keep themselves alive by raising poppies used to make harmful drugs. Consider the United States, where extreme greed and selfishness have contributed to the global economic crisis. Consider Indonesia, Haiti, and Chile, which have suffered from earthquakes and tidal waves. Imagine yourself in the context of those countries, and think which country and which situation would be most appropriate for you. It may be that you are best suited to India, where a new religious conflict may erupt. Or it could be Rwanda, which languishes in drought and hunger.

In setting a goal, students shouldn't be so foolish as to decide that because a country is small, like Korea, it isn't worthy of your goals. Depending on what you do, there is no limit to how large a small country can become in the global arena. Its national boundaries could even disappear. Whether you do good work on the large continent of Africa or in the small country of Korea, your goal should not be restricted by size. Your goals should be about where your talents can have the most impact.

Think of the world as your stage as you decide what you want to do in life. If you do, you will likely find many more things to do than what you were originally dreaming about. You have only one life to live, so use it to do something that the world needs. You cannot reach the hidden treasure on an island without adventure. Please think beyond your own country, and think of the world as your stage in setting your goal.

During the 1980s, I sent many Korean university students to Japan and the United States. I wanted them to leave Korea, where tear gas canisters were being fired almost daily, and let them see a wider world with greater variety. The frog that lives at the bottom of a well does not realize there is a bigger world outside the well.

I was thinking globally before that word even entered the Korean language. The reason I went to Japan to study was to see a wider world. The reason I planned to work for the Manchuria Electric Company in Hailar, China, and learn the Chinese, Russian, and Mongolian languages, even before Korea was liberated, was to enable me to live as a global citizen. Even now I travel by plane to many places in the world.

If I were to visit a different country every day, it would take more than six months to visit all of them.

People live in many countries, and they all live in different circumstances. There are places where there is no water to cook rice with, while other places have too much water. Some places have no electricity, while some countries are not able to consume all the electricity they produce. There are many examples of how something is lacking in one place but overabundant in another. The problem is there are not enough people focused on equalizing the distribution.

The same is true with raw materials. Some countries have an abundance of coal and iron ore in surface deposits. They don't even need to dig into the earth. All they need to do is shovel the coal and iron ore from these deposits which are easily accessed. Korea, however, has a critical shortage of coal and iron ore reserves. To dig out anthracite coal we need to risk our lives to go thousands of feet underground.

Africa has many places where bananas grow naturally in abundance, and they could keep people from starving. But there is a lack of technology and lack of access to productive land, so not enough banana plantations are created. Korea's climate is not suited for growing bananas, and yet we grow them. This technology in Korea could be very helpful in solving the problem of poverty in Africa. It is similar to the way South Korean technology for planting corn has helped relieve starvation in North Korea.

The phrase "global leader" is now in vogue in Korea. People say they want to become fluent in English and become global leaders. Becoming a global leader, however, is not just a matter of a person's fluency in English. The ability to communicate in English is nothing more than a tool. A true global leader is someone who is able to embrace the world in his own bosom. A person who has no interest in the problems of the world cannot become a global leader, no matter how well he might communicate in English.

To be a global leader a person must think of the world's problems as his own and have the pioneering spirit that is needed for finding difficult solutions. A person who is attached to a secure and fixed income, or dreams of having a pension after retirement and a comfortable family life, cannot be a global leader. To become a global leader a person must consider the whole world to be his country and all humanity to be his brothers and sisters and not be overly concerned that he does not know what the future may hold for him.

What are siblings? Why did God give us brothers and sisters? Siblings represent all human beings around the world. The experience of loving our brothers and sisters in the family teaches us how to love our fellow countrymen and love humanity. Our love for our own siblings expands in this way. The family whose members love each other is a model of how humanity can live together in harmony. Love among siblings means that one sibling is willing to go hungry, if necessary, so that his brother or sister can eat. A global leader is someone who loves humanity as he loves his own family.

It has been a while since we first heard the phrase "global village." Yet the earth has always been a single community. If a person's goal in life is to graduate from a university, get a job with a company that will pay him a high salary, and lead a secure life, then that person will have the success of a puppy. But if he dedicates his life to helping refugees in Africa, he will have the success of a lion. The course that is chosen depends on the heart of the individual.

Even at the age of ninety, I continue to travel around the world. I refuse to rest from my mission. The world is like a living organism in that it is always changing. New problems are always arising. I go to the dark corners of the world where these problems exist. These are not the places with beautiful views or comfortable amenities, but I feel happy in places that are dark, difficult, and lonely because that is where I'm fulfilling my mission, my purpose, and my goals.

My hope is that Korea will produce global leaders in the true sense. I hope to see more political leaders who will lead the United Nations to fulfill its purpose and more diplomatic leaders who will stop the fighting in areas of conflict. I hope to see someone like Mother Teresa who will take care of those wandering and dying on the streets. I hope to see peace leaders who will take on my mission of pioneering new solutions from the land and sea.

The starting point is to have a dream and a goal. Please have an adventurous and pioneering spirit. Dream dreams that others dare not imagine. Set goals for yourselves that have meaning, and become global leaders who will bring benefit to humankind.

Everything We Have Is Borrowed from Heaven

P eople say I am one of the richest people in the world, but they don't know what they are talking about. I have worked hard all my life, but I don't own so much as a single house in my name. Everything is for the public. Virtually every adult Korean has his official stamp that he registers with the government and uses to sign legal documents. I don't have such a stamp.

You may wonder, then, what benefit I have received from working hard and not eating or sleeping while others ate and slept. I didn't work so I could be rich. Money has no meaning to me. Any money not used for the sake of humanity, or for the sake of my neighbor who is dying in poverty, is nothing more than a piece of paper. Money earned through hard work should always be used to love the world and carry out projects that benefit the world.

When I send missionaries overseas, I don't give them a lot of money. Yet they survive wherever they go. It takes very little for us to support ourselves. If we have a sleeping bag, that is enough for us to sleep anywhere. What is important is not how we live but the kind of life we lead. Material affluence is not a condition for happiness. It is sad to me that the phrase "to live well" has come to be defined in terms of material affluence. To live well means to live a life that has meaning.

I wear a necktie only for worship services or special events. I don't wear a suit often, either. I generally wear a sweater when I am at home. I sometimes imagine how much money is spent on neckties in Western societies. Necktie pins, dress shirts, and cuff links are very expensive. If everyone stopped buying neckties and used the money instead for the sake of our neighbors who suffer from hunger, the world would be a little bit better place to live.

Expensive things are not necessarily the best to have. Imagine what it would be like if the building were on fire. Who would be the first to get out — I in my sweater, or someone in a suit and tie? I am always ready to go outside.

Some people might think I take conservation to extremes. I'm not in favor of taking a bath every day. Once every three days is enough. I also don't wash my socks every day. In the evening, I take off my socks and put them in my back pocket so I can wear them again the next day. When I am in a hotel, I use only the smallest of the towels that are hanging in the bathroom. I flush the toilet only after I have urinated in it three times. I use only a single square of toilet paper, after folding it in half three times. I don't care if you call me uncivilized or barbaric for this.

The same desire to conserve is true at mealtime. I have no interest in elaborate meals. There may be all sorts of exotic foods and different types of desserts in front of me, but I am not interested in those. I don't fill my rice bowl completely. It's enough if it is three-fifths full.

The shoes I prefer most in Korea cost 49,000 won ($40) at a large discount store. The pants I wear every day are well over five years old. The meal I enjoy the most in America is McDonald's. Some people call it junk food and don't eat it, but I like eating at McDonald's for two reasons. It's cheap, and it saves time. When I take the children out to eat, we often go to McDonald's. I don't know how it came to be known that I often go to McDonald's, but now the chairman of the McDonald's Corporation sends me a New Year's greeting card every year.

The message I give to our members every year is "spend money carefully, and conserve on everything." I don't tell them this so they can save money and become rich. I want them to have a consciousness of conserving in order to help the country and save humanity. We don't take anything with us when we leave this world. Everyone knows this, and yet for some reason people are desperate to get their hands on as many things as possible. I plan to give away everything I have built up during my life before leaving this world. The Heavenly Kingdom has plenty of treasure, and there is no need to take anything there from this world. When we understand that we are going to a place that is better than where we are now, there is no need to become attached to the things of this world.

There is a song I have always liked to sing. It's an old popular song that many Koreans know. Every time I sing this song it sets my heart at ease, and tears come to my eyes. It reminds me of my boyhood when I used to lie in the fields near home.

You may say you will give me a crown with platinum and jewels,
But a shirt smelling of dirt and dripping with sweat is worth more.
A pure heart wells up within my bosom,
I can make a flute out of willow leaves,

And the sparrows sing along with my tune.

You may say you will give me enough gold to buy the world,
But an ox that will till the soil in a barley field is worth more.
The buds of hope sprout in my bosom,
I can talk freely with the rabbits,
And the days go by as I play my tune.

Happiness is always waiting for us. The reason we can't find happiness is that our own desires block the way. As long as our eyes are fixed on our desires, they cannot see the path we should follow. We are so busy trying to pick up the scraps of gold lying on the ground near us that we do not see the huge pile of gold a little way up the road. We are so busy stuffing things into our pockets that we don't realize there are holes in those pockets.

I have not forgotten what it was like to live in Heungnam prison. Even the most terrible place in this world is more comfortable and more materially abundant than Heungnam prison. Every object belongs to Heaven. We are only its stewards.

Happiness Is a Life Lived for Others

Children are born from the flesh and blood of their parents. Without parents there would be no children. Yet people in this world shout out for individualism as though they came into this world on their own. Only a person who receives no help whatsoever from anyone at all would have the right to speak of individualism. There is nothing in this world that comes into being for its own sake alone. All beings are created for one another. I exist for you, and you exist for me.

There is no one as foolish as the selfish person who lives only for his or her own sake. It may appear that a selfish life benefits the individual, but ultimately it is a life of self-destruction. The individual must live for the family, the family for the people, the people for the world, and the world for God.

All the schools I have founded have three mottos. The first is "Live a life that casts no shadows, as if you were under the sun at high noon." A life without shadows is a life with a clear conscience.

When we finish our life here on earth and go to the spirit world, our entire life will unfold before us, as though it were being played back on videotape. Whether we go to heaven or to hell is determined by how we live. So we need to live spotlessly clean lives, casting not even the smallest shadow.

The second motto is "Live shedding sweat for earth, tears for humanity, and blood for heaven." There are no lies in the blood, sweat, and tears that people shed. There is only truth. There is no great meaning or value, however, in the blood, sweat, and tears that a person sheds only for his own sake. This great investment must be shed for the sake of others.

The final motto is "One Family under God!" There is only one God, and all human beings are brothers and sisters. Differences of language, race, and culture account for less than one percent. As human beings, we are more than ninety-nine percent the same.

There are fourteen island countries in the South Pacific. When I visited the Marshall Islands, I asked its president, "This is a beautiful land, but it must still be difficult to lead this country, isn't it?"

The president sighed and replied, "Our population is just sixty thousand, and the land is just two meters above sea level on average. So high waves, or a rise in sea levels of just one meter would flood much of the country. But our most serious problem is education. Children of rich families go to America or Europe to be educated and do not return. Children of poor families have no schools from which to receive a good education, so even the brightest child cannot be trained properly for leadership. The concern for an island country such as ours is that we are unable to raise up leaders who will lead us in the future."

After hearing his lament, I established the High School of the Pacific in Kona, Hawaii, for the sake of the children of these island countries. This school provides secondary education to children from countries throughout the Pacific and helps them apply to college. We provided round-trip airfare to Hawaii, tuition, board, and even computers so they could receive the best education. We attached just one condition to receive this education: Once they finish, they must return to their countries and work in the service of their nation and its people.

Living for the sake of others requires sacrifices from time to time. Some years ago one of our church missionaries was touring South America when the place he was visiting was hit by a major earthquake. His wife came running to me with her face as white as a sheet. "What should I do?" she asked with tears in her eyes. "I'm so worried, I don't know what to do."

You might be surprised by my response. Instead of patting her on the shoulder and comforting her, I shouted at her, "Are you most worried about your husband's safety? Or are you worried about how many lives he may be able to save in that disaster area?"

It was natural for her to be concerned for her husband's safety. But because she was the wife of a missionary, her concerns should have been of a higher order. Rather than only pray for her husband's safety, she should have prayed that her husband could save as many lives as possible.

Nothing exists for its own sake. That is not how God created the world. Man exists for the sake of woman, and woman exists for the sake of man. Nature exists for the sake of humanity, and humanity exists for the sake of nature. All created beings in this world exist for the sake of their counterparts. It is an axiom of Heaven that every being lives for the sake of its partner.

Happiness is possible only in a relationship with a partner. Imagine that some fellow who has lived his life as a singer goes to an uninhabited island and sings as loudly as possible. If there is no one there to hear him, he will not be happy.

To realize we exist for the sake of others is the great achievement that changes our lives. When we realize that our life is not ours alone but is meant to be for the sake of the other, we begin to follow a path different from the one we were on.

Just as singing to yourself will not make you happy, there is no joy without a partner. Even the smallest and most trivial thing can bring you happiness when you do it for another.

Dreaming of a Peaceful World

For years I have called for a world where all religions live together as one, all races live as one, and all nations exist as one. Yet for thousands of years history has seen the continuous increase of divisions. Each time a different religion was adopted or a new regime came into power, more boundaries were drawn and wars were fought. Now, however, we live in an age of globalism. For the sake of the future we must become one.

One way I propose to facilitate that is through the International Peace Highway, a huge undertaking. It will link Korea and Japan by an undersea tunnel and create a bridge or tunnel across the Bering Strait that separates Russia and North America. These great links can unify the world. When the highway is completed it will be possible to travel by car from Africa's Cape of Good Hope to Santiago, Chile, and from London to New York. There will be no roadblocks; the entire world will be interconnected like the way the blood vessels function in the body.

The world will become one integrated community, and everyone will be able to travel freely across international borders. Borders that give free passage to anyone will lose their significance as borders. Something similar will be true for religion. As the frequency of exchanges among religions increases, greater mutual understanding will arise, conflict will disappear, and the walls of separation will crumble.

When different types of people live together in a single global community, barriers between races will come down. Interaction between races will occur despite differences in appearance and language. This cultural revolution will bring the world into one.

The ancient Silk Road was not simply a trade route that people used in order to sell silk and buy spices. It was also a vehicle for the peoples of the East and West to meet and for Buddhism, Islam, and Christianity to meet. These different cultures intermingled and gave rise to a new culture. The International Peace Highway will play a similar role in the twenty-first century.

Rome could thrive because all roads led to Rome. This is a good illustration of the importance of roads. When a road is built, people use it to travel. It is used to transport culture and ideology. That is why when a road is built it can change the course of history. When the International Peace Highway is completed, the world can be physically bound together as one. The road will make this possible.

I cannot overemphasize the importance of bringing the world together. Some may think that this is an idea ahead of its time. Religious people, however, foresee the future and prepare for it. So it is only natural that we are ahead of our time. The world may not understand us and may cause us to suffer, but religious believers must persevere to lead the way to the future.

Completing the International Peace Highway will require the cooperation of many nations. China, which was a victim of Japanese aggression, may not welcome the idea of being connected to Japan by a highway. Japan and Korea, however, cannot connect to the rest of the world without going through China, so we need to make efforts to win China's trust.

Who will do this? Those of us who will take spiritual ownership over the International Peace Highway in the twenty-first century need to take the lead in this effort.

How about bridging the Bering Strait? It will cost a great deal, but this should not cause concern. The amount of money that the United States has spent in Iraq would be more than enough to build such a bridge. We must stop waging war and forcing people to suffer. It is perverse to start wars and squander hundreds of billions of dollars. The time has come for us to beat our swords into plowshares and our spears into pruning hooks.

The International Peace Highway is a project to bring the world together as one. To become one means more than simply connecting continents by tunnels and bridges. It refers to an equalization of the world's standards of living. When someone monopolizes a technology and keeps the profit entirely for himself, the balance of the world is upset.

The International Peace Highway will rearrange the current inequality by creating access to existing natural and human resources. This will bring about a leveling of wealth. Leveling means that a little is taken off places that are high and added to places that are low. As a result, the two have the same height. This will require sacrifice from those with greater material possessions or knowledge. Building a world of peace cannot be done with onetime charitable acts or donations. Only sincere love and continuous sacrifice is capable of creating a world of peace. We must be willing to offer everything.

Building the International Peace Highway does more than just provide the world with a physical means of communication. Human beings are created so that their mind and body become one. Something similar is true for the world we live in. The world can be completely unified only when there is both physical communication and communication of heart.

For this reason, I have been working for the reform and renewal of the United Nations for many years. Of course, the United Nations has done much for world peace. All Koreans are grateful for its efforts in preserving our freedom during the Korean War. However, today, more than sixty years after its founding, it seems to be losing sight of its original purpose and is in danger of becoming an organization that works for the interests of a few powerful countries.

In 2005, I founded the Universal Peace Federation in New York and immediately afterward embarked on a world tour to a hundred cities to deliver a peace message about a new future for the United Nations and the world. The United Nations was created to solve the conflicts that arise in the world, so it must put the world's interests before the interests of one side or the other. It only leads to further conflict when a powerful country insists on its own way and uses force to pursue it. Unfortunately, the United Nations today is unable to do much about such situations.

In this light, I have proposed a restructuring of the United Nations as a bicameral institution. In addition to the General Assembly there should be a religious, or cultural, assembly or council. This body would consist of respected spiritual leaders in fields such as religion, culture, and education. The members of this interreligious assembly would need to demonstrate an ability to transcend the limited interests of particular religions and cultures and to speak for the spiritual and moral purposes of all humanity. I maintain that the two chambers, working together in mutual respect and cooperation, will be able to make great advances in ushering in a world of peace.

Some may oppose this, saying, "Why should religious people become involved in world affairs?" My answer is that the world today is in a period when the participation of religious people is crucial. Those who have achieved deep self-awareness through religious practice are needed now more than ever.

Only truly religious people can stand up to the unrighteousness and evil of the world and practice true love. Only when the knowledge and experience of political leaders are combined with the wisdom of inter-religious leaders will the world be able to find the path to true peace.

Each day, I set out on my path with renewed determination to achieve that goal. My prayer is that every person on earth will be reborn as a peace-loving global citizen, transcending barriers of religion, ideology, and race.

INDEX